WITHDRAWN

Liberal purposes

This book is a major contribution to the current theory of liberalism by an eminent political theorist. It challenges the views of such theorists as Rawls, Dworkin, and Ackerman who believe that the essence of liberalism is that it should remain neutral concerning different ways of life and individual conceptions of what is good or valuable.

Professor Galston argues that the modern liberal state is committed to a distinctive conception of the human good, and to that end it has developed characteristic institutions and practices – representative government, a diverse society, a market economy, and zones of private action – in the pursuit of specific public purposes that give unity to such a state. These purposes guide liberal public policy, shape liberal justice, require the practice of liberal virtues, and rest on a liberal public culture. Consequently, the diversity characteristic of liberal societies is limited by their institutional, personal, and cultural preconditions.

The publication of this book will be of especial importance to all political theorists, be they in departments of philosophy or political science; sociologists; legal theorists; and even general readers concerned with such issues as civic education, cultural diversity, and church–state relations.

Cambridge Studies in Philosophy and Public Policy

GENERAL EDITOR: Douglas MacLean

The purpose of this series is to publish the most innovative and up-to-date research into the values and concepts that underlie major aspects of public policy. Hitherto most research in this field has been empirical. This series is primarily conceptual and normative; that is, it investigates the structure of arguments and the nature of values relevant to the formation, justification, and criticism of public policy. At the same time it is informed by empirical considerations, addressing specific issues, general policy concerns, and the methods of policy analysis and their applications.

The books in the series are inherently interdisciplinary and include anthologies as well as monographs. They are of particular interest to philosophers, political and social scientists, economists, policy analysts, and those involved in public administration and environmental policy.

Mark Sagoff: *The Economy of the Earth*
Henry Shue (ed.): *Nuclear Deterrence and Moral Restraint*
Judith Lichtenberg (ed.): *Democracy and the Mass Media*

Liberal purposes

Goods, virtues, and diversity in the liberal state

WILLIAM A. GALSTON

SCHOOL OF PUBLIC AFFAIRS AND
INSTITUTE FOR PHILOSOPHY AND PUBLIC POLICY,
UNIVERSITY OF MARYLAND AT COLLEGE PARK

CAMBRIDGE
UNIVERSITY PRESS

PUBLISHED BY THE PRESS SYNDICATE OF THE UNIVERSITY OF CAMBRIDGE
The Pitt Building, Trumpington Street, Cambridge CB2 1RP, United Kingdom

CAMBRIDGE UNIVERSITY PRESS
The Edinburgh Building, Cambridge CB2 2RU, UK   http://www.cup.cam.ac.uk
40 West 20th Street, New York, NY 10011-4211, USA   http://www.cup.org
10 Stamford Road, Oakleigh, Melbourne 3166, Australia

First published 1991
Reprinted 1992, 1993, 1995
Transferred to digital printing 1998

Typeset in Palatino

A catalogue record for this book is available from the British Library

Library of Congress Cataloguing-in-Publication Data is available

ISBN 0-521-42250-7 paperback

Transferred to digital printing 2002

To my son Ezra

The first service a child doth
his father is to make him foolish.
—George Herbert

Contents

Contents

PART IV: FROM THEORY TO PRACTICE
IN THE LIBERAL STATE

Acknowledgments

Any author of a book nearly ten years in the making is bound to have incurred numerous debts, and to have forgotten many of them. What follows is at best a partial enumeration; I offer my apologies, in advance, to those inadvertently excluded.

Thanks go to Robin Lovin and Michael Perry for inviting me to write a critique of Roberto Unger's recent work, a portion of which made its way into Chapter 3; to Richard Flathman for asking me to draft a survey of Michael Walzer's *oeuvre*, a portion of which also appears in Chapter 3, and to Michael Walzer for his generous comments; to Flathman, William Connolly, and Susan Wolf of Johns Hopkins University, and to Bernard Yack, Arlene Saxonhouse, and Don Herzog of the University of Michigan for invitations to present early versions of what became Chapters 5 and 13, and for their helpful reactions; to Richard Arneson for crucial advice on the arguments of Chapter 5, and for inviting me to write and then helping me to improve what became Chapter 7; to Charles Larmore, who provided a steady stream of instructive comments on Chapter 5 and on the basic issues of this book; to Benjamin Barber for asking me to write, and then inducing me to expand greatly, an earlier version of Chapter 6; to Frank Lucash and the Leonard Conference at the University of Nevada at Reno for inviting me to present the paper that served as the basis for Chapter 9; to Harvey Mansfield, Jr., Delba Winthrop, and Stephen Macedo for giving me opportunities to present an early version of Chapter 10 at Harvard, and to Judith Shklar for helping me better understand what I was trying to do in that chapter; to Nancy Rosenblum and the Conference for the Study of Political Thought for asking me to comment on Amy Gutmann's views on civic education (a venture that ultimately turned into Chapter 11), and to Amy Gutmann for perceptive reactions that helped me see far more clearly what was at stake; to Alphonso Damico for persuading me to write a version of Chapter 12 and for many helpful comments along the way; and to Jeremy Shearmur and the Institute for Humane Studies for inviting me to present material that found its way into Chapter 13.

I am also grateful to my colleagues at the University of Maryland's Institute for Philosophy and Public Policy for their guidance on Chapters 1 and 2; to Judith Lichtenberg and David Luban for taking on an entire sprawling manuscript and for helping me get through some rough patches; and, in particular, to Luban for a painstaking critique of Chapter 12 that helped me avoid some serious errors.

I owe special thanks to the general editor of this series, Douglas MacLean, for his good judgment and for a confidence in this project far steadier than my own; as well as to the Cambridge University Press executive humanities editor, Terence Moore, for his patience in the face of my many requests, for the generosity and integrity that characterized all his dealings, and for helping me avoid a potentially disastrous choice of titles. (He is of course absolved of blame for the one I eventually selected.) The anonymous reviewers greatly assisted me in eliminating inessentials, plugging gaps, and generally turning this into a much shorter, tighter book than it would otherwise have been (which is not to say that it could not have been shorter and tighter still).

Thanks also to the following journals and presses for their kind permission to reprint materials that served as the bases for portions of this book: to *Political Theory*, for "Community, Democracy, Philosophy: The Political Thought of Michael Walzer" (Chapter 3) and "Moral Personality and Liberal Theory: John Rawls's 'Dewey Lectures' " (Chapter 6); to the

Acknowledgments

American Political Science Review, for "Defending Liberalism" (Chapter 4) and "Liberal Virtues" (Chapter 10); to *Ethics*, for "Pluralism and Social Unity" (Chapter 7); to Cornell University Press, for "Equality of Opportunity and Liberal Theory" (Chapter 9); to Harvard University Press, for "Civic Education in the Liberal State" (Chapter 11); to Rowman and Littlefield, for "Liberalism and Public Morality" (Chapter 12); to *The Responsive Community*, for "A Liberal-Democratic Case for the Two-Parent Family" (Chapter 12); and to *Polity*, for "On Liberalism" (Chapter 13).

WILLIAM A. GALSTON
College Park, Maryland

Part I

Liberalism and political philosophy

Chapter 1

Introduction

I

This is a book about liberalism. Its central thesis is that the modern liberal state is best understood as energized by a distinctive ensemble of public purposes that guide liberal public policy, shape liberal justice, require the practice of liberal virtues, and rest on a liberal public culture. Liberal purposes, so conceived, define what the members of a liberal community must have in common. These purposes are the unity that undergirds liberal diversity; they provide the basis on which *e pluribus unum* ceases to be a raw and shifting balance of contending social forces and becomes instead an ethically meaningful characterization of the liberal state.

This affirmative thesis entails a triple negation. The liberal state cannot be understood along Michael Oakeshott's lines as a purposeless civil association structured by adverbial rules. Like every other form of political community, the liberal state is an enterprise association. Its distinctiveness lies not in the absence but, rather, in the content of its public purposes.[1]

Nor can the liberal state be properly understood as "neutral" in any of the senses in which that term is currently employed. Like every other political community, it embraces a view of the human good that favors certain ways of life and tilts against others.

Nor, finally, can the liberal state be understood as an arena

3

for the unfettered expression of "difference." In the very act of sustaining diversity, liberal unity circumscribes diversity. It could not be otherwise. No form of social life can be perfectly or equally hospitable to every human orientation.

Purposive liberalism is not, however, unresponsive to the underlying concerns that give rise to talk of civil association, of neutrality, and of difference. Liberal purposes are deliberately and doubly partial. They do not fill the total space of public action; much is left to the play of individual and collective choice. Nor do they determine the totality of individual lives; they define only what we, as citizens, must publicly affirm.

A purposive liberalism is consistent with – indeed, gives content and specificity to – the liberal distinction between public and private and the liberal commitment to individual freedom. It comes closer than any other form of human association, past or present, to accommodating human differences. It is "repressive" not in comparison with available alternatives but only in relation to unattainable fantasies of perfect liberation.

II

As I draft this introduction, liberalism is ascendant. From Warsaw to Sofia, activists talk of little save individual rights, independent judiciaries, multiparty democracies, autonomous "civil societies," and free markets. In the Soviet Union, Marxism–Leninism has been supplemented by a tacit liberalism struggling for official affirmation. Faced with demands for liberal-democratic reform, a senescent Chinese leadership can find no reply other than brute force. Throughout the West, orthodox Communist parties continue to wither, while throughout the developing world, market-oriented economies surge forward as command economies stagnate.

These developments cannot simply be accidental. One of the most attractive features of liberal democracy is the wide opportunity it affords individuals to define and lead their

4

lives as they see fit. Contrasts with other societies that use public instrumentalities to promulgate orthodox views, repress dissent, and assign individuals to careers only emphasize the importance of such opportunities. Few who have tasted them would willingly accept public restraint, and (as recent events throughout the Communist world demonstrate) citizens of nonliberal orders cherish the hope that their fetters will soon be removed. After three generations of indoctrination, the failure of such orders to engender compliant belief can only be regarded as stunning.

Despite this euphoric onrush of events, one may doubt that the end is in sight, either for history or for political philosophy. On the most practical level, as reformers in Central Europe and the Soviet Union are discovering, public support for liberal democracy depends on its ability to deliver ever rising levels of material affluence. This relation is hardly confined to societies newly emerging from decades of authoritarian government. We would do well to recall that the economic crisis of the 1930s contributed immeasurably to the appeal of various antiliberalisms throughout the West, and we should avoid overconfidence that our understanding of economics has progressed so far as to preclude a repetition. It would be ironic indeed if the fall of communism were swiftly followed by a crisis of capitalism.

Nor should we overlook the sources – and continuing power – of the various antipathies to liberalism expressed throughout the past two centuries: the longing for community over against "individualism," for stability and security in the face of "progress," for aristocratic excellence in opposition to democratic "leveling"; the embrace of conflict as the venue for heroic self-expression and as the antidote to boredom; contempt for the alleged greed and pettiness of everyday bourgeois existence; the quest for a deeper spirituality, typically counterposed to liberal "shallowness"; an instinctive tribalism that opposes universalism in the name of race, ethnicity, or nationalism and sustains nativist populism or authoritarianism; the resentments, fears, hatreds, and hysterias that have led – and could lead once again – to

5

fascism; and the instinct for cruelty and domination, rooted in human nature, and opposed to liberal mildness, equality, and respect.[2]

While it would be reckless in the extreme to lose sight of these enduring conflicts, there can be little doubt that we are now experiencing a rare liberal opportunity – a period (who knows how long it will last?) in which many of the most critical political issues will be contested within the liberal framework. It becomes, then, a matter of more than ordinary importance to strive for a better understanding of liberal strengths and limitations. I offer this book, the product of nearly a decade of reflection, as my contribution to that endeavor.

Of all the issues facing the contemporary liberal polity, one is of special concern to me here: the relationship between liberal political institutions and practices, on the one hand, and what might be called the moral culture of liberal society on the other. Although much of the argument in this book develops on the plane of theory, it was evoked not so much by theoretical puzzles as by civic experiences: of rising rates of crime, drug abuse, and family breakdown; of the near collapse of effective public education; of greed and shortsightedness run amok in public and private affairs; of a steady decline in political awareness and an equally steady rise in political cynicism; and of what I can only regard as the relentless tribalization and barbarization of American life. My guiding intuition is that the United States is in trouble because it has failed to attend to the dependence of sound politics on sound culture, and that all similarly inattentive liberal polities will eventually experience similar difficulties. My proposal is that the liberal state must become far more aware of, and far more actively involved in reproducing, the conditions necessary to its own health and perpetuation. My thesis is that the public focus on these conditions – the legitimate ground of liberal unity – is fully consistent with the historic liberal commitment to freedom and diversity.

6

III

It might be imagined (indeed, opponents of liberalism have typically argued) that liberal freedom would unacceptably corrode the bonds of social unity. At least since Locke, liberals have turned this argument on its head. They have insisted that civil strife is the product not of diversity but, rather, of public institutions designed to repress it. Acceptance of diversity will produce, or restore, peace; pluralism is compatible with social unity; self-determining individuals will be linked to the accommodating state by bonds of interest and conviction far stronger than a sullen obedience born of fear.

This classic liberal argument was first spawned by the religious wars of the Reformation. "Toleration" would end bloody strife, not by restoring the unity of Christendom but by acknowledging its permanent diremption. Far from being imcompatible with religious liberty, public order now required it. Indeed, argued Locke, the nature of religious faith, rightly understood, rendered public coercion of individual conscience not only damaging but futile.

Contemporary liberal theorists have dramatically expanded the scope of toleration. Thinkers such as John Rawls, Ronald Dworkin, Bruce Ackerman, and Charles Larmore insist that the state must be "neutral," not simply toward religious professions but toward all individual conceptions of the good life. Indeed, they regard this neutrality as the defining characteristic of liberal orders in contrast to the partisanship of all other regimes.

The impulse animating these thinkers is understandable. If the distinctive appeal of liberal societies is the extraordinary scope and protection they afford for individual choices, then any acceptable theory of liberalism must accommodate and justify, if not celebrate, diversity. I want to argue, however, that the current emphasis on neutrality has come at the expense of other key elements of the liberal experience. Whether we examine the intellectual and political history of liberalism, inspect the social practices and beliefs of contemporary liberal societies, or analyze the tacit presuppositions of recent liberal theories, we discover that liberalism is in fact far from fully neutral with respect to conceptions of the good.

There are at least three reasons why the neutrality thesis cannot be sustained. First, it represents a deep misunderstanding of the Lockean argument, which embodies, and requires, consensus concerning the substance and importance of key secular goods such as the minimization of violent conflict. Liberal neutrality toward competing accounts of salvation thus cannot be extended straightforwardly to competing conceptions of the good. Second, it cannot be squared with the reality of liberal politics, which can hardly take a step without appealing to some understanding of the good. Finally, the thesis fails in its own terms: Each of its proponents tacitly relies on a more than formal and more than instrumental conception of the good to move his argument forward.

Nor could it be otherwise. As Richard Flathman has said, "If moral and political life takes its distinctive character from, if moral and political issues and disputes are about, ends and purposes, how can moral and political philosophy do other than address and attempt to resolve questions about ends and purposes?"[3]

One of the main purposes of this book is to reject the neutrality thesis and replace it with another. I shall argue that liberalism does in fact rest on a distinctive conception of the human good. This conception differs from the "perfectionism" of classical antiquity. It does not, for example, culminate in a depiction of the *summum bonum* or of the best way of life for all human beings. It is shaped as much by experiences of deprivation and evil as by images of perfection. It adumbrates a small number of basic goods held to be worthy of special attention in individual and collective deliberation. It offers considerations capable of shaping our judgment in fundamental ways, and it demarcates a capacious but nonetheless determinate sphere of public possibilities. To quote Flathman once again:

If, or to the extent that, such a consensus [about good and bad] can be achieved and maintained, perhaps in part by giving it various institutionalized expressions and embodiments, it may be possible to contain the all but inevitable, and the all but inevitably expressed, disagreements about other questions of value within nondestructive bounds.[4]

In offering this case, I want to associate myself with a native element of American liberalism. In the Declaration of Independence we read:

Whenever any Form of Government becomes destructive of these ends [the securing of certain unalienable rights], it is the Right of the People to alter or to abolish it, and to institute new Government, laying its foundation on such principles, and organizing its powers in such form, as to them shall seem most likely to effect their Safety and Happiness.

And in the Preamble to the Constitution the people institute their government "in order to form a more perfect Union, establish Justice, insure domestic Tranquility, provide for the common defence, promote the general Welfare, and secure the Blessings of Liberty to ourselves and our Posterity." The liberalism I espouse is conceived in this spirit. It is more substantive and purposive, less formal and procedural, than is the currently dominant version of liberal theory. It is committed not to neutrality but to the pursuit of those ends that give the liberal polity its distinctive appeal.

Such a conception is not incompatible, as many neutrality theorists have feared, with classic liberal commitments to freedom and individuality. These theorists have tacitly presupposed a two-value model: Either a society is neutral, or it must be restrictively partisan, even covertly perfectionist. This is much too simple. The good is a continuum, not a dichotomous choice. Some accounts are very constraining, others much more capacious. There is a vast – and vitally important – terrain between Plato and Ronald Dworkin. And therefore, there is a coherent alternative to both liberal neutrality and its communitarian critics. It is possible to argue for a robust understanding of goods and virtues while remaining faithful to liberal insights and accomplishments. Indeed, I want to suggest, it is only on the basis of such an understanding that liberal societies can meet the challenge of forging and maintaining needed unity in the face of the centrifugal forces of diversity. *E pluribus unum* is not merely a geographical and institutional but also a cultural and moral imperative.

To begin with, the liberal conception of the *good* (or *well-being;* I use these terms more or less interchangeably) allows for a wide though not wholly unconstrained pluralism among ways of life. It assumes that individuals have special (though not wholly unerring) insight into their own good. And it is consistent with the minimization of public restraints on individuals: For liberalism, the proposition that "A knows that X is good for B" does not by itself warrant the conclusion that "A is justified in coercing B to do (or be) X."

This is not to say that the liberal conception of the good has no impact on individual and collective possibilities within liberal orders. If X is part of that conception, then the polity will probably be warranted in promoting X through public policy, and in compelling dissenting individuals to support this policy. So, for example, a liberal community may legitimately establish institutions to promote public health and require all citizens, including Christian Scientists and individuals bent on suicide, to maintain them through taxation. It does not follow, however, that a liberal community may compel these dissenters to make use of its public health facilities: Coercion for public purposes is distinguishable from coercion directed at individual ways of life.

Not only does the liberal account of the human good help define the appropriate bounds of public policy; it also undergirds the fundamental considerations on the basis of which individuals can make valid claims of distributive justice within liberal orders. To put it briefly, liberal citizens can make claims on the basis of *need* (i.e., access to certain basic goods, due to all citizens simply in their capacity as citizens); *desert,* defined as an individual's contribution to the good of some part of the community, or to the community as a whole; and *choice*, which reflects the liberal commitment to the good of individual freedom in the domain unencumbered by claims of need, desert, or other duties.

A distinctive conception of the human good is but one of the respects in which liberalism is more substantive, and less formal-procedural, than is widely supposed. Liberalism is committed to equality, but it needs excellence. It is committed to freedom, but it needs virtue. I argue that these sets of terms are not antinomies: An undogmatic inspection of liberal beliefs and practices reveals recognizably liberal excellences and liberal virtues.

To say that liberal orders need their own excellences and virtues is not to say that they reliably generate them. On the contrary, the liberal commitment to equality can all too easily turn into the populist resentment of distinctions, and the liberal embrace of freedom can imperceptibly shift into demands for the loosening of all restraints. One of the purposes of this book is to indicate how, both in theory and in practice, these tendencies may legitimately be resisted.

In speaking of the human good, and of liberal excellences and virtues, I necessarily adopt a critical stance toward the currently fashionable skepticism on these matters. If sufficiently rigorous criteria are employed, we are of course forced to conclude that we "know" nothing. If, however, we adopt criteria appropriate to the subject matter, it turns out that we actually know a fair amount about what promotes our individual and collective well-being. There are important inferences to be drawn from the convergence of opinion, from the winnowing and testing effects of time, from the kinds of beings we are and the circumstances in which we are placed. If it is wrong to presume knowledge when we are ignorant, it is equally wrong to presume ignorance when in fact we know. Much liberal skepticism reminds me of Hegel's remark about Descartes: What initially presents itself as fear of error eventually reveals itself as fear of truth.

The struggle between hope and fear proceeds on planes other than the epistemological. As Judith Shklar has forcefully reminded us, liberalism was born in fear – of cruelty, of bloody conflict, of arbitrary and tyrannical authority.[5] Liberal institutions are designed, therefore, to neutralize insofar as is possible the strength that would otherwise be employed to oppress the vulnerable, and to enhance to the extent feasible the ability of the weak to defend themselves. Liberal rights, and the institutions in which they may be asserted, afford the most effective bulwark against the worst abuses.

But the fact that liberalism was born in fear does not mean that it must necessarily remain there. Especially in America, the fear of tyrannical power has been enriched by the sense of vast possibility. Social ills are not "conditions" but, rather, "problems"; they need not be endured but instead can be "solved." Although such sentiments are subject to cyclical variation, it seems fair to say that American liberalism is optimistic as well as fearful, willing to invest public authority with the power to act even as it congenitally mistrusts those who wield that power.

This dualism creates a dilemma the gravity of which is in no way reduced by its familiarity. A government too weak to threaten our liberties may by that very fact be too weak to secure our rights, let alone advance our shared purposes. Conversely, a government strong enough to be effective may be difficult if not impossible to control.

This dilemma cannot be permanently solved or exorcised. At best it can be vigilantly monitored, and we may hope that temporarily aroused publics will lean against perceived excesses of both weakness and strength. The broader point is that proposals cannot be dismissed as inconsistent with liberal theory simply because they imply a strengthening of central political authority over against individuals. In each case, the risks of public power must be fairly compared with the risks of public weakness.[6]

I have already referred, more than once, to America. It is of course essential to distinguish between what is intrinsic to liberalism as such from what is characteristic of the United States as a special case of liberal thought and politics, a task for which there exists no neat mechanical procedure. I have tried to address this difficulty in part by separating the more purely theoretical arguments from their practical applications to American history and public policy, but I am under no illusions that this constitutes an adequate response. Readers from other countries will have to judge for themselves to what extent my theoretical account of liberalism has succeeded in extricating itself from the particularities of American political culture.

Nowhere is this problem more acute than in the case of religion, because nowhere is American exceptionalism more clearly manifested. By every measure, Americans remain vastly more religious, in both ritual and belief, than are the citizens of the European liberal democracies. This means, in turn, that the question of whether the relation between liberal politics and revealed religion is one of antagonism or mutual support is of special, and more than theoretical, interest for Americans. It also means, I suggest, that the American experience provides exemplary evidence – and perhaps a unique opportunity – for the exploration of this question.

Liberalism may be said to have originated in an effort to disentangle politics and religion. It has culminated in what I see as a characteristic liberal incapacity to understand religion. This incapacity has theoretical implications, for it prevents liberals from fully comprehending what is distinctive (and partisan) in their creed. Nor is it devoid of political consequences: Policies that liberals typically defend as neutral are experienced by many religious communities as hostile. Liberals see themselves as the defenders of our constitutional faith, while many of the religiously faithful see themselves as the victims of secularist aggression.

I do not mean to suggest that this clash is in the last analysis avoidable. Indeed, it may be a shadowy representation of the most important and enduring fault-line in Western culture. But I believe that we must work harder to understand the strained relations between liberalism and religion, and do so in a manner that does not begin by privileging, or derogating, the sentiments of either party. An important purpose of this book is to contribute to such a broadened awareness.

The clash over religion is only one instance of what I regard as a deep and pervasive rift in contemporary American political culture. Many Americans (I shall call them *liberationists*) believe that the state should refrain from coercive public judgments about what constitutes the good life for individuals. Legal, educational, and other institutions that embody preferences for or against different conceptions of the good must be reformed to eliminate "bias." The law should not prescribe a "narrow" definition of the family; the public schools should not be in the business of teaching "middle-class values"; society should relax its strictures against "victimless crimes."

Other Americans vigorously dissent. These *traditionalists* believe that certain core principles and virtues regulating individual choice are essential for the maintenance of social decency and cohesion, and they do not understand why verities that (in their view) have stood the test of time must now be set aside in the name of some vague notion of liberation. From this standpoint, there is no reason why the law cannot tilt toward arrangements that promote the reproduction of the species and the rearing of children; no reason why public schools should not teach honesty, hard work, and patriotism; no reason why judges and juries cannot express the community's sense of outrage in their imposition of criminal penalties.

For more than two decades, this disagreement has exerted a powerful influence on American politics. The conceptual distinction between traditionalists and liberationists has coincided with significant class divisions – in particular, between the working class and upscale professionals engaged in symbolic manipulation. Cultural and class divisions have been reinforced by the dynamics of party competition. Democratic activists have become increasingly liberationist, whereas Republicans have become increasingly traditionalist. The presidential election of 1988 bore witness to the continuing power of this cleavage.[7]

There are signs, however, of increasing ambivalence among both parties to the dispute. Many liberationists are troubled by an apparent breakdown of public order and the evident difficulty of rearing children in an environment that undermines parental discipline. (I would bet that most purchasers of *The Closing of the American Mind* were worried parents and aging baby-boomers, not blue-collar workers and religious fundamentalists.) For their part, many traditionalists are not as confident as they once were that the coercive power of the state should be fully deployed on behalf of what is morally correct. (This is not to say that they have changed their minds about the content of morality.) For example, the Supreme Court's *Webster* decision seems to have sparked considerable soul-searching among the more moderate opponents of abortion, many of whom are apparently moved by the "Who decides?" counteroffensive of the prochoice movement.

The perplexity at the heart of contemporary American culture, then, is this. On the one hand, many feel that we cannot be a well-ordered polity without some limits – some line between good and bad, permitted and forbidden – and that these limits cannot be effective without some kind of public endorsement. On the other hand, our long-standing antipathy toward central political authority causes us to suspect that the state will become dangerous if it is allowed to step unto a morally tutelary, let alone morally coercive, role. It is my thesis that an appropriate understanding of liberal virtues, excellences, and equality can reduce this tension. But I do not pretend that it can be altogether dissolved.

The foregoing observations only reinforce the note of methodological caution earlier introduced. What holds true of America may not be wholly shared by the political cultures of other liberal democracies. Moreover, it ought not be assumed that everything characteristically American can be regarded as liberal. Core American convictions may well be a complex alloy of liberalism and other traditions, such as Protestant Christianity and civic humanism. It will remain a question throughout this book whether the tensions I explore are wholly within liberalism, or between liberalism and other sources of moral authority as well.

However this may be, from beginning to end I shall be forced to engage in cultural interpretation, a task that compels me to confront a pervasive methodological debate within contemporary liberal thought. Some theorists argue that the central task is what might be called *deep description:* the elucidation of basic structures of moral belief within our political culture. This is typically (though not invariably) linked to a fashionable brand of pragmatism, which maintains that the process of justifying belief is (nothing but) tracing it to, placing it within, such cultural structures. Other theorists contend that we must engage in *wide justification* – that is, the traditional philosophical effort to scrutinize the premises of a political culture in light of (the possibility of) transcultural standards.

I argue in Chapter 2 that the wide justifiers have the better case. (I also believe that much of what liberal societies think and do can meet the test of wide justification, but that is a different story.) This does not mean, however, that deep description is trivial or irrelevant. On the contrary, the Socratic practice of moral and political philosophy I espouse takes community belief as its necessary point of departure and progresses by exploring, and trying to overcome, the incompletenesses and contradictions embedded in all such belief. The insights on which wide justification depends can be located only along this dialectical path. So it becomes a matter of considerable importance to do deep description well.

In executing this task, the cultural interpreter is eventually compelled to invoke "what we believe." But who is the "we"? Obviously it is fatuous to suggest that any society can be unanimous about anything. But it is nevertheless possible to identify central tendencies: strong and enduring aggregations of belief that substantially define a political culture, and against which alternative views must contend. Louis Hartz did something like this for the broad sweep of American history; Robert Lane, Jennifer Hochschild, and others have carried the task forward within the canons of contemporary empirical inquiry.[8] (I might add that my own direct involvement in qualitative assessments of public opinion has only strengthened my belief in the existence, and importance, of central tendencies.)

Every political culture, I would surmise, has its own distinctive core. In every society, moreover, such dominant views are generally taken as valid benchmarks for public policy, with the proviso that liberal societies typically make special efforts to reduce the costs to dissenting individuals of disagreement with these benchmarks. It would not be farfetched, in my view, to interpret the past generation of American history as a series of attempts to minimize such costs through ever widening legitimations of difference.

At some point, every political theorist comes face to face with the challenge of significance. Suppose, arguendo, that the thesis I advance in this book is correct; what difference would it make? I offer, in the form of promissory notes, three answers. First, this thesis provides a more morally and humanly attractive account of liberalism, an account that can relieve many thoughtful individuals of the need they now feel to choose between liberal principles and their own moral experience. Second, it contributes to a more usable self-understanding by providing a more explicit account of the judgments and practices characteristic of liberal societies. Third, it provides a better basis for liberal public policy. Not only does it enable us to characterize with greater confidence the zone and course of legitimate public action; it also makes possible a greater degree of accommodation among divergent forces within liberal societies.

In this connection, I should note a parallel (which I discuss in detail later) between developments on the theoretical and practical planes. In the past generation, I suggest, important forces within both American academia and public life have embraced understandings of liberalism perceived, with some justification, as hostile to traditional moral understandings. The result has been a disaster for progressive politics. If self-styled liberals cannot accommodate, and recognize their partial dependence on, the moral restraints espoused by ordinary citizens, liberalism cannot regain in practice the general acceptance needed to guide public life in a constitutional democracy. For even die-hard liberal optimists, the tenor and outcome of the 1988 U.S. presidential election should have been proof enough.

Many liberal theorists believe that the neutrality they advocate provides the best basis for the necessary accommodation. I disagree: The public perceives the liberal embrace of neutrality as part of the problem, not the solution; as a corrosive assault on, not a relegitimation of, ordinary morality. I offer my account of liberal goods, of liberal excellences and virtues, and of the diverse historical sources of the American constitutional order, as a more promising basis of reconciliation. One thing is clear: Absent a renewed partnership between liberal elites and the American public, the prospects for the resumption of progressive politics can only be regarded as bleak.

IV

It remains only to outline what is to come. Let me restate the bare essentials of my thesis. Liberalism cannot, as many contemporary theorists suppose, be understood as broadly neutral concerning the human good. It is rather committed to a distinctive conception of the human good, a conception that undergirds the liberal conception of social justice. To pursue its understanding of justice and the human good, liberal societies have over time developed their characteristic institutions and practices: representative governments, diverse societies, market economies, zones of private action. Sustaining these institutions and practices, in turn, requires of liberal citizens specific excellences and character traits: the liberal virtues. These virtues are by no means natural or innate. Liberal communities must, then, be especially attentive to the processes, formal and informal, by which these virtues are strengthened or eroded.

So much for the whole; now here is how the parts fit together: In the remainder of Part I, Chapter 2 offers a Socratic account of moral and political philosophy that is intended as an alternative to the antitheses of absolutism and relativism, foundationalism and antifoundationalism, universalism and particularism, which now dominate the methodological debate. Chapter 3 discusses in some detail my disagreements with three contemporary critics of liberalism – Michael Walzer, Roberto Unger, and Alasdair MacIntyre.

Part II (Chapters 4 to 7) explores in depth whether liberalism can be understood as neutral with respect to competing conceptions of the good.[9] The focus of my analysis is John Rawls's post–*Theory of Justice* writings, but I consider a range of other authors as well. Chapter 4 takes a general look at recent efforts to construct neutralist theories of liberalism. Chapter 5 distinguishes a number of different senses of neutrality and focuses on neutrality of procedure (neutral dialogue), which has emerged as central in the recent debate. Chapters 6 and 7 examine Rawls's attempt to construct a "political" liberalism that is morally committed on essentials while remaining (or so Rawls supposes) substantially neutral concerning the human good. Key questions are: Can a broadly Kantian understanding of "moral personality" serve as a central element of a moral but neutral liberalism? What are the conditions on the basis of which the unity of liberal politics can be secured in a manner consistent with the diversity of liberal society?

Part III (Chapters 8 to 10) offers my alternative to liberal neutrality. It rests, as I have indicated, on what I take to be a liberal account of the human good, and on the kinds of public purposes and individual claims that seem to me to flow from that account (Chapter 8). I trace the implications of this thesis for such topics as liberal justice – in particular, equality of opportunity (Chapter 9) – and the liberal virtues (Chapter 10).

Part IV (Chapters 11 to 13) moves from theory to practice.

Here I am particularly concerned with the relation between liberal politics, on the one hand, and religion, virtue, and public excellence on the other. If, as I argue in Part III, liberal polities rely on certain moral capacities among their citizens, it becomes necessary to consider both the means – formal (Chapter 11) and informal (Chapter 12) – through which these capacities may be effectively promoted and those aspects of politics and culture that tend to thwart or distort their development. These concerns, the reader will discover, were initially sparked by my extended involvement in presidential politics throughout the 1980s, but they led me to consider some broader structural parallels between liberal theory and the cultural controversies that have shaped American politics over the past generation. I have come to believe that the understanding of the public role of religion, morality, and excellence developed by key figures of the founding period and by Tocqueville offers insights that present-day liberals can ignore only at great cost.

In taking seriously (as I do throughout this book) the arguments of antiliberals and of past generations, I hope to remind today's liberals of what they too often forget: that there are ways other than their own of looking at the world. If liberal political philosophy complacently confines itself to the explication of principles and institutions whose superiority is taken for granted, it will find itself disarmed when (as is inevitable in human affairs) it is confronted with new and unexpected challenges.

This introduction has emphasized (as does the book it introduces) a set of issues that might broadly be characterized as cultural. I do not mean to suggest, however, that these are the only problems with which liberalism must now contend or that this book offers anything like a comprehensive liberal theory. I note, in conclusion, three other key areas of concern.

First, contemporary liberalism faces the problem of reforming its public institutions so as to be more capable of responding sensitively to public needs and judgments and of vigorously pursuing public purposes while safeguarding essential rights and liberties. In both Britain and the United States today, the sense is growing that the balance among these objectives has been disrupted: in Britain, by government actions less respectful than heretofore of minority interests and dissent; in the United States, by public institutions that seem unresponsive to, and incapable of acting effectively in, the public interest.[10]

Second, liberal societies must find strategies for achieving balanced and sustainable long-term economic growth. Whatever may be urged in theory against the value of growth, in practice there can be little doubt that it is required for the health and viability of liberal societies. Adequate savings, sound investment, wise management, a first-class educational system, a productive and dedicated work force – these and other preconditions of growth are appropriate subjects for public as well as private concern in the liberal state.

The third great challenge is that of inclusion. Liberal societies must somehow ensure that each of their members has a full and fair chance to achieve basic material decency, economic self-dependence, and civic competence. This is in part a matter of appropriate distributional norms, vigorously implemented. But it entails as well a general public commitment to treat every citizen as a full partner in a collective venture whose strength is a function of its weakest, not just its strongest, participants.

For the most part, as I noted earlier, this book focuses on the cultural challenges confronting the contemporary liberal state – securing unity amid diversity, fostering the liberal virtues, and strengthening social institutions (such as education and the family) that contribute to unity and virtue. But the reader should not infer from this emphasis that I consider issues of political responsiveness, economic growth, and social inclusion to be less fundamental, or that cultural challenges can be adequately addressed in practice without progress on these other fronts as well.

Chapter 2

Peirce's cable and Plato's cave: objectivity and community in contemporary political philosophy

I

The title of Richard Bernstein's book *Beyond Objectivism and Relativism*[1] neatly sums up a central strand of discussion within contemporary political and moral theory. The guiding idea is this: The kinds of objectivity claims characteristic of the philosophic tradition from (say) Plato to Kant cannot be redeemed, but what is widely taken to be a consequence of this – the relativization of truth claims, both scientific and normative – is unacceptable. There is therefore a felt need for some *via media* or, alternatively, for a redefinition of the alternatives that removes the distress that is frequently felt at the prospect of being compelled to choose between them.

A typical response to this need has been to situate individual propositions and judgments within discursive communities. Assessments of rationality, truth, and validity can be made relative to the constitutive commitments of particular communities. There is, however, no neutral external standpoint from which such assessments can be made across the boundaries of such communities. Thus, Richard Rorty asserts, "There will be no way to rise above the language, culture, institutions and practices one has adopted and view all these as on a par with all the others."[2] To accept this claim "is to give up on the idea that there can be reasons for using languages as well as reasons within languages for believing statements."[3] Alasdair MacIntyre has recently defended a similar position. As Charles Larmore summarizes it:

MacIntyre's principal claim is that rationality – in ethics as elsewhere – is possible only within a tradition. Reasons for belief and action . . . cannot properly be thought to be recognizable by any rational being as such, since the justification of belief and action must always rely upon given commitments that are part of some particular tradition.[4]

This abandonment of the traditionally central philosophic aspiration toward transcendent objectivity is said to pose no problems. For those who can get beyond the metaphysical impulse, Rorty insists, "there is no such thing as the 'relativist predicament,' just as for someone who thinks that there is no God there will be no such thing as blasphemy."[5] On the contrary, it is the misguided quest for transcendence that lies at the heart of the relativist cul-de-sac: "The effort to make rationality consist in a critical distance toward all tradition must end, if consistent, in the loss of the means for any significant form of rational thought."[6]

We all live in Plato's cave, say these contemporary advocates of situated reason. We shall stop trying to escape from it when we realize that there is no outside and no sun, but only an infinity of paths to new caverns. Instead of searching for the way out, then, we shall settle down to the real business of describing the shadows on the walls of the cave, or (if we are Rortean "strong poets") of casting new ones, or (if we are Walzerian "social critics") of trying to make our subterranean abode more decent and commodious.

The trajectory of much recent moral and social theory can be understood in this light. As John Rawls has shifted from theory conducted *sub specie aeternitatis* to theses drawn from, and addressed to, a specific public culture, he insists that there has been no loss – but only a redefinition – of objectivity.[7] In *After Virtue*,[8] MacIntyre at once rejects the metaphysical basis of Aristotelian moral theory and maintains that what remains – an account of the virtues within the context of social practices – is enough to serve as an antidote to the arbitrary subjectivity of emotivism. Michael Walzer argues that views

23

of justice are rooted in "social meaning," which varies from community to community, but that the absence of an external standpoint poses no deep difficulties because principles internal to communities are perfectly adequate to the task of social criticism. In a more radical vein, Rorty seeks to dissolve the opposition between relativism and objectivity, in part by exorcising the impulse to push beyond community solidarity to some transcendental ground.

I argue that the effort to transcend this opposition, although important, has been misconceived in ways that have disfigured it. The methodological discussion has been conducted at a debilitating remove from the actual phenomena of society and of inquiry that it is intended to characterize. When we attend to these phenomena, we cannot help noticing ways in which moral and social thought breaks through the bounds of specific community practices, not in response to some external and exorcisable metaphysical need, but rather in accordance with its own inner and inescapable activity. Social philosophy that begins by seriously attending to the contradictions of everyday social practice necessarily ends by moving some considerable distance from its point of departure.

The very notion of exorcising the impulse to transcendence, rooted in Wittgenstein and Heidegger, has become one of the central dogmas of our times. But it cannot withstand examination. For not only is it oddly, abstractly removed from experiences it purports to defend; but also it rests on the fallacy of attributing to philosophy per se every mistake that one philosopher – Descartes – committed in executing a single, idiosyncratic agenda. It is the drive to exorcise the transcendental impulse that is most in need of exorcism from contemporary thought. As Thomas Nagel has put it, "To redefine the aim [of philosophy] so that its achievement is largely guaranteed, through various forms of reductionism, relativism, or historicism, is a form of cognitive wish-fulfillment. Philosophy cannot take refuge in reduced ambitions."[9]

II

Theorists who seek to situate philosophy within specific social or discursive communities frequently talk as though such communities are spheres within which coherent agreement prevails, and as though the only significant differences of belief lie across community boundaries. This view is not entirely mistaken. There may well be certain core notions to which the overwhelming majority of a particular community subscribes and which help constitute its special identity. But closer inspection always reveals tensions among beliefs held within communities.

These tensions make their appearance in a number of guises. In developing his conception of "social criticism," Walzer has focused on contradictions between social principles and social practices – for example, between the abstract norm of equal citizenship and the concrete denial of voting rights. He suggests – correctly, in my view – that such contradictions exist in every community and that social criticism is therefore always possible.[10] There is, however, a complication. Walzer assumes that the critic appeals to principles in order to undermine practices. But surely the reverse is also an option. In the early days of the Nazi regime, for example, some judges employed traditional legal practices as arguments against the worst excesses of the government's arbitrary decrees. In South Africa today, practices have arisen that represent small chinks of decency in the wall of apartheid, and they are defended as such by many reformers who do not possess (or dare not deploy) a developed counter-ideology. When principles clash with practices, it is not obvious which should give way – a perplexity well captured in the two-way revisability of Rawlsian reflective equilibrium. What is obvious is that such clashes represent problems – for individual thought as well as social policy – that cannot easily be ignored.

Another important form of intrasocietal tension arises when core principles or commitments contradict, not practices, but one another. Consider the First Amendment to the

Constitution. The Supreme Court is now wrestling with the fact that its efforts to apply the free-exercise clause have collided with the establishment clause, and vice versa. Or consider equality of opportunity. In an important analysis, James Fishkin has shown that three widely held American (and liberal) principles – merit-based social assignment, equal life-chances for individuals, and substantial family autonomy – contradict one another in a wide range of actual cases.[11] Consider, finally, the well-known debate between Rawls and Robert Nozick over the proper role of individual desert and entitlement in a theory of justice. Rawls appeals to the intuitive idea that individual endowments are the fruits of nature and chance, hence arbitrary from a moral point of view. (This is *our* idea; it would be rejected, for example, by a range of Eastern religions.) Nozick appeals to the counterintuition that these endowments are an important part of what makes us separate and distinctive individuals and that to reject their moral significance is to undermine an important part of the individualism that makes liberalism attractive (to liberals, anyway). Once again, this is a clash between commitments widely held within one and the same community.

A third source of contradiction arises in the effort to interpret and apply principles not themselves seen as controversial. For example, the Fourteenth Amendment guarantees the equal protection of the laws to all persons. But who, exactly, are "persons"? Some philosophical and religious traditions insist that fetuses are persons, whereas others deny it, and both enjoy substantial support within our community.

Yet another kind of contradiction arises in the course of what might be called *first-order reflection on common maxims* – the kind of reflection that arises in the ordinary course of daily life or in the normal operation of a legal system. At the outset of Plato's *Republic*, for example, Cephalus suggests that justice consists in paying one's debts and telling the truth. Socrates quickly persuades him that matters are not so simple: One wouldn't, for example, return a weapon to a friend who had gone mad. The appeal is to a background understanding of justice as standing in some relation to the human good as well as to rules.

Finally, I should note the phenomenon of *multiple membership*, easily overlooked if the focus of analysis is citizenship. One and the same person may well be a parent, child, professional, religious congregant, and possessor of a racial or ethnic identity – all these alongside membership in the political community. It frequently happens that the moral requirements of differing memberships come into conflict, and it is by no means obvious how they are to be rank-ordered. This is the stuff of tragedy, and also the source of provocatively unusual commitments: Recall E. M. Forster's famous comment that in case of conflict between friendship and politics, he hoped he would have the courage to betray his country.

III

This analysis of social contradictions could be lengthened, but I have said enough to make the basic point. The next step is to insist that for all practical purposes, such contradictions are inevitable within each and every community.

There are many reasons for believing this to be the case. To begin with, the sheer diversity of individual human types guarantees differences of outlook, no matter how strong the homogenizing force of public socialization may be. (Some would add that gender-based differences of social and moral outlook are fundamental and ineradicable.)

Second, reasonable individuals exercising their judgment on common problems will inevitably arrive, in many cases, at differing conclusions. The explanation is to be found in what Rawls calls the "burdens of reason": complex and conflicting evidence; vague concepts; a multiplicity of relevant considerations whose relative weighting is disputed; and so forth.[12]

A third source of contradiction lies in the clash of interests among groups, classes, regions, sectors of society, or whatever. To the extent that social conflict is settled by means other than force, each contending social party will press its interests in part by generalizing its claims. The resulting bodies of more or less systematic argumentation will reflect, though not precisely mirror, the diversity of interests that engendered them. To this may be added the observation that no effort to expunge social diversity – or, for that matter, multiple membership – in the name of totalitarian citizenship has ever succeeded or ever could do so.

Finally, political communities develop and change over time, growing through accretion as well as design. But although the initial strata of practice and belief may be overlaid by social responses to succeeding challenges, the residue of earlier history does not simply disappear. It remains generally present in the form of cultural memory, and more specifically present in the consciousness of particular social groups. (An example of this would be the persistence of Jeffersonian agrarianism as an element in our understanding of democratic virtues.)

IV

If social contradictions are inevitable, so is the consciousness of them among at least some reflective members of each community. This creates an existential problem. For reflective individuals will experience contradictory imperatives as imposing demands on them that by definition cannot all be honored, at least not fully and simultaneously. It is this experience of practical contradiction that in part gives rise to the demand for increased coherence of both practice and belief.

I say "in part" because something else is also at work. The drive for what might be called bare or formal rationality – that is, noncontradiction within a system of belief – can be observed among members of cultures whose substantive commitments vary widely. The Rawlsian conception of reflective equilibrium as a coherent scheme within which consistency is achieved among principles, and between

28

principles and individual cases, is simply the expression of this drive in a particular philosophic idiom. As a general matter, we feel that if our beliefs on issues of any importance clash with one another, matters cannot simply be left as they are. (This is *not* to say that at the end of the day, all such clashes will be resolved.) Contradictions on the level of thought are distinguishable from, but are no less intolerable than, contradictory imperatives of action.

Political philosophy as I understand it is in the consequence of the interaction of the two basic phenomena just described: the inner contradictions of social life, and the commitment to noncontradictory systems of practice and belief on the part at least of reflective individuals within particular societies.

If this is correct, there are two kinds of circumstances in which political philosophy would lose its motive, or its point. A society might conceivably come into being in which all inner contradictions have been overcome; this is the classic Marxian scenario for the withering away of philosophy (and much else besides).

Alternatively, one might imagine a society whose members were no longer moved by criteria of formal rationality, that is, who were simply not bothered by contradictions among beliefs or between beliefs and practices. On my account, anyway, this would amount to a fundamental change in the meaning of being human. Nevertheless, this is what the call for the exorcism of the metaphysical impulse reduces to.

The exorcists, of course, have a different view of the matter. Rorty's understanding seems to be that political communities are collections of what he calls (borrowing a term from Sellars) "we-intentions": roughly, things we (all) believe to be valid and binding (on all of us). Within liberal communities, anyway, everything is in reasonably good order. But within this generally cheerful picture of consensus is a superfluous but potentially disruptive force: the "metaphysical" need to justify social institutions and beliefs through appeal to transcultural, generally valid principles or facts. This need is superfluous because there is no problem to which it is the solution; potentially disruptive because it cannot be satisfied but undermines what ought to be, and would otherwise be, our sense of satisfaction with what we already have and know.

My objection to this way of looking at things is twofold. First, as I have already argued, absent heroic assumptions about the coherence of political communities, reflection is prompted not by some exogenous and dispensable metaphysical itch but by the inner contradictions of daily life. It is possible, I suppose, to imagine a world in which those contradictions would not be experienced as problematic. But it would be a science-fiction world, not ours, and it would be a world in which philosophy (on virtually *any* understanding) would lose all point.

My second objection is that even if, against all odds, one's own community achieves inner coherence, reflective citizens cannot help becoming aware of other communities resting on very different principles and containing very different ways of life. (The Greeks already had this awareness in ample measure, and we do too.) Even if (and this is counterfactual for us) particular communities do not make universal claims that conflict with one another (e.g., freedom of speech versus the punishment of blasphemy), the experience of other societies typically leads reflective individuals to doubt the full adequacy of their own.

The reason is straightforward: No society is fully universal; every society picks out some favored goals and ways of life while discouraging or repressing others. No matter where one lives, some arguably valuable collective objectives are not pursued and some arguably admirable human traits are not developed. Acquaintance with other societies forces upon us an awareness of the partiality and cost of our own. Wherever it may lead, such reflection asks us to take seriously standards of social justification other than the ones we ordinarily employ. And even if we end up by reaffirming our point of departure, it can no longer be on the basis of simple habit or loyalty.

Our consciousness is changed, as well, by the effort to

30

cope with contradictions internal to our own society. At least three different kinds of possible responses may be discerned. The first is to affirm a multiplicity of relevant considerations but to deny that any one of them is of general validity. Conflicts between free exercise and establishment of religion, or between family autonomy and the best interests of the child, or whatever, are to be resolved by giving to each competing consideration the weight for which the features of a particular situation seem to call. Of possible strategies, this response stays closest to prereflective consciousness, but it nevertheless requires two important innovations. The balancer must at least deny the claims of the many citizens who will seek to accord one or another competing principle absolute weight. The balancer must also be prepared to defend some account of judgment on the basis of which the particular balances he or she strikes can be rendered more broadly compelling – an account that by its very nature must invoke considerations not fully reducible to any one of the competing principles, or to all of them together.

A second response to social contradiction is to select from among the conflicting principles some subset for special privileged status: A is the *summum bonum;* B has lexical priority over C; D trumps E; and so forth. Clearly this selection cannot be made on the basis of the competing principles themselves. Some appeal must be made to considerations outside the immediate sphere of conflict. It is possible that such considerations could be other features of what we already say or do within our community. But this move depends on the assumption that these latter features, unlike the former, are not socially contested. For if they are contested, this strategy produces a regress rather than a resolution.

A third response to social contradiction moves from the truism that *all* the contradictory propositions cannot be true to the suspicion that *none* of them is – at least not straightforwardly and simply. This suspicion gives rise, in turn, to a dialectical process that searches for some basis on which the initial competing views can be understood as partial and incomplete descriptions of a more comprehensive truth.

(This is the sort of process one sees at various points in Platonic dialogues, and somewhat differently in Hegel.)

I don't want to dwell on the important and interesting differences among these three responses but, rather, on what they have in common. Each represents some kind of break with ordinary consciousness, some felt need to judge that the world of everyday belief is not well (enough) ordered. Each of them gestures toward the Platonic characterization of quotidian moral and social life as the cave and to the implied contrast with something outside it. Each of them, that is, tacitly embraces some distinction between opinion and knowledge. Their motive, to repeat, is not any illicit, destructive, expungible metaphysical impulse but, rather, the presuppositions and desires of consciousness itself.

V

Note that at the outset, and perhaps much longer than that, the distinction between knowledge and opinion is not based on an affirmative understanding of what it means to know something, let alone "criteria" of knowledge. There is a strong but vague negative sense that contradiction, one-sidedness, and instability are unsatisfactory, and that it would be a fine thing if our understanding could become more consistent, comprehensive, and secure. It does not follow that we can offer a compelling definition of knowledge (as anything other than other-than-opinion), that we can adequately characterize the relation between knowledge and opinion, or that we can attain the other-than-opinion for which we strive.

In Plato's dialogues, for example, we find three quite different representations of what it means to reach consciousness of other-than-opinion. In the *Apology*, among other places, we find Socrates expressing the view that transcendence of opinion is the knowledge of ignorance – a well-founded judgment about the inadequacy of opinion, a negation not however wholly barren of affirmative consequences (at least for the inquiring mind).

In the *Gorgias*, there is a further step. Responding to Cal-licles, Socrates declares: "My position has always been the same: though I have no real knowledge of the truth of these matters, yet just as on the present occasion, I have never encountered anyone who was able to maintain a different position and not come off covered with ridicule. Accordingly, I must assume that matters stand as stated" (509a). Justified belief, then, is opinion that has survived the most rigorous process of dialectical testing in contestation with the available contrasting views. Although it is always possible that some-body will devise a new and conclusive refutation of the So-cratic position, or a more attractive alternative to it, tested belief nonetheless enjoys a cognitive and practical status dif-ferent from – and higher than – unexamined opinion.

Finally, of course, there is the full-blown "metaphysics of presence" of the *Republic* and the *Symposium*. At the end of our long, wearying journey through the contradictions of cognition and craving, there is an end to doubt and a satisfaction of desire: our direct apprehension of what is "be-yond being" and is "in a certain way" the ground of all beings – that is, of their existence, mutual coherence, and collective intelligibility. To be sure, as Socrates announces this meta-phorical possibility in the *Republic*, he frames it with the aside that "A god doubtless knows if it happens to be true" (517b). Still, this picture has held a powerful attraction for, and has exercised an extraordinary influence on, wave after wave of Western philosophers who agreed on little else.

What unites these conceptions of knowledge as other-than-opinion is the presumption that the road to knowledge starts from, and goes through, opinion. The Socratic–Platonic stance toward the realm of opinion was far from totally neg-ative. That tradition saw opinion not simply as the source of error and uncertainty but also as the repository of dim but suggestive apprehensions of the truth. The movement to-ward truth occurs – can occur *only* – when these apprehen-sions are compared with one another and tested against the evidence of logic and experience. For Socrates and Plato (Ar-istotle is squarely in this camp as well), it would have seemed counterproductive, almost crazy, to begin the quest for truth by discarding all doubtful opinions. This would have been like denying ourselves the use of our senses in scientific inquiry just because the raw evidence they furnish can sometimes lead us astray.

This line of argument indicates that accepting the distinction between knowledge and opinion does not require us to embrace the denigration of opinion characteristic of Descartes and the tradition he inspired. This conclusion is of particular importance for the conduct of moral and political inquiry. The Greeks viewed the moral and political realm as standing in the most intimate possible connection with opinion. The effort to approach that realm "scientifically," by denying opinion as the point of departure, was in that view to lose touch with the phenomena to be explicated. If knowledge is understood in the Cartesian way, therefore, one is forced to choose between a set of abstract propositions far removed from the real experience of moral–political life and the conclusion that ethics and politics are matters of opinion which can at best be interpreted but to which judgments of truth and falsity do not apply. (Contemporary relativism is thus an understandable response to this restricted set of alternatives. It is, so to speak, Cartesianism with a minus sign, and it remains within the same horizon of presuppositions.) But if knowledge is understood in the Greek way, then moral–political inquiry – the systematic comparison and testing of opinion – can be seen as a legitimate branch of philosophy.

This brings me to a second important contrast between the Greek and Cartesian understandings of the distinction between knowledge and opinion. Even if knowledge is understood, along the lines of the *Republic* and *Symposium*, as direct apprehension of what is certain, stable, and ontologically fundamental, it does not follow that philosophical argument takes the form simply of logical reasoning from such direct apprehensions. A portion of philosophy may (see *Republic* 511b–c), but the process of dialectical argument leading to direct apprehension is equally, or perhaps more, important.

34

Philosophy, then, is not simply mathematical in form, and the working model of truth generation is not simply derivations from the most parsimonious possible set of basic axioms. Nor is philosophical argument construed as a single strand leading from premise to conclusion, but rather as a multiplicity of mutually reinforcing considerations jointly (though perhaps not individually) capable of determining the intellect.

We are led, then, to Peirce's view that philosophy ought to "trust rather to the multitude and variety of its arguments than to the conclusiveness of any one. Its reasoning should not form a chain which is no stronger than its weakest link, but a cable whose fibers may be ever so slender, provided they are sufficiently numerous and intimately connected."[13] This view suggests, in turn, that philosophical reasoning is not as far removed from moral and political deliberation as is often supposed. For in both cases we are engaged in a process of scrutinizing opinions in order to arrive at descriptions (of what is the right thing to do or say) that have withstood every test we can devise and which are therefore candidates for informed agreement. Philosophy, like deliberation, is the collective effort of preparing ourselves to recognize what is worthy of our assent.

A standard theme of much recent philosophy has been the critique of Cartesian "foundationalism." The burden of the preceding argument is that it is perfectly possible to reject Descartes root and branch while holding fast to the distinction between knowledge and opinion and to the conception of the philosophic enterprise to which it is linked. Knowledge need not be understood as clear and distinct perception; opinion need not be regarded as the enemy of knowledge; philosophy need not be conducted on the model of mathematics.

There is a further point. Cartesian foundationalism is often thought to embody a singular "first philosophy" on which all other parts of philosophy depend. The rejection of foundationalism seems therefore to entail the rejection of such dependence.

In an important paper ("The Independence of Moral Theory") written more than a decade ago, John Rawls applies this logic to the Cartesianism of analytic philosophy. We do not, or so he argues, have to do theory of meaning, or epistemology, or metaphysics, or the philosophy of mind, or anything else, as propaedeutics to moral and political philosophy. On the contrary, the logical starting point is our "substantive moral conceptions." If anything, moral epistemology is dependent on those conceptions rather than the reverse: "Just as the theory of meaning as we now know it depends on the development of logic from . . . Frege to Godel, so the further advance of moral philosophy depends upon a deeper understanding of the structure of moral conceptions and their connections with human sensibility."[14] There are, then, many (perhaps indefinitely many) possible points of departure for inquiry, the choice among which will be relative to the particular subject under consideration.

This argument seems correct as far as it goes, and it has certainly buttressed a welcome return of moral and political philosophy from its Babylonian exile. But it has also led to a widely shared conclusion that does not seem to me to follow from its premises, namely, that moral and political philosophy are wholly independent of, and unaffected by, other branches of philosophical inquiry. This has licensed an outbreak of Kantian social philosophy without transcendental idealism, of Aristotelian practical philosophy without metaphysical biology, and so on.

All of this strikes me as a mistake. Moral and political philosophy may well *begin* with inquiry into their own characteristic phenomena, but they cannot *continue* indefinitely without bumping into premises characteristic of other parts of philosophy. There may not be any kind of hierarchical relation between the moral and the extramoral, but the two kinds of considerations are linked and stand or fall together. So, for example, Rawls's rejection of desert as a principle of social justice turns out to be connected logically to a particular view of the core identity of persons. To the extent that this notion of identity seems unattractive, we have a good reason for questioning the expulsion of desert from justice (and vice versa, of course). Similarly, it does not seem possible that moral and political philosophy can remain unaffected by developments in the natural sciences, even though most contemporary social philosophy proceeds as though it were totally autonomous from such mundane considerations.

Beginning from everyday opinion, then, the dialectic of social inquiry breaks through the boundaries of the "social" and generates a rich network of philosophical connections. Far from being a problem, this is in fact a great advantage, because it generates multiple points at which an overall point of view (which integrates, say, moral, natural-scientific, and epistemological propositions) can be evaluated. "Wide reflective equilibrium" seems to me to rest on an adequate degree of coherence not just between moral intuitions and moral principles but also across the full range of considerations implicit in a particular view, as well as on the appeal of any one of them considered in isolation from the rest.

The force of this thesis cannot be evaded by the late-Rawlsian assertion that good social theory (good liberal theory, anyway) is "political, not metaphysical." For even if the conception of free and equal moral personality, which Rawls links with liberal social principles, is understood relative to our culture rather than to transcendental idealism, it is always possible to criticize that understanding of personality in the name of some contrasting moral or religious conceptions, many of which are present as minority or dissenting strands within our culture. The adequacy of "external" propositions to which a social philosophy turns out on reflection to be linked is always relevant to our judgment of that philosophy.

In short, social philosophy has its characteristic point of departure and set of concerns, but it is not in the full sense independent of the rest of philosophy. The rejection of Cartesian foundationalism does not then lead, as some have supposed, to the practice of social philosophy as a self-enclosed activity, descriptive of its own domain and self-justifying with reference only to the adequacy of that description.

37

VI

While social philosophy, for the reasons sketched, must begin from and drive beyond local opinion, it would be misguided to suppose that this inner telos can be wholly realized. Two countervailing forces are crucial: Morality is in part local, particular, community-based, historical; and reason may not be fully competent to resolve contradictions among considerations relevant to the rational determination of moral judgment.

To begin with, it is surely a mistake to insist that all meaningful norms are somehow universal. There are of course many simply (and properly) local customs. The normative force of the observation that "this is the way we do it in our family" does not rest on the tacit assertion that "all families should do it this way." My point, rather, is that there are discernible limits to localism. Most recent theorists who have flirted with localist arguments have concluded that local variety is overlaid on, and is constrained by, a moral understanding that we are prepared (indeed, find it necessary) to generalize.

This bedrock morality is defended, not metaphysically, but rather with reference to the general features of human beings and of the circumstances in which they are ordinarily placed. Michael Walzer, for example, espouses a "minimal code" common to different communities and valid across, not merely within, their boundaries. Although the outlines of prohibitions against "murder, deception, betrayal, gross cruelty" must be filled in with the details of a particular culture, they nonetheless "provide a framework for any possible (moral) life."[15] H. L. A. Hart's description of the "minimum content of natural law" may be understood in similar terms: "We could not subtract the general wish to live and leave intact concepts like danger and safety, harm and benefit, need and function, disease and cure."[16]

It is some version of the minimal code that gives Judith Shklar's recent emphasis on injustice, vice, and victimization its special force. We may argue interminably about distributional entitlements, but the violation of basic decency – of the rules that make human life possible and tolerable – is an undeniable affront. The victim's cry – it isn't right, it isn't fair – is not so much claiming a share as it is expressing fear, suffering, and humiliation. Once our attention is sufficiently engaged for us to be capable of "rational empathy," of understanding what it must be like to be *that* person undergoing *that* indignity, our response must be one of distress and indignation. And rights are to be understood in the first instance as individual protections against breaches of the minimal code, whether by government or by concentrations of private power.[17]

It is, I think, Stuart Hampshire who has best captured the complex relation between the local – particular, historical, community-based – and the universal elements of moral philosophy. He writes:

The dependence of very young children on adult nurture, the onset of sexual maturity, the instinctual desires associated with motherhood, the comparative helplessness of the old, are all biological features and a standard outline of human life, which may be appealed to as imposing some limits on moral requirements at all times and in all places. [Moreover,] some moral injunctions and prohibitions are explained and justified, when challenged, by reference to the unvarying dispositions and needs of normal human beings, living anywhere in any normal society: for example, the requirement not to cause suffering when this can be avoided. On the other hand, some injunctions and prohibitions, as in duties arising from kinship, duties of politeness, of many kinds of loyalty, are in fact traced back, when challenged, to a particular way of life in which these duties are essential elements.[18]

It is only necessary to add that arguments from local custom are not irrevocably and hermetically sealed off from external critique. It is hardly satisfactory for child abusers to defend their practices by pointing to established multigenerational patterns of behavior within their families, or even within their entire society. In all such cases, the critic properly appeals to the limits of moral possibility that are defined by the basic framework.[19]

The extent to which philosophical reflection can move beyond the minimal code remains an open question. There is no guarantee that the desire for consistency and intelligibility animating moral and political philosophy can be gratified in the process of inquiry. It need not, for example, lead to a fully articulated rule-morality in the Kantian mode but may instead vindicate a wide scope for *phronesis*. It need not lead to the identification of a single highest good in the Platonic (and in some readings Aristotelian) fashion but, rather, may leave us with some version of intuitionism across a range of basic normative considerations. Nor need it lead to the elimination of fundamental moral conflict: The outcome of inquiry may well be the heightened sense of tragic choices articulated by Bernard Williams and Martha Nussbaum or of moral complexity by Charles Larmore.[20]

David Mapel has argued that the heterogeneity of our conception of the good (and, more broadly, of what is morally relevant to social decision) means that we cannot move beyond "commonsense pluralism." Either we abstract so far from heterogeneity (Bruce Ackerman's manna) that our philosophical conclusions are all but useless in practice, or we acknowledge that, at least within very broad limits, moral conflict can be resolved only politically, by and within each community.[21]

James Fishkin has offered a similar proposal – intuitionism, "ideals without an ideal" – as his version of the *via media* between objectivism and relativism:

> Such a position . . . lacks any general priority relations among its conflicting parts. How its principles are to be balanced remains an open question, to be faced in particular cases as they present themselves. It leaves unclear how much one conflicting principle is to be emphasized, compared to another.[22]

Now it may turn out that this is the best that we can do. Still, it seems to me worthwhile to explore a possibility that stands between intuitionism and what Fishkin calls "rigorism" – the application of objective principles without exception or overriding. Brian Barry has sketched this intermediate possibility in his discussion of incommensurability. The idea is this: It is not necessary to (be able to) reduce competing moral considerations to a common measure in order to make publicly defensible choices: "One can sensibly speak of rational choices on the basis of principles which are not all reducible to a single one provided only that the (actual or hypothetical) choices made show a consistent pattern of preference."[23] I suggest that there are widely shared, and well-founded, views as to the appropriate shape of social indifference curves: for example, that only an emergency threatening national survival could possibly justify the temporary suspension of fundamental rights such as habeas corpus. In Chapter 8, I explore the hypothesis that the rankings we are apt to establish "at the margin" among valued goods can be understood as flowing from a consistent social philosophy, even though there is no common unit of value (utility, primary goods, manna, or whatever) in light of which these goods can be rendered commensurable.

Even if successful, this strategy in no way entails the embrace of full-blown Platonic objectivism. For all the reasons sketched in this chapter, I am persuaded that the inner movement of the reflective consciousness engenders a philosophically significant distance from local perspectives. It does not follow that this initial gesture of negation will be succeeded by any adequate affirmation. Nor does it follow that the dialectical movement from community A will necessarily converge on the point reached by the comparable path from community B. The outcome of moral and political philosophy as I conceive it cannot be deduced from its formal features but can become known only through the process of inquiry itself.

Chapter 3

Contemporary critics of liberalism

The primary purpose of this book is to reject a pervasive theoretical understanding of liberalism as neutral regarding human goods and to replace it with an alternative understanding of liberalism in which specific goods and virtues figure centrally. My project, then, unfolds as a disputation within the liberal tradition, broadly defined.

But there is an impediment to the execution of this project. Even though events in Europe, the Soviet Union, and China have significantly undercut the credibility of Marxism, the critique of liberalism continues unabated. Today's critics appeal not to discredited ideas such as the dictatorship of the proletariat and the withering away of the state but, rather, to aspirations alive and potent within the contemporary public culture of the West. Readers may well feel that a dispute remaining within the ambit of liberalism is bound to be a somewhat scholastic affair unless these far-reaching criticisms of liberalism are addressed.

This is by no means a simple task. The literature of criticism is vast, and it assumes no one canonical form. Still, certain characteristic political themes may be discerned. Liberalism is said to undermine community, to restrict unduly opportunities for democratic participation, to create inegalitarian hierarchy, and to reinforce egoistic social conflict at the expense of the common good. Community, democracy, equality, virtue – these constitute the mantra of contemporary antiliberalism.

Beyond this core, as we shall see, the critics diverge. Some, for example, view liberalism as constricting personal freedom, whereas others regard the liberal emphasis on freedom as thwarting a fuller human identity that can transpire only within communities of tradition. Some argue that the universalism characteristic of liberalism is both false and dangerous and should be replaced by an endorsement of local particularism; others believe that liberal universalism is correct in form (as a mode of argument) but mistaken in content.

In this chapter, I do not try to deal comprehensively with the contemporary criticism of liberalism.[1] Rather, I discuss at some length three of its important representative figures: Michael Walzer, Roberto Unger, and Alasdair MacIntyre. My purpose is twofold. First, I want to argue that the criticism misfires. Liberalism does not undermine community; it is a form of community. Liberalism does not reject virtue; indeed, it needs a wide range of virtues to maintain itself. Liberalism does not thwart democratic participation; it contends only that democracy must be situated within a broader moral framework that includes both collective purposes and individual rights. Liberalism does not deny equality; it proposes an understanding of moral equality compatible with differences of individual endowment and social outcome.[2]

My second purpose is at once personal and philosophical. Some readers of my previous work have classified it as skeptical of liberalism, or even as antiliberal. Jeremy Waldron has filed me under the heading of "The New Communitarianism," whereas Nancy Rosenblum labels me a "theorist of latent community" and discusses me in parallel with Walzer and Unger.[3] Will Kymlicka, by contrast, regards me as a "worried liberal," which is closer to my own intention (and self-understanding).[4] In this chapter, I explain my disagreements, which I regard as fundamental, with contemporary critics of liberalism. In so doing, I offer some preliminary indications of how the concern for community and virtue, for example, is not only not antithetical to liberalism but perfectly consistent with liberalism rightly understood. That is, I provide grounds for believing that the debate (and alleged need to choose sides) between liberal neutrality and

43

antiliberalism is poorly framed. For there is a third way: a nonneutral, substantive liberalism committed to its own distinctive conception of the good, broadly (though not boundlessly) respectful of diversity, and supported by its own canon of the virtues.

I

Most commentators have stressed the importance of community (or the "common life") in Walzer's thought. Nancy Rosenblum has remarked that while his argument begs for the theory of community, he does not supply one.[5] I would put it slightly differently: Walzer tacitly offers two accounts of community, which do not altogether cohere. One is the notion of the *moral* community in which individuals are conjoined by their shared understandings of social goods. The other is the notion of the *legal* community in which individuals come together through specific acts of consent that create and delimit sovereign authority. Walzer's guiding, but questionable, assumption is that moral and legal communities are congruent, that the community of shared meanings is also the sovereign nation-state.

There are, to be sure, important examples of such a congruence – Japan, for instance. But there seem to be at least equally important examples of dissonance: the Basques, Tamil separatists, African tribalism, and warring religious groups in Lebanon and Northern Ireland. Or consider Soviet Jews, many of whom found new individual and collective identity in the rediscovered precepts of a religious-historical community, an identity that solidified their opposition to the Soviet state. Walzer is not unaware of this possible disjunction between legal and moral communities, remarking at one point that the adjustment of the resulting tension "must itself be worked out politically, and its precise character will depend on understandings shared among the citizens about the value of cultural diversity, local autonomy, and so on."[6] But what if there are no such shared understandings?

Walzer is willing to push the idea of moral community a

very long way. He explicitly rejects Marx's dictum that a community's ruling ideas are nothing more than the ideas of the ruling class, forcibly imposed on subordinate classes: "A people's culture is always a joint, even if it isn't an entirely cooperative, production."[7] Still, he does admit a limited case in which moral community vanishes: "Slaves and masters do not inhabit a world of shared meanings. The two groups are simply at war."[8] Within this schema, then, it becomes in each individual case an empirical question whether Gramsci's account of hegemony or Hegel's account of slavery provides the more appropriate understanding of actual relations between dominant and dominated social groups.[9]

This modification of strict congruence between moral and legal community moves us some distance toward reality. But it is still too starkly dichotomous. Consider the classical account of the origin of liberalism in response to seventeenth-century wars of religion. In this account, the doctrine of toleration is an agreement that permits disagreement; or, to put it slightly differently, it provides the basis for a political community in which some meanings are shared and others are not. Aristotle was surely right to say that individuals who share nothing cannot constitute a community. But it does not follow that in order to be a community, individuals must have everything in common.

Liberalism is an account of the manner in which diverse moral communities can coexist within a single legal community. Because (in a well-ordered liberal polity), the different moral communities jointly acknowledge the force of liberal legal principles, the relationships among these communities can be mediated by persuasion rather than force. And in Walzer's own terms, a rich, complex political community can emerge from the clash of interpretations as to the "meaning" of juridical liberal principles. It does not follow, however, that every difference within a liberal community can be traced back to varying interpretations of shared principles. Some differences are bedrock.

Liberalism is not the antithesis of community but, rather, a conception of community framed in response to the particular circumstances of modern society. Walzer's account of community has the merit of forcefully reraising the question whether the liberal account is empirically and normatively adequate. But he has not as yet resolved that question in his own favor.

Of the many important features of Walzer's recent thought, none has proved more controversial than his alleged "relativism." Methodologically, this relativism opposes the stances of Plato and Descartes: We should neither leave the cave nor impatiently dismiss the opinions that constitute our everyday world.[10] Substantively, it appears at first glance to abandon the chief goal of traditional political philosophy, the comparative evaluation of regimes and ways of life: "There is no way to rank and order these worlds with regard to their understanding of social goods."[11]

Though sweeping in its claims, Walzer's relativism is actually quite constrained. To begin with, he deploys a non-contextual, universalistic, and thoroughly traditional conception of philosophic truth. His entire theory of justice is presented as a transcontextual metatheory, structurally valid for all communities (though substantively different for each). And the nerve of his relativism – the assertion that it is not possible to rank-order social worlds – is itself put forward not as an interpretation of *our* experience but as a universal truth. (If this assertion were understood as relative to our culture, there would be no obvious way of adjudicating between it and the competing nonrelativistic claims advanced by other cultures.)

Walzer's philosophic traditionalism emerges clearly in comparison to the characteristic stances of "postmodern" thinkers. Richard Rorty, for example, distinguishes between two ways in which reflective human beings try to give sense to their lives: telling the story of their relation to their community ("solidarity"), and describing themselves as standing in immediate relation to some transcommunal reality ("objectivity"). As a pragmatist, Rorty rejects the coherence – indeed, the very possibility – of objectivity.[12] Walzer does not go nearly so far. For the most part, he works within a

46

tacit distinction between spheres of discourse that are solidaristic in Rorty's sense and spheres in which objectivity may
well be possible. Walzer's point, I suggest, is that objectivist
philosophy has at most limited relevance for, and authority
within, solidaristic communities.

The universalism lurking beneath Walzer's relativism is not
confined to metatheory. The assertion that social worlds cannot be rank-ordered turns out to be the key premise of the
argument that "we do justice to actual men and women by
respecting their particular creations," and hence, "to override those understandings is (always) to act unjustly."[13] But
experience suggests that some societies are inclined to respect
– and others to invade – the self-understandings of foreign
societies. It would seem to follow, on Walzer's own grounds,
that the self-understanding of respectful societies is superior
to the self-understanding of invasive societies. (That is, if
justice is preferable to injustice. If not, why bother with
a theory of justice at all?) And, to pile complexity on
complexity, the maxim "Do not override a society's self-
understanding" itself overrides the self-understandings of
invasive societies. Walzer's argument thus reproduces, par-
adoxes and all, the logic of the liberal doctrine of toleration.

Walzer's universalism also expresses itself, as we have
seen, in his espousal of a "minimal code" common to different communities and valid across, not merely within, their
boundaries. His theory of just and unjust war explicitly rests
on individual rights to life and liberty that are "somehow
entailed by our sense of what it means to be a human
being,"[14] a thesis explicitly reendorsed in his more recent
work.[15] And within all (or nearly all) communities, there are
prohibitions against "murder, deception, betrayal, gross cruelty." Although the outlines of these prohibitions must be
filled in with the details of a particular culture, they nonetheless "provide a framework for any possible (moral) life."[16]
Walzer straightforwardly acknowledges that this minimal
code may provide a valid basis for outsiders to intervene in
local practices – as, for example, when Vitoria invoked natural law in opposition to Aztec human sacrifice.[17]

A third element of Walzer's universalism emerges in his account of human nature. We are, he asserts, "culture-producing creatures; we make and inhabit meaningful worlds."[18] We are driven to act in this manner by a "passion for justification": At the heart of every culture are standards of "virtuous character, worthy performance, just social arrangements" in light of which its practices can be validated[19] – and criticized. Filtered through Gramsci's theory of hegemony, Walzer's account of the universal justificatory impulse leads to his remarkable portrait of the "social critic" as the marginal but deeply committed citizen who scrutinizes the practices of his or her community in the stringent light of its professed standards.

Two aspects of Walzer's portrait are especially noteworthy. First, because social criticism is to be a public activity and not merely a private judgment, it presupposes certain enabling conditions. It requires the ability to speak and be heard, which implies some community commitment to freedom of expression. It rests on the proposition that contradictions between principles and practices are a social (not merely logical) problem, which implies some public commitment to rationality. And if social criticism is to have any effectiveness, it must be addressed to public authorities and dominant groups that are not, in the last analysis, willing to rule by force alone. Thus, while all societies are equally in need of social criticism, not all are equally hospitable to it. One might even say, in the spirit though not the letter of Walzer's argument, that societies that afford substantial public space for social criticism enjoy a certain superiority to those that do not.

The second noteworthy aspect of Walzer's portrait is the evident high regard in which he holds the social critic, both as committed and as marginal. Walzer goes so far as to acknowledge in his description a "certain idealism of my own" and asks why value should be attached to the critic's commitment to his or her own society. Walzer's answer, rooted in the historic conflict between Bolshevism and social democracy, goes as follows:

The problem with disconnected criticism, and thus with criticism that derives from newly discovered or invented moral standards [rather than existing community standards] is that it presses its practitioners toward manipulation and compulsion. . . . [I]nsofar as the [disconnected] critic wants to be effective, he finds himself driven to one or another version of an unattractive politics.[20]

This passage reveals with utmost clarity that Walzer's understanding of social criticism – and of "attractive" politics – rests on a deep antipathy to coercion in any form. His core commitment is to a politics purged of force and directed by a process of mutual persuasion.

These strains of universalism raise the question of the relation between Walzer's methodological commitment and the substance of his thought. What standing can he claim for broad propositions about justice, the minimal code, human nature, and social criticism that could conceivably be consistent with his professed anti-Platonic relativism – that is, with his insistence on remaining inside the cave and his conviction that there are many diverse caves?[21]

There are, it seems to me, three ways of relaxing this tension. The first is to observe that Walzer's framing of the methodological choice as the opposition between situated, particular thought (the view from somewhere) and disembodied universalism (the view from nowhere) is not exhaustive. There is another possibility – call it the view from everywhere. Suppose that the denizens of the various caves, though divided on many issues, converge in their understanding of core social and moral propositions. This kind of universality would be rooted not in transcendental metaphysics but in certain empirical commonalities: the kinds of beings we are and the kinds of circumstances in which we find ourselves. Walzer seems to endorse just this notion of nontranscendent universality in his Humean account of the minimal code.[22]

A second way of relaxing the tension between substance and method is to note that Walzer is by no means as distant from Platonic philosophizing as he supposes. Socrates, after all, is not Descartes. He begins not by sweeping away the opinions of his community but, rather, by taking them as his (indispensable) point of departure. On inspection, it turns out that there are contradictions between the community's principles and its practices, and even among its principles. Moreover, the latent logic of core concepts often diverges startlingly from their standard unexamined interpretation. What then? The Socratic/Platonic suggestion is that sustained reflection on the contradictions inherent in one's community leads inexorably to a standpoint in some respects external to that community. One does not choose to leave the cave; one is forced to leave. Of course, Walzer does not accept this last step, but some of his own arguments nonetheless exemplify it. Recall, for example, that his effort to forge a description of justice equally respectful of the internal life of every community leads to assertions that transcend the self-understanding of many, perhaps most, communities.

The final way of relaxing the tension between universalist substance and relativist method is to remember that Walzer practices a highly traditional form of philosophic argumentation. Inherent in this practice are a number of substantive commitments: to rationality and consistency, to public persuasion, to the resolution of social differences through means other than force. In Walzer's recent work, I find echoes both of the Socratic maxim that the unexamined life is not worth living and of the Enlightenment belief that the unexamined society is not worth living in. Behind each of these stances is a set of universal commitments that constrain – and ultimately trump – Walzer's relativistic professions.

Of all Walzer's general commitments, the most pervasive is to democracy. During the past decade, Walzer has offered three quite different kinds of argument in support of democratic self-government. In *Radical Principles*, he puts forward a perfectionist case: Moral self-development toward freedom requires an appropriate arena for human activity, which only a democratic community can provide.[23] In "Philosophy and Democracy," he invokes Rousseau: The people "are the subjects of the law, and if the law is to bind them as free men and women, they must also be its makers."[24] And in *Spheres of Justice*, his claim is drawn from the intrinsic nature of the political sphere itself:

> Once we have located ownership, expertise, religious knowledge, and so on in their proper places and established their autonomy, there is no alternative to democracy in the political sphere.... Democracy is ... *the political way* of allocating power. Every extrinsic reason is ruled out. What counts is argument among the citizens. [The democratic citizen] can't use force, or pull rank, or distribute money; he must talk about the issues at hand.[25]

Among the many competitors to democracy, Walzer takes the claims of philosophic knowledge most seriously. Indeed, he says that only two answers to the question "Who should rule?" are intrinsic to the political sphere: "first, that power should be possessed by those who best know how to use it; and second, that it should be possessed, or at least controlled, by those who most immediately experience its effects."[26] Thus, to defeat the Platonic argument for the rule of the wise is to vindicate the rule of the people.

Walzer offers two kinds of arguments against the rule of knowledge. The first is that transcendental philosophy – philosophy that pushes beyond the limits of community consciousness – in fact generates no politically relevant knowledge except through a covert appeal to the very community beliefs it claims to have surpassed.[27] There can be technical knowledge – the science of means – but there can be no rational science of ends. Navigators know how to steer a ship, but their knowledge cannot tell them where to go. That is for the passengers to determine: "The proper exercise of power is nothing more than the direction of the city in accordance with the civic consciousness or public spirit of the citizens."[28]

Walzer does not quite commit himself to the full-blown antitranscendental view (he says that he is "tempted" by it), and we have already seen considerable evidence of universalism in his own thought. But even if this position were correct, it would not in itself suffice to rule out a privileged political place for nontechnical knowledge. At one point, Walzer concedes that a majority of citizens "might well misunderstand the logic of their own institutions or fail to apply consistently the principles they professed to hold."[29] There may, then, be a kind of knowing that is neither the technical science of means nor the transcendental knowledge of ends – call it expertise in the understanding of civic consciousness – that cuts against simply majoritarian institutions and democratic procedures. In *Brown* v. *Board*, for example, the U.S. Supreme Court rendered a decision that at the time would almost certainly have been rejected by majority vote. Yet this decision was ultimately recognized by the community as an authoritative interpretation of our civic principles. Thus, while Walzer's animadversions against the expansion of judicial power in a democracy contain much that is true and important, they give short shrift to the respects in which – by the logic of his own argument – judicial review can be legitimate and even on occasion necessary.[30]

Walzer's second, and in many ways more central, anti-Platonic argument is that whatever universalistic knowledge philosophy may provide, that knowledge has no special political authority beyond the assent it can win through the process of democratic discussion. The philosopher contends that it can never be right to do wrong; the democrat replies that the people have a right to act wrongly. The philosopher looks for reliable ways of putting his or her ideas into practice, and thus philosophical founding "tends to be an authoritarian business." The democrat, by contrast, worries about the resort to force implicit in any effort to reshape particular institutions in light of universal claims: "That particularity can be overcome . . . only by repressing internal political processes." At bottom, Walzer's defense of democracy against philosophy rests on the same motivation as does his preference for committed social criticism over external revolutionary action – namely, on a deep antipathy to coercion.[31]

52

Yet an untrammeled democratic majority – like any other form of power – can itself become coercive, a threat traditional liberal institutions are in part designed to ward off. Walzer acknowledges this fact: "The limitation of power is liberalism's historic achievement."[32] And he himself defines an extensive list of acts that no sovereign political authority, including (especially) the people, can rightly perform: not only Rousseau's formal strictures against particularity in legislation and against the alienation of the popular will, but also enslavement, censorship, invasion of religious conscience, and more.[33] More generally, Walzer derives limits to political power from its very status as only one "sphere" among many:

> Political power is the regulative agency for social goods generally. It is used to defend the boundaries of all the distributive spheres, including its own, and to enforce the common understanding of what goods are and what they are for. (But it can also be used, obviously, to invade the different spheres and to override those understandings.) . . . [P]olitical power is always dominant – at the boundaries, but not within them. The central problem of political life is to maintain that crucial distinction between "at" and "in."[34]

But how is that problem to be solved? The traditional liberal answer includes a publicly supported doctrine of private individual and institutional rights, a judiciary dedicated to the enforcement of those rights, a system of representation designed to mute the excesses of popular passions, a constitutional framework that impedes the hasty translation of public impulses into sweeping changes of fundamental law, and, above all, a private sphere diverse and capacious enough to mount a stern defense against public encroachment. I think it is fair to say that Walzer is skeptical of all these liberal contrivances. Yet it is far from clear what he would put in their place. He asks, "What if some political majority misunderstands or overrides the autonomy of this or that institutional setting?" And he replies, "That is the unavoidable risk of democracy."[35]

Liberals are willing to restrict democratic authority in order to reduce the risk of democratic tyranny. For Walzer, the reverse is true: He is willing to risk democratic tyranny to avoid restricting democratic authority. It is by no means evident, at least to me, that the protection of untrammeled direct democracy is a good so dominant as to justify making more likely what Walzer himself characterizes as the public evil most to be avoided: the tyrannical overstepping of boundaries.

II

In the mid-1970s, in *The Cultural Contradictions of Capitalism*, Daniel Bell argued against what he termed the monolithic view of society. Whatever may have been true of classical and medieval communities, Western industrial societies are characterized not by integration but by disjunction. There is no single spirit that animates these societies. Rather, they are divided into different realms, each guided by its own principle: the technoeconomy, whose operating principle is efficiency; the polity, whose legitimacy is based on the concept of free and equal citizens; and culture, increasingly dominated by the modernist ideal of unlimited self-expression. Within this frame, Bell suggested, one can discern the structural sources of tension in modern societies

> between social structure (primarily technoeconomic) which is bureaucratic and hierarchical, and a polity which believes, formally, in equality and participation; between a social structure that is organized fundamentally in terms of roles and specialization, and a culture which is concerned with the enhancement and fulfillment of the self and the "whole" person. In these contradictions, one perceives many of the latent conflicts that have been expressed ideologically as alienation, depersonalization, the attack on authority ... [36]

Roberto Unger's project in his opus *Politics*[37] is to argue that these contradictions can be overcome. Specifically, the principle of what Bell calls culture – the enhancement and

54

fulfillment of the self – is the axis around which all of society must be reconstructed. Economic roles and hierarchies that constrain self-expression must be dismantled. Legal–constitutional forms that restrict the free play of the human imagination must be reconstituted. Fortunately, Unger argues, to accord normative primacy to self-assertion is not to surrender other desirable features of modern life. Plastic, nonhierarchical economic institutions are not only compatible with but actually necessary for the attainment of material prosperity. Rights-based political institutions can be redesigned to accommodate the democratic clash of imaginative projects while preserving individual security against tyranny. We need neither embrace the rigors of republican civic virtue to achieve democracy nor accept the repressiveness of the Protestant ethic to ensure prosperity; the modernist ideal of personal liberation is functional in every sphere of life. We can, in short, realize the old Enlightenment dream of a rational society in which our most treasured goals are no longer in ultimate conflict.

From this normative vantage point, Unger launches a vigorous attack on contemporary liberal polities. Western societies are, he asserts, frozen into rigid individual roles and collective hierarchies. The political system of checks and balances impedes both democratic self-expression and egalitarian social reconstruction. A combination of social rigidity, political gridlock, and imaginative stultification locks liberal politics into futile cycles of reform and retrenchment. Even European social democracy – the fullest realization of liberal aspirations – fails to liberate individual practical, emotional, and cognitive capacities. For these reasons, we cannot be satisfied with a program of incremental changes pursued within current institutions. Rather, we must seek to destabilize these institutions in order to move toward their radical transformation.

Unger's *Politics* is an ambitious attempt to combine the synoptic explanatory claims of modern social theory with the normative aspirations of traditional political philosophy. While each of these elements deserves a full exploration, it is the complex relation of Unger's thought to the normative philosophical tradition that serves as the focus of my remarks.

Three key features of Unger's thought express his fidelity to the classical project. Against the strictures of Machiavelli and Marx, but in line with the thinkers of antiquity, he insists that normative social theory culminates in a concrete vision of a good society (in classical terms, a "utopia"). Like Aristotle, he argues that the good society is justified through its propensity to permit and promote individual *eudaemonia*. And like Plato, he suggests that the structure of society mirrors the structure of the self, that the political community is the human soul writ large.

At the same time, Unger contemptuously rejects the classical account of human nature and, with it, the classical depiction of the good society. "The classical moralizing doctrines of the virtues and the vices," he declares, are a species of "superficial sentimentality."[38] The decisive break with these doctrines – the revolutionary view of human existence developed by the great modernist artists and authors – is "one of the most important events in the history of modern culture. . . . Compared with this modernist view of the self, earlier images of man look shoddy and unconvincing."[39] Correspondingly, the classical conception of society, which culminated in an account of natural order and hierarchy, must be supplanted by forms of social organization compatible with the modernist revolution.

The isomorphism between self and society rests on the troubled relation between formative structures and formed activities. Unger rejects the primacy of character – fixed, habitual patterns of behavior – in favor of a fluid capacity to act on imagination and desire. Similarly, he rejects a sharp distinction between stable constitutional institutions and the vagaries of ordinary politics in favor of a continuum characterized throughout by openness and revisability. To be sure, he tempers modernist iconoclasm with the antiskeptical claim that some individual virtues and collective institutions can be rationally defended. But the defense rests on the modernist premise that infinite personality can never be adequately contained in any set of rules, roles, or structures.

For Unger, the essence of human personality is that it is "infinite." It has the capacity to transcend all contexts: traits of character, moral rules, political institutions, cognitive structures, and so forth. No one context is hospitable to the full range of practical, passionate, political, or philosophic projects that personality can imagine. This infinity is not just an abstract capability but, in the old language of teleology, an immanent impulse as well.

The health of each individual personality, Unger believes, is incompatible with its acceptance of the constraints inherent in specific contexts. Indeed, vice, psychological illness, and simple unhappiness are all consequences of the failure to relieve the tension between personal desire and contextual constraint. Modernist visionaries identified and struggled against this tension. Their struggle may have taken the form of an artistic fringe in conflict with bourgeois society, but its inner meaning is a universal truth about the human condition. The vague but spreading apprehension of this truth, Unger argues, is now evoking disquiet and longing among men and women everywhere.

Unger's modernist account of personality rests on a sharp distinction between "character" and "self." Character is the set of routinized habits and dispositions that channel individual behavior into fixed patterns. Selfhood, on the other hand, is the dual capacity both to reject routine patterns of conduct and to imagine and act on alternatives to them.[40]

This distinction provides the point of departure for my critique of modernism, so understood. That individuals have a capacity to question and revise settled features of their existence cannot be denied. But Unger's separation of self and character is far too sharp. His thesis is reminiscent of Kant's bifurcation between phenomenal and transcendental consciousness, and it is exposed to the same difficulties. Our traits of character are not related to our existence in the mode of external possessions or physiological stimuli. These traits are not what we *have* and *feel*, but rather what we *are*. Our

57

identities as persons are largely constituted by learned or inherited patterns of behavior. The consciousness that struggles against these patterns is nevertheless implicated in them. Personal change results not from a struggle of self against character but, rather, from a mobilization of some traits of character against others. Ambition can be made to counteract sloth; courage can overcome shame.

Even if we grant Unger's disjunction between routinized character and fluid self, it does not follow that the latter is to be given normative preference. The mere fact that we are able to upset settled patterns in favor of new experiences does not mean that we should do so. The fact that the imagination can counterpose itself to moral rules does not mean that these rules should be transgressed. At one point, Unger characterizes the view of individual behavior underlying his proposed political institutions as "the ability to entertain fantasies about possible forms of self-expression or association and to live them out."[41] To this I reply that there is no more solace to be found in the total liberation of fantasy than in its total repression.

This point may be broadened. Unger projects a boundless hostility to the "vast spiritual sloth" and "overwhelming apathy" that allegedly characterize ordinary human experience.[42] Rejecting solace most of us find in ordered existence, he insists that to understand deeply "is always to see the settled from the angle of the unsettled."[43] He even finds in the forcible destruction of everyday patterns the fount of moral insight:

> The growth of the transforming and ennobling passions . . . and the ability of these passions to penetrate the crust of everyday perception and habit seem to depend upon loss and sacrifice. . . . [T]he primary form of loss and sacrifice is the sacrifice and loss of your settled place in the settled world. This is the event that allows you to distinguish the gold from the tinsel, the opportunities of human connection from the forms of established society, and the disclosures of incongruous insight or disobedient desire from the distraction and the narcosis of habit.[44]

So workers are ennobled by unemployment? Husbands and wives are ennobled by shattering divorces? Parents are ennobled by the death of children? Lebanon's citizens were ennobled by civil war? The most charitable response to Unger's proposition is that disaster strengthens some of these unfortunate human beings but destroys the others. A franker response is that his proposition is a classic example of theoretical deduction swamping experiential truth. As for the alleged pharmacological properties of habit, the relentless modernist quest for peak experiences is more of a narcotic than the stable patterns of daily life could ever be.

The preference for the unsettled over the settled, the impulse to imagine and to act out context-smashing transgressions, is indeed characteristic of modernist artists, authors, and revolutionaries. But Unger mistakes the part for the whole. His critical error is to assume that the motives and satisfactions of a tiny elite somehow constitute the (hidden) essence and desire of all human beings. A world restructured to accommodate the iconoclastic cravings of modernist visionaries is a world from which everyone else would recoil in dread. Most human beings find satisfaction within settled contexts and experience the disruption of those contexts not as empowerment but, rather, as deprivation. The everyday life for which Unger has such contempt is not an oppressive imposition by the few on the many. It retains its customary form precisely because it is the mode of existence best suited to the overwhelming majority of the human race.

Modernists typically represent themselves as the vanguard of broad popular movements. In reality, however, modernism is an elite doctrine and practice masquerading as populism. Modernist novels and music have failed to attain any measurable mass influence, spawning instead a split between the iconoclastic tastes of a narrow elite and the enduring popular demand for naturalism and tonality. Modern art, sculpture, and architecture have achieved a greater measure of acceptance, but only by shedding their adversary stance toward bourgeois culture and becoming either economically functional or visually decorative. In no instance has modernism transformed the broad public outlook, which remains aesthetically and morally conservative.

To the extent, therefore, that modernism craves transformative efficacy, it is driven toward "revolution from above" – that is, toward coercion. It is no accident that in its rage against the stolid persistence of bourgeois society, modernism has repeatedly flirted with fascism. Nor is it an accident that Unger's political modernism, ostensibly justified in the name of the greatest possible openness to individual expression, culminates in the forcible destruction of traditional ways of life. Unger is admirably – if chillingly – candid on this point:

> People have . . . always put their sense of basic security in the maintenance of particular social roles, jobs, and ways of life. Any attempt to indulge this conception of security would prove incompatible with the institutions of the empowered democracy and with the personal and social ideals that inspire them. . . . [P]eople can and should wean themselves away from a restrictive, rigidifying view of where they should place their sense of basic security.[45]

> They and, if not they, their children will discover that the security that matters does not require the maintenance of a narrowly defined mode of life. They do so in part by awakening to a conception of the personality as both dependent upon context and context-smashing.[46]

To summarize Unger's thesis, modernist social theory rests on a normative conception of personality valid for, and binding upon, everyone. Today, some of us accept this conception while others stubbornly resist it. Within suitably constructed institutions, we all (eventually) come to experience the correctness of the modernist vision. But what happens in the interim, while our generation has not yet been reeducated – or replaced by suitably socialized children? We certainly are not "indulged." Instead, we are shaken out of our narcoleptic trance and purged of stubborn habits. We are forced to be free.

Unger anticipates a certain resistance to this proposal on the part of the "classical liberal": Modernist social theory culminates in totalitarian interventions in areas that even traditional despots are content to leave alone. While accepting the factual accuracy of this accusation, Unger seeks to transvalue its moral meaning:

> The classical liberal is wrong to think . . . that an institutional order can draw a watertight distinction between the public institutions of a people and the forms of close association or intimate experience to which the people are drawn. . . . The authority of the radical project lies in its vision of the individual and collective empowerment that we may achieve by cumulatively loosening the grip of rigid roles, hierarchies, and conventions. . . . But it does not claim to be indifferent to the choice among alternative styles of associations.[47]

Would it not be more honest to say that we have a *choice* of constructing society in accord with the traditionalism of the many or, alternatively, with the iconoclasm of the few? The former alternative propels the modernist elite to the fringes of society, where it assumes an adversary stance toward established institutions. But the latter alternative evokes a traditionalist counterreaction to the practices of advanced culture, a response that (depending on circumstances) can take the form of either a relatively benign conservatism or a far more virulent fascism. Unger is systematically – almost willfully – blind to the origins and dangers of contemporary "populist" movements. The false universality of his conception of personality obscures the dominant cultural clash of our time. Ironically, a social philosophy that takes as its point of departure the unmasking of suppressed strife ends by smothering genuine strife in a theoretical structure that suppresses some of the most fundamental human differences.

The chief virtue of political institutions, Unger believes, is to be maximally open to the infinite variety of practical and emotional arrangements human beings may devise. All social contexts are restrictive to some extent. But unalloyed modernist iconoclasm, Unger argues, overlooks differences among contexts in the degree of constraint they impose. Institutions go astray when they needlessly constrict human possibilities by freezing society into rigid roles and hierarchies. Restrictive polities are thus characterized by a sharp distinction between basic structures, which are highly resistant to revision, and the routine activities that occur within these structures. The good society, on the other hand, builds opportunities for challenge and change into its basic institutions. In so doing, it narrows the breach between contexts and routines, and it enables each individual to participate as a self-determining personality in the reconstructions of fundamental social arrangements. Unger's proposed constitution is thus a "structure-denying structure" that "preserves in its determinate existence the marks of an original indefinition" and is "designed to prevent any definite institutional order from taking hold in social life."[48]

No brief discussion can adequately confront the complex development of Unger's institutional argument. Out of necessity, I set aside the details and focus on what I take to be his basic premises, offering in each instance a counterproposal.

Unger Thesis 1: Far from resting on, or reflecting, a natural order, society is a pure artifact originating in, but freezing, struggle among human beings.[49]

Counterthesis: Society is neither purely natural nor purely artificial. Human beings are naturally drawn together into political communities, whose goals include such natural ends as survival, security, and material adequacy. These facts impose certain constraints on the possible range of institutional arrangements and political programs. At the same time, the specific forms such communities may assume are determined largely by differences of human belief and will. Social theory goes astray if it understands society either on the analogy of determinate natural growth or in the image of unconstrained artistic creation – the latter being Unger's error.

Unger Thesis 2: All hierarchies – rigid structures that thwart human flourishing and lack rational justification – are unnatural. For that reason, to open up hierarchies to the possibility of scrutiny and revision is to initiate the process of their dissolution.[50]

Counterthesis: Some hierarchies are both rationally justifiable and conducive to individual self-assertion: the authority of parents over children, teachers over students, skilled artisans over apprentices, and, more generally, the authority of those who have special knowledge or competence that promotes the attainment of shared ends. If members of a society agree on certain ends, and if the achievement of those ends is in part a function of knowledge or competence, there can in principle be rational social and political authority.

Unger Thesis 3: All contexts that resist revision thwart human flourishing. The more revisable the context, the better: "Over the long run, the practical, moral, and cognitive advantages to be won by disentrenching formative contexts outweigh in the strength and universality of their appeal the benefits to be gained by entrenching these contexts further."[51]

Counterthesis: Rather than constraining us, some revision-resisting contexts actually liberate us. In the arts, such conventions as baroque harmony, the sonnet, and the blues have provided enabling structures within which explosions of creativity have occurred. In social relations, such institutions as indissoluble marriage may promote intimacy and personal growth – a point even Unger ultimately concedes.[52] In politics, similarly, relatively stable contexts may provide arenas within which conflicting proposals and ways of life may be tested against one another without risking the escalation of conflict into community-threatening bitterness and violence.

Because circumstances change unpredictably and dramatically, the structural context of political life – the "constitution" – must of course be open to revision. But the art of constitution making is not, as Unger would have it, to maximize revisability. It is rather to locate the appropriate mean between rigidity and anarchy. So, for example, the U.S. Constitution does not require unanimous consent of the states to pass constitutional amendments, but it does require more than a bare majority. One may argue (as some did after the defeat of the Equal Rights Amendment) that this requirement gives excessive power of veto to relatively small minorities. But few believe that constitutional amendments should be as easy to pass as ordinary legislation.

The critique of Unger's norm of maximal revisability rests on logical as well as prudential grounds. If political strife is to be resolved through means other than force, and if political dialogue cannot produce unanimity, then some structure of decision rules is needed to determine when the views of a portion of the community are deemed to have become binding on the entire community. Within this structure, institutions, laws, and social arrangements may be exposed to revision. But the structure itself cannot be challenged, at least not in the same way, as long as the prohibition on the use of force is maintained. Every effort to alter the structure must respect the laws of revision that structure embodies. The constitutional provision by which proposed constitutional amendments require a three-quarters majority of the states for passage can be changed only through an amendment that itself receives a three-quarters majority. The only alternative to respect for basic structures is the resort to revolutionary force, which may indeed be justified in some instances. But the point is that no structure can be made so comprehensively revisable as to rule out the need for revolution in certain extreme circumstances. The distinction between context and routine cannot be wholly effaced without at the same time effacing the distinction between peaceful and violent settlement of political disputes.

Unger Thesis 4: Political change is properly conceived as isomorphic with scientific change. The ideal of maximal institutional revisability "is the political counterpart to an ideal of objectivity in science that relies not on the incorrigibility of self-evident propositions but on the universal and accelerated corrigibility of an explanatory practice, including the very conception of what it means to explain something. This comparison represents more than a vague parallel; it is . . . a precise and revealing convergence."[53]

Counterthesis: This comparison represents a failure to understand the fundamental difference between scientific and political change. At their best, scientists form a rational community. That is, the authority of particular scientific propositions rests solely on their ability to withstand skeptical scrutiny. To be sure, habitual beliefs and practices can impede the operation of scientific inquiry and retard the acceptance of new propositions. But the sway of tradition is, strictly speaking, a perversion of science. In a political community, on the other hand, the authority of particular propositions rests in part on familiarity and habit. Of course, mere existence should not sustain the status quo. But reason is not enough either. Without the practical familiarity born of habit, political propositions cannot be rendered effectively binding for a community. Excessive openness to revision undermines the very foundation of law and, with it, the very possibility of community not ruled by force. The realistic political alternative to habitual practices is not pure reason, but a destructive oscillation between anarchy and tyranny.

As a critique of liberalism, in short, Unger's argument misfires completely. "Bourgeois" habits are consistent with the interests and desires of most members of liberal societies, and liberal-democratic institutions strike a reasonable balance between stability and change. Unger's preference for fluidity represents the illegitimate transposition of an already questionable aesthetic stance into the political domain. It is hard to imagine how the benefits of full fluidity, taken as the basis of a public program, could possibly outweigh its risk: As Unger unmistakably (if inadvertently) reveals, any serious attempt to implement this program will inevitably turn toward tyranny.

III

Alasdair MacIntyre rightly observes that we do not fully understand the claims of any moral philosophy "until we have spelled out what its social embodiment would be."[54] To this I would add: Neither have we fully understood it until we have seen the kind of social criticism to which it gives rise.

MacIntyre's own case is instructive. The point of departure for his moral philosophy is a premise with which I agree: Contemporary political thought has been weakened by its neglect of the Aristotelian tradition of the virtues. But MacIntyre arrives at a conclusion that I cannot accept: Morally and humanly, there is little to choose between Stalinism and liberalism, for they are kindred forms of "barbarism."[55] *Both* ways of life, he insists, "are in the long run intolerable."[56]

MacIntyre's hostility to liberalism – which he calls "bureaucratic individualism" – stems from what he sees as a fundamental opposition between the theory and practice of liberalism and the Aristotelian tradition of the virtues. In that tradition, the virtues are part of a threefold scheme:

> [T]here is a fundamental contrast between man-as-he-happens-to-be and man-as-he-could-be-if-he-realized-his-essential-nature. Ethics is the science which is to enable men to understand how they make the transition from the former state to the latter. Ethics therefore on this view presupposes some account of the existence of man as a rational animal and above all some account of the human *telos*. The precepts which enjoin the various virtues and prohibit the vices . . . instruct us how to move from potentiality to act, how to realize our true nature and to reach our true end.[57]

This moral tradition is called into question at the very beginning of the modern era by Protestant/Jansenist Catholic theology and by Hobbesian/Cartesian natural philosophy. The new theology asserts that human reason is not competent to discern essences or ends. The new natural philosophy altogether denies the existence of essences.

By itself, MacIntyre insists, the destruction of Aristotelian metaphysics need not have undermined the teleological theory of the virtues. The teleological concept of man

> is rooted in the forms of social life to which the theorists of the classical tradition give expression. For according to that

tradition to be a man is to fill a set of roles each of which has its own point and purpose.

The teleological thesis finally collapses "only when man is thought of as an individual prior to and apart from all roles."[58] This is the liberal–individualist concept of the self: the product of the early modern revolt against all the forms of social organization that were perceived as outmoded, illegitimate restrictions on freedom of philosophical reflection and political action.

The difficulty, in MacIntyre's view, is that moral discourse as such is meaningless unless it rests on some conception of the human telos. With the denial of both metaphysical and social teleology, the possibility of rationally grounded morality disappears. Modern moral theory thus consists either in the bad-faith pretense that moral meaning exists when it does not or in the frank assertion that moral principles are subjective and arbitrary. Liberalism in the broadest sense is the form of social life that embodies and expresses these false moral modes. But, MacIntyre continues, false theories cannot eradicate our enduring need for a morality in which we can rationally believe. The failure of the liberal social order to requite this need is at the root of profound political pathologies of our time.

MacIntyre is at pains to argue that liberal individualism is not just *one*, but rather *the* social philosophy of modernity. Nietzsche and Marx are frequently seen as alternatives to liberalism. But, MacIntyre contends, the Nietzschean stance "turns out not to be a mode of escape from or an alternative to the conceptual scheme of liberal individualist modernity, but rather one more representative movement in its internal unfolding."[59] Nor can the defects of liberal individualism be overcome through Marx, because Marxism has no moral content other than the liberal moralities of utilitarianism and no institutional forms other than bureaucracy, which is liberal through and through.[60] In the last analysis, "the crucial moral opposition is between liberal individualism in some version or other and the Aristotelian tradition in some version or other."[61] If, then, liberalism is a historical cul-de-sac, we have no choice but to return to Aristotle's theory of the virtues. And we *can* return, MacIntyre believes. Aristotle's metaphysical teleology may well be untenable, but some version of his social teleology is perfectly defensible. And that is all the theory of the virtues requires.

Central to MacIntyre's thesis is the contention that the alleged impasse of liberal theory, which progressively unfolds from its initial rejection of the virtues, is reflected in the progressive degeneration of liberal society. Indeed, he asserts, "What we discover is a single history and not two parallel ones."[62] It is at this point that the argument goes off the rails, for he is able to sustain his position only by looking at modern society through the prism of his own theoretical expectations while ignoring important but (for him) inconvenient phenomena.

In the following discussion, I consider four strands of MacIntyre's treatment of liberal society: emotivism, conflict, bureaucracy, and the nature of the virtues. Uniting these topics is MacIntyre's belief that liberal society makes virtuous life impossible. I believe, and I shall argue, that this belief is in large measure false.

1. *Emotivism:* Virtuous activity, MacIntyre argues, presupposes forms of cooperative endeavor in which each of us views at least some others as full and equal partners in the quest for some good. But liberal society, he asserts, is the social embodiment of emotivism, a moral philosophy that is systematically incapable of distinguishing between manipulative and nonmanipulative social relations – indeed, a philosophy that reduces moral discourse to a form of manipulation.

This is, to say the least, an extraordinarily one-sided view of liberal society. To be sure, liberal theories and practices of manipulation are plentiful, as the experience of daily life and a glance at the *New York Times* best-seller list will attest. But there are countervailing forces. The language of respect for human rights, dignity, and individuality is extraordinarily prevalent in our culture, and not without force. On the more

68

theoretical plane, there has been a remarkable resurgence, during the 1970s and 1980s, of liberal social theory inspired by Kant, the philosopher MacIntyre cites as having articulated a defense of nonmanipulative human relations.[63]

I might add that this duality of manipulation and non-manipulation is hardly confined to modern liberal societies. As Plato's *Gorgias* and Thucydides' narrative graphically reveal, much the same split existed in the political culture of classical Greece.

2. *Bureaucracy:* Within emotivist societies, MacIntyre argues, institutions must take the form of Weberian bureaucracies – that is, of organizations that cannot distinguish between power and authority and that legitimate themselves through appeals to managerial effectiveness in manipulating others in the pursuit of exogenous and arbitrary ends. In our culture, MacIntyre asserts, "we know no justifications for authority which are not Weberian in form."[64]

MacIntyre's thesis is patently false. Alongside the kind of power that stems from effectiveness stands the authority that comes from consent. Whatever the abuses in practice, the democratic rhetoric and theory of popular sovereignty are deeply embedded in our culture, for they flow naturally from widely-held liberal conceptions of history and of the self. Indeed, it would not be farfetched to view our recent history as a complex struggle between managerial and democratic views of authority.

3. *Conflict:* The virtues, MacIntyre argues, can flourish only within genuine communities, which rest on a shared recognition and cooperative pursuit of some good. But liberalism rejects the very possibility of a shared good. Leading liberal theorists identify as the very essence of liberalism the denial that there exists any rationally justifiable conception of the good life on which we can or should agree. Liberal society embodies this very denial: "Modern politics is civil war carried on by other means."[65]

MacIntyre's characterization of modern liberal theory is not wholly inaccurate. But, as I argue in Chapter 4, these theories are neither internally consistent nor true to the facts of liberal societies. Every society – and liberal society is no exception – rests on some shared perception of the good to be achieved through collective endeavor. The goals of our own society are expressed in a document that begins "We the people" and speaks of a "more perfect union" and of the "common defense" and the "general welfare" – a document representing a solemn and explicit mutual undertaking.

Now it is perfectly true that the American view of the common good deviates in significant respects from the classical view. It is not a *total* good, because many parts of the human good are regarded as falling outside the purview of the political community. And it is not expressed primarily in the vocabulary of the virtues.[66]

This raises a more general point. To argue, as MacIntyre does, that the virtues are genuine goods is not to argue that they are the *sole* goods. Toward the end of *After Virtue*, MacIntyre finally gets around to admitting that "external goods [objects of competition that can be individually appropriated and held] genuinely are goods."[67] But he never incorporates this admission into his theory of society, which is thus radically unbalanced. It emphasizes a vision of community as engendering and providing an arena for the virtues while virtually ignoring the role of the community in producing, distributing, and guaranteeing the security of external goods. It is this imbalance that in large measure underlies MacIntyre's misinterpretation of and studied contempt for liberal societies which (to say the least) have come somewhat closer to solving the problems associated with external goods than did the classical societies he so admires. Extremism in the defense of virtue is no virtue.

4. *The nature of the virtues:* MacIntyre advances a tripartite theory of the virtues. They furnish internal goods by sustaining the practices, the cooperative activities, that engender those goods; they sustain the narrative unity that gives individual lives coherence and meaning; and they nourish tradition, which gives individual identity and endeavor its indispensable point of departure. But liberal societies, he contends, undermine each of these elements of the virtues.

Because they embody conflict rather than cooperation, they make genuine practices impossible. The theories of self and narrative characteristic of liberal societies, as well as practical diremptions within those societies, fragment human life into a jumble of disconnected roles and episodes. And liberal individualism is at war with the very concept of a tradition that provides us with inherited identities and obligations.

I speak to these points more fully in Chapter 10. Here I respond only briefly. Because there is cooperation as well as conflict in liberal societies, there *are* practices – public as well as private – and therefore a place for the virtues. (Indeed, there are practices even within the bureaucratic organizations MacIntyre so despises.) The forces of fragmentation in liberal societies are not strong enough to prevent most of us from experiencing and living our lives as narrative unities, in our professions as well as our families. And liberal societies, far from being hostile to tradition, embody a vibrant tradition of whose progressive unfolding they are the scene.

It is one thing to imagine an emotivist society, quite another to identify that imagined society with our own. MacIntyre devotes a great deal of energy to the first task, virtually none to the second. He assumes that when he presents us with the product of his imagination, we experience a spontaneous shock of recognition.

I for one do not. Where MacIntyre sees a seamless unity of anti-Aristotelian moral theories and anti-Aristotelian societies, I see a gulf between the moral doctrines of many elites and the moral sensibilities of most ordinary citizens. The virtues are by no means dead in liberal society. Courage, justice, self-restraint, prudence, and many others are widely prized. That they are more prized than practiced is not a problem confined to our own historical moment.

MacIntyre reaches the opposite conclusion because of a persistent error of method. When he seeks to describe liberal society, he examines the responses of writers and intellectuals to that society. To say the least, these reactions are not always the soundest guide to social reality. From Sartre's nauseated depiction of bourgeois society we learn more about

71

Sartre than we do about the bourgeoisie. From Solzhenitsyn's fulminations against liberal anarchy we learn with sorrow how in tyrannies the psychology of tyranny can come to permeate even its staunchest opponents. And so on.

MacIntyre constantly confuses the reality of liberal society with the vagaries of contemporary thought. Only on this basis can he possibly assert that "people now think, talk, and act *as if* emotivism were true, no matter what their avowed theoretical stand-point may be."[68] On the contrary, it would not be misleading to interpret American politics of the 1970s and 1980s as a kind of moral class conflict – a swelling revolt of antiemotivist citizens against elites that appear to abet, if not espouse, the prejudices and practices of emotivism.[69]

One of the most perplexing features of MacIntyre's argument is his stance toward moral conflict. His critique of liberal societies rests heavily on the proposition that these societies lack the cultural resources for resolving internal conflict through means other than force, overt or disguised. Yet his own views on the preconditions of social conflict resolution seem barely distinguishable (if at all) from those of his liberal targets. To illustrate, let me venture a brief comparison between MacIntyre's thesis and that of Isaiah Berlin, an arch-liberal by any measure.

Berlin and MacIntyre seem to agree on a number of essential points. Both argue that it is possible to speak of the human good in a way that is not simply arbitrary, subjective, or relative. But both insist that the good is radically heterogeneous. There is no Platonic–monistic idea of the Good from which all particular goods can be deduced or through which they can be justified. Nor is there any rational principle for ranking all goods. Nor is there a way of life through which we can synthesize and attain all goods. Genuine goods conflict with one another. To live, therefore, is to pursue some goods at the expense of others, while recognizing that other individuals may defensibly embark on courses of action very different from one's own.

It is easy to see how Berlin moves from this pluralist view

of the good to a defense of liberal society. It is more difficult to understand why MacIntyre does not. He rests his case on an alleged distinction between Berlin's pluralism and his own, which he bases on an interpretation of Sophoclean tragedy. According to MacIntyre, we are subject to rival and incompatible claims. But "our situation is tragic in that we have to recognize the authority of both claims . . . [T]o choose does not exempt me from the authority of the claim which I chose to go against."[70]

MacIntyre seems to argue that both Berlin's theory and liberal society depend on a concept of *nontragic* choice that, unlike his own, rejects the authority of the spurned claim. He is wrong on both counts. Here is what Berlin has to say:

> If, as I believe, the ends of men are many, and not all of them are in principle compatible with each other, then the possibility of conflict – and of tragedy – can never wholly be eliminated from human life, either personal or social.[71]

Much the same is true of liberal societies. Take the issue of abortion, which MacIntyre cites as a prime example of interminable moral dissonance in our culture.[72] It seems to me that this controversy fulfills, and is viewed by thoughtful observers as fulfilling, MacIntyre's criterion of tragic choice: All of the alternatives "have to be recognized as leading to some authentic and substantial good."[73] To be sure, there are fanatics at the fringes. But the anguished tone of recent public debate testifies to the widespread recognition that every course of action necessarily surrenders some significant good. I might add that this feature of moral debate is the norm rather than the exception in liberal societies. MacIntyre charges liberal societies with moral subjectivism. It is more accurate to say that they believe in certain goods but cannot discern any universally valid principles for ranking and choosing among them when they come into conflict.[74]

These reflections raise a more general point. MacIntyre begins *After Virtue* by castigating contemporary moral argument – and contemporary society – for intractable disagreements over crucial issues of public issues of public policy. The premise implicit in his critique is that a satisfactory theory of morality would enable us to overcome such disagreements. It is striking, then, that his own theory does not and cannot do so. As MacIntyre states, the tragic protagonist "has no *right* choice to make." Rather, his moral theory – the theory of the virtues – is what I would call "adverbial." It judges not what we do but how we do it. Thus, the moral task of the tragic protagonist "may be performed better or worse, independently of the choice between alternatives that he or she makes. . . . The tragic protagonist may behave heroically or unheroically, generously or ungenerously, gracefully or gracelessly, prudently or imprudently."[75] To this Berlin and thoughtful liberals in general will reply: Granting what you say, even a society that agrees on the virtues will be divided on goals and on the nature of the good life. The real choice is between societies that attempt to accommodate, and those that strive to repress, this unexpungible disagreement.

But MacIntyre has one more arrow in his quiver. The liberal/Berlin theory of choice among incompatible goods is defective because it rests on a false view of the "free" or "autonomous" self making such choices. According to the modern view, the self must be seen as independent of any particular place, role, or tradition. The self's choices must be wholly unconstrained if they are to be regarded as truly free. But, MacIntyre retorts, this notion of radical autonomy actually destroys the identity of the free agent. From the standpoint of the Aristotelian tradition, such freedom of choice of values appears "more like the freedom of ghosts – of those whose human substance approached the vanishing point – than of *men*."[76]

There is indeed a modern tradition of freedom, with its roots in Kant and fullest expression in Sartre, that corresponds to MacIntyre's description. And it is at least arguable that this concept of freedom is vulnerable to MacIntyre's critique. But this is not to say that liberal theory requires, or that liberal society embodies, such an extreme view. The revolt against traditional authority in which liberalism originates does *not* entail repudiation of all social determination of individual identity. Human beings choose as they do, Berlin says, because "their life and thought are determined by fundamental moral categories and concepts that are . . . a part of their being and thought and sense of their own identity; part of what makes them human."[77] Characteristically, MacIntyre can make his case only by taking a certain form of modernist theory as the essence of liberal practice.

MacIntyre proffers the concept of tradition as an antidote to liberal individualism. But it seems to me that liberalism *is* a tradition, in precisely MacIntyre's sense: a historically extended, socially embodied argument about the goods that constitute a specific form of human existence. I see no other way to interpret the New Deal, *Brown* v. *Board*, or indeed the *Bakke* case, which MacIntyre appears to view as the definitive proof that Americans have no moral principles in common.

MacIntyre's condemnation of moral disagreement within liberal societies is profoundly paradoxical. He urges us to heed the Australian philosopher John Anderson's advice "not to ask of a social institution 'What end or purpose does it serve?' but rather 'Of what conflicts is it the scene?'" But when he characterizes the *Bakke* case as "an engagement whose antecedents were at Gettysburg and Shiloh" and on this basis condemns American politics as "civil war carried on by other means," he refuses to take seriously Anderson's dictum. Preoccupied with conflict in liberal societies, MacIntyre is oblivious to the underlying agreement in these societies, an agreement that permits most conflict to be waged and resolved peaceably. It is precisely through a history of political conflict that Americans have deepened their sense of shared goods. Conversely, the one conflict that could not be peacefully resolved was a struggle not within liberalism but between liberalism and a way of life (slaveholding) that over time came to define itself in opposition to liberal equality, liberty, and moral universalism.

IV

Much more could be said (indeed, has been said)[78] on these thinkers and on contemporary antiliberal thought. But I believe I have said enough to validate the opening contention of this chapter: The critique of liberalism in the name of democracy, community, equality, and virtue misfires. Liberalism is open to its own forms of virtue and community, and the qualifications it imposes on equality and participation are amply justified by the range of heterogeneous goods pursued by liberal societies. Liberalism is capable of embracing what is true in its critics' views and of offering principled reasons for rejecting the rest.

But to say that liberalism *can* do this is not to say that it always *does*. On the contrary, the most influential liberal theories of the 1970s and 1980s have sought to rest their case on the widest possible neutrality concerning conceptions of a choice-worthy human existence, and this stance has been paralleled by developments in American jurisprudence and social life. It is my contention that this neutralist liberalism is incapable either of meeting the concerns of liberalism's critics or of doing justice to the lived experience (and highest possibility) of liberal life. It is essential, therefore, to offer a comprehensive critique of the neutralist interpretation of liberalism to clear the path for a more adequate and substantive account. I now turn to this task.

Part II

Liberalism and neutrality

Chapter 4

Liberalism and the neutral state

The contemporary revival of political theory in the Anglo-American intellectual community has for the most part been a revival of liberal theory. This should not have come as a great surprise. Most Anglo-Americans are, in one way or another, liberals; all are deeply influenced by the experience of life in liberal societies.

Although this revival of liberal theory has been much discussed, it is less often noted that in one decisive respect it remains rooted in the climate of moral skepticism that it has supplanted. Most contemporary liberal theorists are deeply mistrustful of what John Rawls has called "perfectionism" – the philosophic attempt to identify superior aspects of human existence or traits of character and, once having identified them, to use them as goals of political life. Contemporary liberal theory consists of the attempt to combine this skepticism about theories of the good life with the belief in philosophically defensible principles that regulate relations among individuals.

It is my thesis that this defense of liberalism is fundamentally misguided. No form of political life can be justified without some view of what is good for individuals. In practice, liberal theorists covertly employ theories of the good. But their insistence that they do not reduces the rigor of their theories and leaves the liberal polity unnecessarily vulnerable to criticism.

I

There are, broadly speaking, two strategies for justifying the liberal state. The first begins by arguing for the worth of the way of life characterized by distinctively liberal or (as some say) bourgeois virtues and goals. The liberal state is justified, according to this view, because it is designed to foster liberal virtues, and to permit, insofar as possible, the unhindered pursuit of liberal goals.

This form of justification has its roots in classical antiquity. Aristotle, for example, virtually defined the *polis* as a tutelary community, based on a shared moral understanding, and directed toward a specific way of life. In our day, substantive justification has been defended by Brian Barry, who insists that every political partisan "must take his stand on the proposition that some ways of life, some types of character are more admirable than others. . . . He must hold that societies ought to be organized in such a way as to produce the largest possible proportion of people with an admirable type of character and the best possible chance to act in accordance with it."[1] Liberalism, Barry asserts, rests on the worth of the Faustian vision: a life of self-mastery, self-expression, active pursuit of knowledge, unhesitating acceptance of moral responsibility.

The second strategy for justifying liberalism is very different. According to this view, the liberal state is desirable not because it promotes a specific way of life but precisely because it alone does not do so. The liberal state is "neutral" among different ways of life. It presides benignly over them, intervening only to adjudicate conflict, to prevent any particular way of life from tyrannizing over others, and to ensure that all adhere to the principles that constitute society's basic structure. Thus, in John Rawls's view, "the liberal state rests on a conception of equality between human beings as moral persons, as creatures having a conception of the good and capable of a sense of justice. . . . Systems of ends are not ranked in value."[2] For Ronald Dworkin, the liberal state "must be neutral on . . . the question of the good life [and] political decisions must be, so far as is possible, independent of any particular conception of the good life, or of what gives value to life."[3] Bruce Ackerman has advanced the "Neutrality Principle" as the centerpiece of liberal theory. It constrains the kinds of reasons that may validly be offered in defense of social arrangements, much as the Rawlsian veil of ignorance limits the considerations available to the denizens of the original position. According to the Neutrality Principle:

No reason [that purports to justify a social arrangement] is a good reason if it requires the power holder to assert (a) that his conception of the good is better than that asserted by any of his fellows, or (b) that, regardless of his conception of the good, he is intrinsically superior to one or more of his fellow citizens.[4]

These defenders of the liberal state, then, assert that liberalism rejects – and can get along without – any substantive theory of the good as a determinate end for human endeavor. This position is, of course, compatible with a theory of the good as neutral universal means; in this vein, Dworkin speaks of "resources and opportunities," and Ackerman of infinitely malleable "manna."[5] It is also compatible with – indeed, is thought by many (though not all) liberal theorists to require – moral principles governing our attitudes toward, and relations with, other human beings: fairness, equal respect, noncoercion, or rational dialogue, for example. In cases of conflict with individual ways of life, moreover, these principles are thought to take precedence. So the neutrality in question need not be a comprehensive moral neutrality but, rather, a wide neutrality concerning the worth of ways of life that individuals may define and pursue.

In Chapter 5, I look more systematically at the different conceptions of neutrality, so understood, and the role they may play in public life. Here I focus on the general concept of public neutrality among individual ways of life. Assuming for the moment that such neutrality is possible, why is it desirable? How does neutrality provide a justification for the liberal state?

There are three answers. First, it may be argued that there is in fact no rational basis for choosing among ways of life. Assertions about the good are personal and incorrigible. State neutrality is desirable because it is the only nonarbitrary response to this state of affairs. Second, it may be argued that even if knowledge about the good life is available, it is a breach of individual freedom – the highest value – for the state to impose this knowledge on its citizens. Of course, the best outcome occurs when individuals freely choose to pursue the good. But freely chosen error is preferable to the coerced pursuit of the good. Neutrality is justified because it is the practical expression of this priority of freedom over the good. Third, it may be argued that diversity is a basic fact of modern social life and that the practical costs of public efforts to constrain it would be unacceptably high. Just as the post-Reformation religious wars could be ended only by adopting policies of public toleration, present-day disagreements can be decently and peaceably accommodated only by a state that refrains from throwing its support to any of the contending parties.

Contemporary theorists of liberal neutrality typically rest their case on one or more of these arguments. In Chapter 5, I consider the third in detail. Here I argue that the first and second – the arguments from skepticism and from the lexical priority of freedom – both fail.

II

Kant offers the model argument for the liberal state based on the priority of freedom over the good. In *The Metaphysical Principles of Virtue*, he develops an account of the good life – the intellectual and moral perfection that each of us has a duty to pursue – and he argues that every individual is obligated to promote the well-being or happiness of others. Yet in his political writings, especially *The Metaphysical Elements of Justice* and "Theory and Practice," he propounds a full-blown and intransigent doctrine of the neutral state. The state is not in the business of teaching or enforcing morality, nor can it promote a specific conception of happiness. A paternalistic government, Kant insists, is the "greatest conceivable despotism." The substance of politics is not virtue, not happiness, but rather "freedom in the mutual external relationships of human beings." And the leading principle of politics is right: "the restriction of each individual's freedom so that it harmonizes with the freedom of everyone else."[6]

The difficulty is that Kant does not and cannot simply posit external freedom as a value. Rather, he seeks to derive it from what is for him the unconditional value: moral autonomy. Kantian moral autonomy is (to adopt Isaiah Berlin's terms) a kind of *positive* freedom. We are morally free when our will is open to, and determined by, moral rationality. But Kantian external freedom is a kind of negative freedom. We are externally free to the extent that we are not constrained by other human beings in the pursuit of our individual purposes. Kantian practical philosophy is the attempt to combine an ethics of positive freedom with a politics of negative freedom.

The attempt fails. External freedom cannot be derived from moral freedom because the two freedoms have different logics and lie in different spheres. They have different logics because while one individual's exercise of moral freedom can never conflict with another individual's moral freedom, the exercise of political freedom can – indeed, must – engender conflict. Thus, unlike moral freedom, the political freedom of each individual must be limited if the multiplicity of wills is to be harmonized. They lie in different spheres because the dignity, the infinite worth, of Kantian moral freedom consists in its elevation above the world of natural necessity, whereas external freedom is an aspect of that world. Thus, the dignity of moral freedom cannot be transferred to external freedom. To assign moral worth and inviolable priority to external freedom is to shift the ground of moral worth in a manner not merely unwarranted by, but actually impermissible within, the overall structure of Kantian theory.

This tension between positive and negative freedom is inevitably reflected in Kant's theory of the state. The strain shows in two ways: First, state policies compatible with negative freedom are nevertheless ruled out if they contradict positive freedom. Kant asks, for example, whether a people can impose on itself an ecclesiastical constitution "whereby certain accepted doctrines and outward forms of religion are declared permanent, [thus preventing] its own descendants from making further progress in religious· understanding or from correcting any past mistakes." No, it cannot, he asserts: "It is clear that any original contract of the people which established such a law would itself be null and void, *for it would conflict with the appointed aim and purpose of mankind*."[7]

With this ringing declaration, Kant breaks through the limits of external freedom and of the neutral state. He appeals not just to historical tendencies but also to the teleological understanding of individual rational perfection that he develops in *The Metaphysical Principles of Virtue*. If human beings cannot, as individuals, deliberately undercut their potential for development, then they cannot, as citizens, do so collectively.

Second, Kant's arguments against the paternalistic state turn out, on close inspection, to constitute no real barrier to the tutelary state, directly engaged in the moral education of its citizens. Kant defines paternalism as state enforcement of an arbitrary conception of happiness, but given his sharp distinction between happiness and virtue, this definition can have no bearing on the issue of moral education. Equally, his insistence that morality cannot be coerced is irrelevant, for he distinguishes between coercion and education. And in spite of his emphasis on moral conscience, Kant affirms the possibility and necessity of moral education: "The fact that virtue must be acquired (and is not innate) is contained already in the concept of virtue.... That virtue can and must be taught follows from the fact that it is not innate."[8]

We come, finally, to what I take to be Kant's official argument. The state cannot act for the people when the people cannot impose that action upon themselves, and, if no individual can so act, then the people as a collectivity cannot do so either. Kant argues:

> It is a contradiction to make the perfection of another my end and to deem myself obligated to promote his perfection. For the perfection of another man as a person consists precisely in his being able to set his end for himself according to his own concepts of duty. And it is a contradiction to require (to make it a duty for me) that I ought to do something which no one except another himself can do.[9]

But this argument seems to rest on a confusion. To say that perfection consists in the capacity for autonomy is not to say that this capacity can be achieved autonomously. Kant appears to conflate perfection as an end state with the process whereby it is realized, a distinction clearly presupposed by his contention that virtue can and must be taught.

In the end, then, Kant gives no good arguments against a tutelary liberal state. This is not terribly surprising, for, as George Kelly has pointed out, there is a tutelary ideal at work in Kantian politics. Entrance into civil society is not a deduction from self-interest but, rather, a direct duty. Membership in civil society and participation in an advancing culture discipline our natural inclinations even as they help us to attain our ends. Political life, especially in a polity that heeds the precepts of republican legitimacy and liberates the life of the mind, is a preparation for morality.[10] Kant's belief in a substantive doctrine of human perfection exerts an irresistible pressure on the limits of the neutral state.

This result is not just an idiosyncrasy of Kantian theory. To say that rational knowledge of the good life is available is to imply both that one ought to strive to lead that life and that one is harmed by deviating from it. It is to open up the possibility that B may understand what is good for A better than A does. It is to concede that negative freedom is not the only value and that its exercise may impede the pursuit of the good.

Still, the defender of negative freedom may seek to blunt

the force of this concession by assigning negative freedom an absolute, lexical priority over the good. Freedom is inviolable in the sense that it may be restricted only by the requirements of others' freedom, never by teleological considerations.

These are two kinds of arguments that might be used to support this contention. First, one could reject Kant's strategy of deriving negative freedom from some more fundamental value and argue instead that negative freedom is an end in itself that does not require – indeed, cannot receive – external justification. Nothing is more important than pursuing my purposes, doing what I want, with a minimum of interference.

The difficulty with this line of argument is that it disregards the nature of freedom. Charles Taylor has reminded us: "Freedom is important to us because we are purposive beings."[11] We are purposive in that we have goals whose attainment seems desirable and attainable – in some measure, anyway – through our striving. And freedom is valuable because it permits us to pursue our good.

But, *ex hypothesi*, the real good and the apparent good are not identical. Negative freedom allows us to pursue the apparent good even at the cost of losing the real good. But the real good is what we really want. It is the goal we would pursue if we had full intellectual clarity and emotional receptivity. To invade negative freedom in the name of the real good is to promote the individual's benefit over his or her harm, rationality over irrationality, truth over error. In practice, such invasions can be wrong *in principle* only if the mere fact that the impetus toward the good is external somehow negates the worth of the good end so achieved, that is, only if the consciously willed pursuit of a goal is a necessary condition of the value of attaining it.

As recent discussions of paternalism have shown, this proposition cannot be defended.[12] Freeing an individual from heroin addiction is good even though the afflicted individual may not consciously will his or her liberation. Indeed, it may well be that the individual cannot affirm the worth of non-addiction before having been coerced to attain it. Similarly, the outcome of education may be worthwhile, and students may retrospectively affirm its worth, even if the process of education frequently thwarts the exercise of their own inclinations.

This is not to deny, but rather to affirm, the superiority of the noncoerced over the coerced pursuit of the good. It is to deny that the noncoerced pursuit of the bad enjoys priority in principle – that is, in every case – over the coerced pursuit of the good. With this denial, the lexical priority of negative freedom vanishes.

We turn, then, to the second defense of the priority of negative freedom, which we may call the Kantian strategy. According to this view, negative freedom is not an end in itself. Its priority stems, rather, from its relation to what is in fact an end in itself – a relation either of instrumentality or of logical entailment. Kant's attempt to ground negative freedom in moral freedom failed. But, it may be argued, this was a product of Kant's faulty execution, *not* a necessary consequence of the strategy itself.

There are two difficulties with this argument. First, the most obvious grounding principles cannot be deployed. As we saw, the path from positive freedom to negative freedom is obstructed, and a substantive doctrine of the good is equally unsuited to serve as a foundation for negative freedom.

Second, even if such a grounding principle could be provided, the argument for the priority of negative freedom would still fall, unless this principle itself enjoyed a lexical priority over the good, and this is an implausibly strong requirement. The good is clearly an end in itself, in the sense that it provides adequate warrant for approving that of which it is predicated, without either the need or the possibility of recourse to "higher" principles. To defend the inviolability of negative freedom, then, we require a grounding principle that is (1) at least as strongly an end in itself as is the good, (2) independent of the good, and (3) dominant over the good in every case of conflict between them.

Now it may seem that such a principle is immediately available. After all, ascribing goodness to X (my neighbor's property, my neighbor's spouse) gives me adequate warrant to *value* X but not necessarily to *pursue* X. To say that X is good is not to say without further ado that the pursuit of X is good; that is, the proposition "the pursuit of X is unjust" trumps the proposition "X is intrinsically good." We may conjecture, then, that justice is a principle satisfying our three criteria and suitable, therefore, as a ground for affirming the priority of negative freedom over the good.

But there are two difficulties with this suggestion. In the first place, it presupposes what nearly every theory denies: that the substantive principles of justice do not themselves conflict with the exercise of negative freedom. And second, the relation between justice and the good is not one of unequivocal lexical priority. Justice is not obviously an end in itself, not obviously self-justifying. We can meaningfully ask, indeed, cannot avoid, the Platonic question: Why should we act justly? The answer, I suggest, rests both on our conception of justice and on our conception of the good. If we believe that justice is a subset of rational action, the value of justice is a corollary of the value we attach to rationality. If we believe that justice is beneficial, its value stems from the worth of the benefits it confers on the just agent or on those affected by that agent's actions. Whatever the specific content of the justification, it implies not an unequivocal priority of justice over goodness but, rather, a complex relation of mutual dependence between them.[13]

Perhaps further investigation will disclose some other grounding principle for negative freedom, but in the absence of plausible candidates, it seems sensible to conclude that the Kantian strategy for justifying the priority of negative freedom over the good is no more successful than was the direct strategy of justifying negative freedom as an end in itself. We are, therefore, warranted in generalizing the conclusion to which the discussion of Kant's argument led us: Every substantive doctrine of the human good, or of human perfection, exerts irresistible pressure on the limits of the neutral state.

To avoid misunderstanding, let me state here what I argue at some length in Chapter 8: Negative freedom has a substantial, and legitimate, role within liberal theory. This is so because the liberal theory of the good is at most a partial account, one that leaves a considerable portion of life up to each individual's discretion. Freedom allows us to pursue this discretionary aspect of our lives, and it gains its worth from its contribution to the ends of life we have properly defined for ourselves. From this standpoint, a suitably constrained interpretation of negative freedom becomes an element of our good.

I should also repeat what I asserted in Chapter 1 (and defend in Chapter 8): What is distinctive about liberalism is not the absence of a substantive conception of the good, but rather a reluctance to move from this conception to full-blown public coercion of individuals. There are, I think, some excellent considerations of both prudence and principle that support this reluctance, and these considerations go some way toward staking out a sphere of individual freedom. My point is only that they do not add up to the kind of come-what-may defense of negative freedom that many liberals believe (wrongly, if I am right) is indispensable to their creed.

III

Contemporary liberal theorists, many of whom have been inspired by Kant, have endeavored to avoid the tension between individual perfection and state neutrality that we found at the heart of Kant's political theory and in every theory that contains these two elements. Many contemporary theorists are deeply skeptical about the rational status of any account of perfection or of the good life. For them, the defense of the neutral state rests in part on the unavailability of knowledge of the good, and they argue that liberal theory requires no substantive theory of the good whatever, but at most a "thin" or instrumental theory.

This argument takes two forms. The first is familiar: Ignorance about the good implies relativism, which mandates tolerance, which in turn requires the neutral state.[14]

The fallacy of this chain of inference is equally familiar. Relativism, taken by itself, does not entail tolerance. B seeks to impose his way of life on A; A protests that B has no rational justification for his action; B replies, "What do I care about rational justification?" or (more moderately) "My way of life requires as a necessary condition a society in which others think and behave as I do." A can continue the argument only by appealing to some principle beyond ignorance of the good. Full skepticism about the good leads not to tolerance, not to liberal neutrality, but to an unconstrained struggle among different ways of life, a struggle in which force, not reason, is the final arbiter.[15]

The second line of defense is more subtle but not more successful. Human beings, it is argued, must be judged and treated as equals unless there is some good reason to do otherwise. The only good reason would be a philosophic demonstration that some human beings are better than others, either in their moral character or in their conception of the good life, but we know that no such demonstration is possible. We must therefore treat all individuals as equals, and in a manner that neither presupposes nor imposes what we lack – a rational theory of the good. It is because individuals are morally equal that the state must be morally neutral.

This is a coherent argument as far as it goes, but it does not bring us to the liberal state. Liberals, after all, cannot be satisfied to say that all human lives are *equally* worthy. They must also say that each life has *positive* worth, greater than zero. So, for example, before Ronald Dworkin can arrive at his fundamental principle of liberalism – equality of concern and respect – he must assert that government is obligated to treat those whom it governs "with concern, that is, as human beings who are capable of suffering and frustration, and with respect, that is, as human beings who are capable of forming and acting on intelligent conceptions of how their lives should be lived."[16]

It is not my purpose here to object to these contentions, but only to point out the grounds on which they rest. Our "respect" is for human existence itself, the ability to form and act on purposes, whatever they may be, taken as a positive good. Our "concern" is for the fulfillment of human purposes – the avoidance of pain, the achievement of our goals, whatever they may be – taken as positive goods. And we move from these positive valuations to equality of concern and respect through the commitment to rationality: Differences of moral weight among individuals can be justified only if they rest on relevant reasons, which are (by hypothesis) absent.

These features of Dworkin's argument are hardly idiosyncratic. The participants in Ackerman's neutral dialogue, from which all special conceptions of the good have allegedly been expelled, in fact share a conception of the good. They argue that life itself is preferable to death: "[None] of us is willing to starve to death while the other takes all the manna." They agree on the worth of human purposiveness, and on the worth of fulfilling purposes: "each of us is prepared to say that our own image of self-fulfillment has *some* value." And they agree that reason is preferable to force, as a guide for the constraint on action. They choose the rational life, and in so doing they endorse a specific conception of what is truly good for beings who wish to be human.[17]

Matters are much the same in Rawls's theory. The distribution of primary goods takes on moral significance only if the fulfillment of the disparate individual purposes they serve is assumed to have intrinsic worth, that is, only if we as social theorists begin by accepting the evaluative standpoint of purposive agents. And clearly, the movement from individual purposiveness to principles of social justice rests on individuals' shared commitment to abide by the dictates of rationality in a suitably defined choice-situation. The formal constraints on possible principles reflect this commitment to rationality as well.[18]

This conclusion is confirmed and reinforced by Rawls's argument in the Dewey Lectures. Human beings are, he contends, characterized by "two moral powers and by two corresponding highest-order interests in realizing and exercising these powers. The first power is the capacity to understand, to apply, and to act from (and not merely in accordance with) the principles of justice. The second moral power is the capacity to form, to revise, and rationally to pursue a conception of the good."[19] The gap separating this conception of moral agency from the perfectionism Rawls elsewhere castigates is exceedingly narrow. (In Chapter 7, I offer an extended discussion of this point, as well as of the broader issues raised by his conception of moral personality.)

We can discern a recurrent pattern. Each of these contemporary liberal theories begins by promising to do without a substantive theory of the good; each ends by betraying that promise. All of them covertly rely on the same triadic theory of the good, which assumes the worth of human existence, the worth of human purposiveness and of the fulfillment of human purposes, and the worth of rationality as the chief constraint on social principles and social actions. If we may call the beliefs in the worth of human existence and in the worth of purposes and their fulfillment the root assumptions of humanism, then the theory of the good presupposed by these neutralist liberals is the theory of rationalist humanism.

In many ways this result is not terribly surprising, for it merely reemphasizes the line of descent from Enlightenment assumptions to present-day liberalism. Nor is it clear at first glance what the critical force of this finding may be. "Very well," we may imagine these theorists to retort, "we do have a more than instrumental theory of the good. Still, it is gratifyingly capacious and undemanding. To begin with, it expresses something like the minimum presuppositions of social philosophy, the convictions that all serious participants

92

in discussions of social principles must hold. Liberalism is the theory not of the neutral state but of the minimally committed state. Moreover, much the same is true on the level of political practice. The liberal state rests solely on those beliefs about the good shared by all its citizens, whereas every other state must coercively espouse some controversial assumptions about the good life."

This is a powerful and important argument. On the theoretical plane, it calls our attention to a crucial ambiguity in the notion of neutrality. Strong neutrality implies the expulsion of any and all conceptions of the good from liberal theory. Weak neutrality, on the other hand, implies the rejection only of those theories that entail moral distinctions among individuals – that is, that preach the superiority of specific types of character and ways of life. But not all conceptions of the good imply hierarchical distinctions among individuals. In particular, neutralist liberals may argue, their theory of the good – the theory of rationalist humanism – does not do so. It is therefore neutral in the only sense that their thesis requires, and in the only sense that they ever intended, even though occasional linguistic infelicities may have led readers to expect that their thesis would be neutral in the strong sense.

But this clarification raises a new difficulty. It is one thing to propound a full-blown skepticism about the possibility of knowing the good in any philosophically or intersubjectively valid manner, and to endeavor to build social theory on this parsimonious foundation. It is a very different matter to assert that we can have usable knowledge of the good, but only up to a point. If we can proceed on the assumption that existence is preferable to nonexistence, that fulfillment of purposes is referable to nonfulfillment, then why are we not free to enter into a fuller range of traditional arguments about the good life? On the basis of what considerations do we draw the line between objectivity and subjectivity just where most contemporary liberal theorists wish to draw it? In the absence of more explicit supporting arguments, the partial skepticism characteristic of neutralist liberalism has the appearance of an arbitrary arrangement of convenience rather than a principled position.

Versions of this problem have bedeviled liberal theory all the way back to Hobbes, whose robust skepticism gives way at the crucial point to the doctrine of the *summum malum*. Good and evil are relative to the individual, and variable within each individual,

> whence arise disputes, controversies, and at last war. And therefore so long as man is in the condition of mere nature, which is a condition of war, as private appetite is the measure of good, and evil: *and consequently all men agree on this, that peace is good*, and therefore also the [moral virtues,] as the means of *peaceable, sociable, and comfortable living*.[20]

The difficulty is dual. Hobbes's skepticism comes to an abrupt end when he accepts the humanist theory of the good – the worth of existence and of the orderly pursuit of individual purposes – that he ascribes to all human beings. On the other hand, he does not and cannot simply appeal to an existing consensus. As he admits, many men – proud aristocrats, reckless desperados, religious fanatics, benighted fools – do not act on the belief that death is the worst of all evils. Liberal humanism is not only a substantive theory of the good but also an eminently contestable theory. The liberal commitment to individual existence and purposes can be challenged not solely by genocidal regimes but also by the traditions of secular heroism and, as we have rediscovered in the case of Iran, by the tradition of religious martyrdom as well.

Moreover, the liberal commitment to moral rationality is far from minimal in its implications for the scope and content of state activity. In Rawls's construction, for example, those who are to decide on general social arrangements are assumed to be able to reflect and to act in compliance with the dictates of rationality. Nevertheless, in formulating these arrangements, they must take into account the certainty that extensive moral education is essential if citizens of actual societies are to obtain the capacity for acting "on principle." A member of a well-ordered liberal society cannot object to state-governed tutelary practices designed to inculcate a sense of justice, for "in agreeing to principles of right the parties in the original position consent to the arrangements necessary to make these principles effective in their conduct."[21] The more seriously liberalism takes its commitment to practical rationality, the more blurred becomes the line separating the liberal state from the tutelary, "perfectionist" state committed to a fuller theory of the good.

The path to defensible clarity in these matters leads *through*, not *around*, a direct consideration of the understanding of well-being on which liberalism rests. In Chapter 8, I argue for a liberal conception of well-being (of which the rationalist humanism just discussed is a part) that makes possible both liberalism's shared public commitments and its characteristic defense of social pluralism and individual agency.

Moving from the theoretical to the practical plane, we must ask whether the minimally committed state is truly hospitable to all ways of life and conceptions of the good (an issue to which I return in Chapters 5 and 6). Rawls concedes that under liberal conditions certain forms of life – those that require control of the machinery of state – are likely systematically to lose out. Does this mean that liberal society is, contrary to its professed principles, systematically biased? No, he replies,

> a well-ordered society defines a fair background within which ways of life have a reasonable opportunity to establish themselves. If a conception of the good is unable to endure and gain adherents under institutions of equal freedom and mutual toleration, one must question whether it is a viable conception of the good, and whether its passing is to be regretted.[22]

But (we may in turn reply) our fears cannot be allayed merely by invoking the sacred ghost of John Stuart Mill.

Social competition is no more reliably benign than economic competition. Indeed, a kind of social Gresham's Law may operate, in which the pressure of seductively undemanding ways of life may make it very difficult, for example, for parents to raise children in accordance with norms of effort, conscientiousness, and self-restraint. The easy assumption that only "undeserving" ways of life lose out in a liberal society is unworthy of serious social philosophy. The line between ways of life that can flourish in the midst of social heterogeneity and those whose viability depends on a more hospitable homogeneity does not neatly divide valuable from worthless, or generous from repressive, conceptions of the good. The destruction of homogeneous and relatively self-contained subcommunities through the subtle corrosion of liberal society or through the direct assault of liberal social policy is not always to be welcomed. But this is not to say that, taken as a whole, we may not rightly choose the characteristic biases of the liberal polity over the biases inherent in the alternative forms of political organization actually available to us. It is not to say that these biases cannot be further ameliorated by more carefully distinguishing between what is and is not required for liberal public order. (See, for example, my discussion of liberal civic education in Chapter 11.) And it is certainly not to say that the bias of liberalism is as systematically constraining, as hostile to full human diversity, as are other forms of political life. Indeed, the relative capaciousness of liberal orders is an important element in the case for their relative superiority.

We need not look to the indirect effects of social heterogeneity to deny the full neutrality of the liberal state. There is a wide range of controverted issues over which, as a matter of both logic and practice, the contending parties cannot simply agree to differ and must instead arrive at binding determinations. Whatever its decision, the polity unavoidably commits itself to specific views of human personality and right conduct as well as to a range of external effects on other institutions and practices. In such cases, neutrality is never violated, because it is never possible. Every polity, then, embodies a more than minimal conception of the good that establishes at least a partial rank-order among individual ways of life and competing principles of right conduct.

Chapter 5

Liberalism and
neutral public discourse

Chapter 4 was structured around a basic distinction between neutral and nonneutral defenses of liberalism. In this chapter I add two layers of complexity to this dyad: first, by distinguishing two variants of neutral defense, the "pragmatic" and the "political"; second, by unpacking and examining the various understandings of neutrality employed by the "political" theorists of liberalism.

I

Broadly speaking, three quite distinct approaches to liberalism have emerged in the past generation. At one end of the spectrum we find *perfectionist* liberalism – the thesis that liberalism finds its justification, and its point, in a distinctive vision of the human good. In Joseph Raz's view, for example, liberalism "regards personal freedom as an aspect of the good life. It is a view of freedom deriving from the value of personal autonomy."[1]

At the other end of the spectrum lies what may be called *pragmatic* liberalism – the thesis that liberalism can be understood as an agreement struck by symmetrically situated, self-interested individuals animated solely by prudential or strategic considerations. This is the view that John Rawls calls "modus vivendi"; it is represented most comprehensively and persuasively in our time by David Gauthier.[2]

Between these two views lies what Charles Larmore has

called *political* liberalism, represented most conspicuously by Rawls (and by Larmore himself). As I cannot improve on Larmore's summary, I simply quote it. Political liberalism "is a conception at once *moral* and *minimal*. It holds that the liberal principle of political neutrality toward controversial ideals of the good life finds its justification in certain moral commitments. But it also claims that these commitments are themselves compatible with a wide range of ideals of the good life."[3]

The problems associated with perfectionist and pragmatic liberalism are well known. Perfectionist liberalism secures authority for liberal politics at the cost of taking sides in normative controversies that are bound to rage within liberal polities under modern circumstances. Perfectionism limits diversity, but wide diversity seems to be at the heart of what we mean by (and cherish in) liberal societies. (As should be clear already, I regard this as a cautionary note rather than a decisive reason for rejecting all perfectionist arguments. Some limits on diversity are not only compatible with, but required by, a liberal order.)

For its part, pragmatic liberalism seems to leave social institutions and policies vulnerable to changes in the relative bargaining position of contending forces. As Rawls has remarked, "To each according to his threat advantage" is not a very attractive principle of justice. Even more fundamental, no one has shown how agents moved by prudence alone would have adequate motivation to comply with cooperative rules, or to invest them with the distinctive authority we associate with the concept of the "moral."[4]

In part for these negative reasons, and in part because it speaks to our felt needs for a defense of liberty and diversity at once moral and consensual, political liberalism has emerged in this decade as a powerful philosophical force. I do not believe that this proposed *via media*, and in particular the special account of public neutrality on which its viability depends, has received the scrutiny it deserves. It is to this task that I now turn.

II

The analyses of Ronald Dworkin, Joseph Raz, Charles Larmore, and Rawls himself have made it clear that liberal neutrality has a number of different senses, which it is essential to distinguish.

The first may be called *neutrality of opportunity* – the thesis that liberalism alone is capacious enough to allow all ways of life to exist, and that it is on that basis the preferred form of political organization. We need not tarry long at this sense of neutrality: It is inconsistent with any account of liberalism that gives pride of place to general principles of justice or rights, for the simple reason that these principles directly rule out certain ways of life. (Rawls gives the example of life plans requiring the repression or degradation of certain persons on racial or ethnic grounds.)

The second sense is *neutrality of outcome* (sometimes also called neutrality of effect or of influence). According to this understanding, a state is neutral, and justifiable, only if the operation of its characteristic principles, institutions, and policies has no tendency to favor certain ways of life and hamper others. Proponents of neutrality by and large repudiate this interpretation of neutrality as well as the first. Thus Rawls: "It is surely impossible for the basic structure of a just constitutional regime not to have important effects and influences on which comprehensive doctrines endure and gain adherents over time, and it is futile to try to counteract these effects and influences."[5] Similarly Larmore: "It is a general truth that what the state does, the decisions it makes and the policies it pursues, will generally benefit some people more than others, and so some conceptions of the good life will fare better than others."[6]

The third and fourth senses, closely related, may be called *neutrality of aim* and *neutrality of procedure*. According to neutrality of aim, state policies should not strive to promote any permissible way of life or conception of the good over any other. According to neutrality of procedure, state policies should be justified "without appealing to the presumed intrinsic superiority of any particular conception of the good life."[7] Richard Arneson has offered an instructive discussion of the difference between these two conceptions:

> An example of a state policy that satisfies neutrality of procedure but not neutrality of aim would be a policy of state establishment of religion based not on the judgment that the favored religion is intrinsically superior to its rivals but rather on the estimate that promoting one religion over its rivals will facilitate the maintenance of civil peace. An example of a policy that satisfied neutrality of aim but not neutrality of procedure would be a policy of broad religious toleration that aims to favor no religion over another and that is justified by appeal to the judgment that Quakerism is the true religion and among the tenets of Quakerism is the principle that there should be broad religious toleration and no tilting by the state in favor of any one religion.

(As Arneson points out, it is perfectly possible to combine these two forms of neutrality into a single, more demanding, criterion, and to describe a range of policies in compliance with it.)[8]

III

The issue of patterned outcomes in liberal society is of great intrinsic interest, and it recurs later in this book. Neutrality of aim, for its part, has had a substantial impact on constitutional jurisprudence, particularly in the context of the First Amendment. But the center of the philosophical debate since the 1980s has been elsewhere. Since the publication of Ronald Dworkin's "Liberalism" and Bruce Ackerman's *Social Justice in the Liberal State*, attention has increasingly focused on neutrality of procedure as what is most distinctive, and attractive, about liberalism.

Neutrality of procedure, to recapitulate, consists in a special constraint on reasons that can be invoked to justify public policy. It stands in roughly the same relation to political deliberation as do rules of evidence to trial advocacy. Specifically, a reason is not publicly valid if it appeals to, or rests upon, the presumed superiority of any particular conception of the good life. A policy is illegitimate if such a conception is an ineliminable element of its proposed justification.

Procedural neutrality, so understood, offers an ingenious translation of key liberal concepts. It can be linked to liberal equality, as an expression of the equal respect due to every individual in his or her public capacity. It helps redraw the line between what majorities may rightly do and what must be reserved, as rights, to even small minorities. Relatedly, it reinvigorates the classic liberal distinction between the public and the private. Finally, it forcibly reiterates liberalism's deep-seated antipathy to what might be called moral coercion: Individuals should not be forced, with either their words or their resources, to lend their support to policies based on conceptions of the good to which they are conscientiously opposed.

The redescription of majority powers versus minority rights, and of the public versus the private, in the language of neutral procedure does not leave these concepts wholly unaltered. Two shifts are especially significant. First, the focus on prohibited reasons for policies rather than on the policies themselves means that descriptive issues become very important, in much the same way that identifying appropriate maxims for proposed deeds becomes critical for Kantian moral theory.[9] Second, the focus on reasons opens up a potential gap between public utterances and private intentions. For example, recent Supreme Court litigation on "moment of silence" legislation has raised the question whether facially neutral justifications are merely cloaks for underlying sectarian aims. The larger question, then, is whether liberal theory attempts to specify a normative relation between reasons and intentions or, rather, confines its attention to the character of public discourse.[10]

In a cogent article, Bruce Ackerman has propounded a particularly blunt and unadorned version of neutrality of procedure. The guiding idea is of a society divided into groups, each of which embraces a distinctive set of moral propositions. These groups differ on many points. Ackerman's proposal is that the moral component of public dialogue should be confined to those propositions on which all groups happen to agree:

> When you and I learn that we disagree about one or another dimension of the moral truth, we should not search for some common value that will trump this disagreement; nor should we try to translate it into some putatively neutral framework; nor should we seek to transcend it by talking about how some unearthly creature might resolve it. We should simply say *nothing at all* about this disagreement and put the moral ideals that divide us off the conversational agenda of the liberal state.[11]

Ackerman recognizes that this conversational restraint, or "selective repression," will prove "deeply frustrating," for it will prevent each of us from justifying our political positions by appealing to what we hold to be most deeply true. But he has a plausible response to this difficulty. Our social life is divided into a number of roles, each of which is guided by special norms of speech as well as action: "Each social role can be understood as a set of conventional restraints upon acceptable symbolic behavior."[12] Whether one is acting as a lawyer, a teacher, a business manager, or whatever, there are certain types of discourse that are held to be off limits, not because they are (necessarily) false, but because they are for some reason inappropriate to the matter at hand. As Ackerman says, "Truth is not necessarily a defense for stepping out of role."[13] Thus, unless we assume that politics is a total activity that transcends all roles and boundaries, an assumption that is bound to prove troubling to liberals of all stripes, the notion of conversational restraints in politics has at least prima facie plausibility. (Whether Ackerman has identified the correct restraints is another matter altogether, as we shall see.)

The true difficulties with this account lie elsewhere. First, as a simple empirical matter, in a society of any significant size and diversity, it is overwhelmingly likely that there will be no moral propositions on which all groups agree, or that the range of agreement will be far too narrow, skewed, and odd to provide an adequate basis for public policy. (A thought experiment: Can you name one moral proposition that would pass Ackerman's overlap test in contemporary America?)

Second, it is far from clear why Ackerman invokes conversational restraint so early in the deliberative process. He insists that when confronted with moral disagreement, members of conflicting groups should not even try to convince each other to change their minds. We should rather assume that the disagreement will be "ongoing" and accordingly sidestep it altogether. The motivation for imposing restraints at the threshold of public discussion rather than at its conclusion seems arbitrary, at least to me. (But perhaps Ackerman is tacitly resting his case on pessimistic empirical propositions about the impact of rationality on personal belief.) Why not begin by exploring the extent to which intractable differences may be narrowed? If moral progress occurs, so much the better; the pool of shared – hence practically usable – premises has been expanded. And if the public conversation leaves matters as they were, nothing has been lost, because procedural neutrality can still be invoked at the decision stage: No policy can be adopted the justification of which rests on moral premises that remain disputed.

This perplexity only deepens when we inspect Ackerman's justification for his brand of procedural neutrality: "Our mutual act of conversational restraint allows all of us to win a priceless advantage: none of us will be obliged to say something in liberal conversation that seems *affirmatively false*."[14] This does not seem to me to be as uniformly advantageous as Ackerman supposes: Perhaps it is a good thing to compel bigots of all stripes to mouth principles they privately believe false; maybe they will even come to believe them to be true.

But even granting Ackerman's point for the sake of the argument, I don't see how it applies to the issue at hand. In the course of public discussion, I deny that fetuses are persons; you say that they possess all essential attributes of personhood. How has either of us been compelled to say something false?

Suppose our society eventually votes on the issue and my side wins. Simply by virtue of its minority status, has your side been compelled to *say* anything it deems false? I think not. The real compulsion lies elsewhere: If your side wishes to remain within the community, it must comply with laws permitting individual acts with which it morally disagrees, and it may even be forced to pay taxes for programs (e.g., public funding for abortions) directly supporting goals it finds abhorrent.

Now I don't mean to deny that these forms of compulsion are very real and that there may be very good reasons for seeking to minimize their occurrence. Indeed, procedural neutrality invoked at the point of public decision (or, that failing, during judicial review of legislative acts) might make sense as a strategy for reducing such compulsion. But (to repeat), I don't see how procedural restraints imposed on discussion prior to decision serves in any meaningful way to limit coercion.

Charles Larmore offers an account of neutrality that at first glance closely resembles Ackerman's. His case rests (in part) on what he believes is a universal norm of rational dialogue:

> When two people disagree about some specific point, but wish to continue talking about the more general problem they wish to solve, each should prescind from the beliefs that the other rejects, (1) in order to construct an argument on the basis of his other beliefs that will convince the other of the truth of the disputed belief, or (2) in order to shift to another aspect of the problem, where the possibilities of agreement seem greater.[15]

This position lacks neither plausibility nor respectable antecedents. It bears a family resemblance to both Socratic dialogue and Aristotle's account of rhetoric, and it maps important features of the practice of persuasion. Still, it seems to me to embody an excessively rationalistic account of ar-

gumentation, and certainly of public discourse. The point of
much dialogue is to invite one's interlocutor to see the world
the way you do, or at least to understand what it is like to
see the world the way you do. One way of doing that is the
reverse of "prescinding" from disputed issues: namely, stubbornly bearing witness to one's stance at the precise point
of difference. This process is more analogous to art criticism
than to mathematical reasoning. The critic invites others to
focus on specific aspects of the work and to see them in a
particular way. Good criticism is capable of changing minds
on very fundamental points. (I know that my basic response
to movies and paintings – what they are "about," whether
they succeed or fail – has frequently been shifted 180 degrees
by individuals whose gifts of perception and description ex-
ceed my own.)

Now clearly the critic is not coercing me to change but, on
the contrary, is appealing to something we have in common.
But that something is not a *premise;* it is, rather, an *experience.*
The implicit logic goes like this: "We may disagree at the
level of abstract concepts. But if you see what I see, your
judgment will converge on mine." This, I take it, is why
prolife advocates display disturbing pictures of second-
trimester fetuses, and why prochoice defenders respond with
graphic accounts of back-alley abortions. The point is to
widen the sphere of shared experiences in order to evoke
the evaluative judgments that seem closely linked to them.

As this example makes clear, if the experiences underlying
public policy issues are themselves diverse and contradictory, the appeal to shared experience will not necessarily
narrow disagreements at the level of discursive premises.
My point is only that the appeal to experience at the point
of difference is an ineliminable element of dialogue, one that
tugs against the norm of prescinding.

To be sure, Larmore's conception is more permissive than
Ackerman's, in the sense that prescinding becomes man-
datory only when it appears that the further airing of differences is unlikely to resolve them. Still, history suggests
that some controversies may persist for very extended pe-

riods before achieving resolution. In the case of such issues, the norm of prescinding may deprive the polity of morally important opportunities for self-improvement.

As Larmore recognizes, the commitment to resolve public disputes through rational argument is not itself morally neutral. It rests in part on a commitment to civil peace, that is, to the resolution of disputes through means other than force. It is this commitment, Larmore insists, that marks the boundary between good liberals and what he terms "fanatics and would-be martyrs."[16] Although the focus on civil peace is not morally ultimate – it can be trumped by the requirement of equal respect – it figures prominently in Larmore's thesis.

This turn in the argument is hardly surprising. Most accounts of liberalism embrace, tacitly or explicitly, the premise that life is too valuable to jeopardize in conflicts over how to lead it and that conflicts over the good life must therefore be muted in the name of life.

(In some accounts, this premise is buttressed by the suggestion that even the conflicts we take most seriously are pretty laughable. A classic example of this can be found in my son's favorite bedtime story, Dr. Seuss's *Butter Battle Book*, whose silent but unmistakable subtext that the differences between liberal democracy and communism are no more important than those between Yooks, who eat their bread butter side up, and Zooks, who eat it butter side down – certainly nothing worth dying for.)

At this juncture, a disagreement emerges between Ackerman and Larmore, for Ackerman rejects as unacceptably nonneutral the focus on civil peace. Ackerman says:

> I would refuse to participate in a political conversation that began: "However much you and I disagree on other matters, we both accept the supreme importance of self-preservation." Rather than provide me with a neutral starting point, a Hobbesian political conversation would constantly oblige me to say things I found morally demeaning, despicable, false. If the point of liberal conversation is to enable me to talk to you without affirming moral propositions I think are false, the Hobbesian line goes nowhere.[17]

This riposte raises the question of whether any liberal theory can get along without some basic agreement on what is good. I think not, and Ackerman's latest offering has done nothing to dissuade me. He begins by formulating the liberal problem of public order: "how people who disagree about the moral truth might nonetheless reasonably solve their ongoing problem of living together." And, he continues, "I do not propose to base my case for public dialogue on some assertedly general feature of the moral life, but upon the distinctive way liberals conceive of the problem of public order. This means, of course, that my argument will not convince people who reject the underlying liberal problematic."[18] Generally, one might say, Ackerman's argument will not persuade anyone who believes that coercion is part of an appropriate response to the fact of moral disagreement. And specifically, it will not persuade anyone who believes that there are on occasion human ills worse than being compelled to affirm publicly things one privately believes to be false. Recall that Ackerman labels the avoidance of such compulsion a "priceless advantage." *This* is what functions as the indispensable *summum bonum* for his whole theory.

However this may be, Larmore recognizes that the neutral dialogue in the name of civil peace will seem far more imperative in the case of interlocutors who are strong enough to threaten, or enough like us to evoke our sympathy, than for those who are "strange and weak." To extend the reach of dialogue to these more difficult cases, he invokes the norm of *equal respect for persons:*

> What is prohibited by the norm of equal respect is resting compliance only on force. If we try to bring about conformity to a political principle simply by threat, we will be treating people solely as means, as objects of coercion. We will not also be treating them as ends, engaging directly their distinctive capacity as persons. . . . We will not be making the acceptability of the principle depend on their reason just as we believe it draws on our own. To respect another person as an end is to insist that coercive or political principles be as justifiable to that person as they are to us.[19]

Larmore (and Ronald Dworkin before him) may well be right that the norm of equal respect for persons is close to the core of contemporary liberalism. But while the (general) concept of equal respect may be relatively uncontroversial, the (specific) conception surely is not. To treat an individual as person rather than object is to offer him an explanation. Fine; but *what kind* of explanation? Larmore seems to suggest that a properly respectful explanation must appeal to beliefs already held by one's interlocutors; whence the need for neutral dialogue. This seems arbitrary and implausible. I would suggest, rather, that we show others respect when we offer them, as explanation, what we take to be our true and best reasons for acting as we do.

For example, when we arrest, try, and convict criminals, we show respect for their moral personality by offering the reasons embedded in the law: The harms to individuals the law seeks to prevent would, if unchecked, damage our interests or violate our rights; to breach these prohibitions is to harm both the individual and the community; the community is entitled to protect its collective determination with the threat, and if need be the reality, of coercive sanctions; and so forth. The convicted criminal may reject each and every one of these premises. He or she may suffer from a sociopathic disconnection from all other human beings and from society at large. But we do not explain our actions to the criminal on the basis of his or her own beliefs. Indeed, to do so would be insulting and manipulative. We rather show respect by treating the criminal as we would anyone else, as someone capable of acting in accordance with a sound understanding of justice and of being motivated by a sense of justice.

I do not mean to imply that individuals who happen to be on the losing side of a democratic vote are on all fours, morally speaking, with convicted criminals. There is a critical difference between those who affirm, and act upon, the principle of respect for fellow citizens and those who flout that principle. The point is rather that any generalized link between coercion and breach of respect is untenable. The point is only strengthened when we note (as Thomas Nagel and Gerald Dworkin have argued) that we can accept paternalistic interventions in a range of circumstances without believing that this benevolent coercion contradicts equal respect for persons. Thus I cannot agree with Larmore that "coercion, or force, [is] the only clear-cut case of treating someone as a means."[20] It can be that, but it needn't be.

In two important respects, Larmore's position is more realistic than Ackerman's. Larmore concedes that under modern conditions in free societies, the overlapping moral consensus required for full state neutrality is most unlikely to exist. He also acknowledges that neutralist noncoercion cannot be the liberal's only desideratum, because it is also necessary to come to some collective decision about the community's structure of liberty and distribution. "So the liberal must be willing to consider tradeoffs between these two goals."[21] And, as Larmore further acknowledges, there is no one obviously correct way of balancing them, even if the metaprinciple is that one should abridge neutrality only to the extent needed to make social decision possible. We are left, then, with the familiar if somewhat indeterminate clash between the individual's resistance to coercion and the community's need to constitute its basic structure in circumstances of nontrivial moral division.

Thomas Nagel's account of liberal public discourse also takes as its point of departure the familiar fact of deep disagreement. He quickly observes, though, that not all disagreements are of the same type: "We need a distinction between two kinds of disagreement – one whose grounds make it all right for the majority to use political power in the service of their opinion, and another whose grounds are such that it would be wrong for the majority to do so."[22] The need for such a distinction immediately generates a series of basic questions:

> When can I regard the grounds for a belief as objective in a way that permits me to appeal to it in political argument, and to rely on it even though others do not in fact accept it and

even though they may not be unreasonable not to accept it? What kinds of grounds must those be, if I am not to be guilty of appealing simply to my belief, rather than to a common ground of justification?[23]

Nagel answers his questions with an account of what distinguishes "public justification" from the "bare confrontation between incompatible personal points of view." Public justification means, first, the willingness to submit one's reasons to criticism in light of a shared critical rationality and understanding of what counts as evidence, as distinguished from "personal faith or revelation." That an understanding of rationality and evidence is shared means that your interlocutor can come to share the grounds on which you have formed your judgment and can judge your judgment on that basis. Public justification means, second, that you can explain the failure of others to share your view in a noncircular fashion – inadequate evidence, faulty reasoning, poor judgment, and so forth – rather than through the unmediated assertion that they don't believe the truth. Thus, Nagel concludes:

> The appeal to truth in political argument requires an objective distinction between belief and truth that can be applied or at least understood from the public standpoint appropriate to the argument in question. Disagreements over the truth must be interpreted as resulting from differences of judgment in the exercise of a common reason.[24]

In a recent paper, Rawls defines a conception of "free public reason" very much along Nagel's lines. It consists of four elements: principles of logical inference; rules of (admissible) evidence; the criteria and procedures of "common sense"; and the "methods and conclusions of science when not in dispute."[25]

The Nagel/Rawls thesis is exposed to three kinds of objections. First, the whole of science is in dispute, at least from the standpoint of religious fundamentalism. A number of religious groups, for example, object to public school curricula that teach the Darwinian theory of evolution but not

Biblical creationism. The notion that scientific rationality is what our public culture has "in common" cannot survive even casual inspection. Nor is it the case that religious alternatives to scientific rationality can be shown to be "irrational" through an appeal to any common ground that would be recognized as authoritative by the faithful.

Second, the proponents of revealed religion would be compelled to reject as tendentious the distinction between evidence-based propositions and religious faith. Many believers insist that their faith is based on evidence – indeed, on personal experience – that is communicable to others. Indeed, they typically try to share it with others, frequently with success. And they have a range of noncircular explanations for the failure of others to agree with them: explanations bearing in many cases at least a formal similarity to the explanations offered by psychiatrists for their patients' "resistance" to hard truths about themselves. Nor can advocates of public reason make much of the fact that faith-based appeals frequently fail to persuade, because arguments based on secular evidence frequently fail to do so as well.

This brings me to the third point. Nagel acknowledges that "moral disagreements which fall within the public domain may nevertheless be irresolvable in fact. That there is common ground does not mean that people will actually reach agreement, nor does it mean that only one belief is reasonable on the evidence." Still, he insists, "I do not believe this makes the distinction between a disagreement in the common, public domain and a clash between irreconcilable subjective convictions too rarified to be of political significance. Judgment is not the same as faith, or pure moral intuition."[26]

Perhaps not. But what exactly is the difference? One possible account is this: Public argument delimits the bounds of reasonable disagreement by defining, in each arena of controversy, the kinds of considerations that are relevant to determining judgment. Nonetheless, the relative priority or weight to be attached to the various considerations is frequently underdetermined by the totality of available evidence and argument. It is the role of personal judgment to affirm the importance or unimportance, significance or insignificance, of the reasons commonly acknowledged as relevant. So far so good. But this approach does not draw the line where Nagel wants it to be. As Kent Greenawalt has argued:

> There are many issues concerning borderlines of status (such as the valuation of fetuses and animals), complicated factual assessments, and conflicts of values as to which shared premises of justice and ordinary modes of reasoning and determining facts are radically inconclusive. Everyone on such questions must rely finally on deepseated feelings that are not subject to convincing interpersonal argument.[27]

The problem is this: If most public problems allow for differing judgments, and if the exercise of personal judgment is guided by the sorts of private, incommunicable beliefs Nagel wants to exclude from the public sphere, then most of what we understand as public argument will be ruled out by Nagel's criteria of publicity. This cannot be the right result: The point of the entire enterprise was to draw the line between legitimate and illegitimate instances of majority coercion, not to justify the proposition that majority coercion can never be right.

Amy Gutmann and Dennis Thompson have offered a useful distinction between two ways of coping with deep moral disagreement. Principles of *preclusion* serve to exclude certain kinds of issues from the political agenda. Principles of *accommodation*, by contrast, govern the conduct of moral disagreement for controversial issues that cannot and should not be excluded from public deliberation. They argue (correctly, in my view) that Nagel's principle of preclusion goes much too far in ruling out public deliberation not only on religion but also on a host of morally charged issues such as abortion and our treatment of animals. They contend (also correctly, I think) that any plausible principle of preclusion has a far less extensive scope than contemporary neutralist liberals would like.[28]

The Gutmann–Thompson entry in the preclusion sweep

stakes is the familiar concept of a "moral position." To be admissible for public deliberation, an argument must satisfy the formal requirements of a moral position. First, it must presuppose a disinterested perspective that could be adopted by any member of a society whatever his or her particular circumstances (race, class, gender, and so forth). Second, "any premises in the argument that depend on empirical evidence should be in principle open to challenge by generally accepted methods of inquiry." Third, "premises for which empirical evidence or logical inference is not appropriate should not be radically implausible ... either by implying the rejection of other significantly more plausible beliefs widely held in the society, or by appealing to authorities whose claims cannot be challenged by those who doubt them."[29]

As attractive as this position may appear, it encounters a number of difficulties. The first emerges at the threshold: Why should we assume that every publicly admissible argument must be a *moral* argument? What about arguments that rest candidly on individual or group self-interest? Granted, such arguments are not likely to gain the support of those individuals or groups whose interests would not be served by the proposed policy. But many political utterances are intended to be declaratory rather than persuasive. For example, an elected representative may well justify his or her position by pointing to the advantages that would accrue to the denizens of his or her district. (One could even construct a not obviously crazy moral defense of the proposition that elected officials *should* seek to advance the interests of those they represent.)

Even if we grant the threshold premise, significant problems remain. To begin with, as we have already seen in our discussion of Rawls and Nagel, there may be no methods of inquiry "generally accepted" by all parties to the dispute. Or, to put the point differently, controversy over what counts as admissible evidence and appropriate procedures of inquiry can be intrinsic to the substantive dispute (as it certainly is in the case of "creation science" versus the theory of evolution).

Second, one can point to important and (I would say) clearly admissible public arguments that violate both parts of the third Gutmann–Thompson criterion. For example, in the decades immediately prior to the Civil War, abolitionists and radical Republicans argued that slavery was unjust because blacks are just as human as, and are therefore fundamentally the equals of, whites. The argument was not primarily evidence-based; indeed, the social "evidence," skewed as it was by two centuries of oppression, probably pointed in the other direction. The argument was rather a moral argument that appealed to authority in at least one of two ways: Human equality could be understood as following directly from the "brotherhood of man under the fatherhood of God," or it could be intuited immediately as one of those truths "we hold to be self-evident." In neither case was the appeal to authority, religious or secular, intended to be open to challenge or test. Nor was an appeal being made to widely held beliefs, for at least during the 1850s the belief in the inequality of the races was far deeper and more pervasive (so much so that even Abraham Lincoln felt compelled to acknowledge it in his debates with Stephen Douglas).

One of two conclusions would seem to follow from the example. If the third Gutmann–Thompson criterion is correct, then the abolitionists were wrong to make their public case as they did. Conversely, if the abolitionists were justified, this criterion must be significantly modified, for as we have seen, the radical antislavery argument both appealed to incorrigible authority and went against the grain of social beliefs widely regarded as plausible.

Gutmann and Thompson characterize their "moral position" argument as a generalization of John Locke's case for religious toleration, which they properly see as nonneutralist in origin and intention. But in at least two respects, the Lockean thesis suggests conclusions quite different from those implied by the moral position. First, Locke focuses on the specific character of politicized religious conflict. History shows that religious coercion yields not agreement and civil concord but, rather, discord, war, and social devastation. The policy of religious toleration rests in part on the dreadful consequences of the alternative. If other kinds of moral disagreement are less generative of bloody conflict, the case for public coercion may well be stronger. Any proposed generalization from religious toleration must therefore attend to the special role that post-Reformation religion has played in our individual and social life.

Second, the anticoercive implications of Locke's argument are remarkably limited. To be sure, inner faith cannot be produced by compulsion, and it is therefore self-contradictory even to try. But outward acts of religious observance and practice are susceptible to coercion and become legitimate targets of public restraint whenever they threaten the survival or good order of civil society.

Precisely this distinction was echoed by Thomas Jefferson, no great friend of religious persecution. The "operations of the mind," he asserted, could not be subject to the coercion of the laws, but matters were entirely different in regard to the "acts of the body."[30] Jefferson therefore viewed the "free exercise" of religion as properly remaining within the bounds of civil order – that is, as trumped by basic public necessity in cases of conflict. From this standpoint (but not that of contemporary neutralist theory and jurisprudence), such public restraints as those on the free exercise of Mormon polygamy become defensible.

Note that this approach is nonneutral in at least three senses: The first, just discussed, is the explicit preference given to civil considerations whenever religious practices come into conflict with them. The second is the implicit tilt toward religions characterized more by internal faith than by external observance – or, to put it the other way around, against religions in which piety is centrally expressed through obedience to a system of law, as in Orthodox Judaism and Islam. Finally, as suggested earlier, in our discussion of Rawls's "common-sense sociology," the Lockean distinction between faith and observance tends to screen out forms of religion whose viability depends on state mechanisms or endorsement.

These biases are the subject of a paper by the theologian Jon Gunneman. He notes that the Lockean-liberal account of religion means "holding religious beliefs as a *private* matter, not as a matter of primary identity and not as public claims about truth. [But] this view of religion is counterfactual, it is not what serious religious people think religion is."[31] Speaking as a Christian, Gunneman asserts that the wholehearted endorsement of liberalism (or indeed, of any secular order) would require him to make an unacceptable spiritual sacrifice:

> The liberal state, like any state, is not and cannot be fully legitimate. The liberal state in particular is illegitimate insofar as it insists on seeing my beliefs as my individual preferences rather than as public truth-claims about the world, truth-claims deeply embedded in a social tradition that gives those of us in it our primary identity and limits all other claims of authority. What will you do with us?[32]

I do not cite Gunneman's argument to undermine liberal legitimacy. The point is, rather, that from certain religious standpoints, the stance of liberalism is bound to seem partisan and hostile. As Locke well understood, this conflict cannot be altogether eliminated. The challenge, on the levels of both theory and practice, is to restrict it to the minimum needed for the peace and good order of society.[33]

Chapter 6

Moral personality and liberal theory

In Chapter 5, I distinguished three variants of contemporary liberal theory – perfectionist, pragmatic, and political – and I explored one important strand of political liberalism, its conception of neutral public dialogue. In this chapter and the next, I continue the discussion of political liberalism by focusing on the recent work of its prime exponent, John Rawls.

Recall that, as Charles Larmore put it, political liberalism is a theory at once minimal (in that it allows wide scope for free choice and diversity) and moral (in that it appeals to individual motivations other than self-interest). Some interpreters of *A Theory of Justice*[1] regarded it as "pragmatic" in the sense in which I am using the term, that is, as an effort to derive a conception of justice simply from the rational calculations of self-interested agents. Since the beginning of the 1980s, starting with the Dewey Lectures, Rawls has made it clear that he does not wish to be viewed in this fashion. Justice as fairness, he now insists, has at its core a moral conception, an (allegedly Kantian) understanding of moral personality. By fleshing out this idea, he says, he hopes to prevent misinterpretations of his theory,

> for example, that it is intended to be morally neutral, or that it models only the notion of [instrumental] rationality, and therefore that justice as fairness attempts to select principles of justice purely on the basis of a conception of rational choice as understood in economics or decision theory. For a Kantian

118

view, such an attempt is out of the question and is incompatible with its conception of the person.[2]

In this chapter, I focus on the content and implications of moral personality, taking Rawls's Dewey Lectures as my text.[3] My overall suggestion is that his conception is at once too narrow and too broad: too narrow, because it rules out elements that partisans of many positions think essential; too broad, because it includes elements that many others find debatable or even unacceptable. In Chapter 7, I extend this thesis to several other features of Rawls's emerging theory of political liberalism.

I

Rawls's reconstructed theory in the Dewey Lectures radiates from a single core: his conception of moral personality. To bring out the force of this fact, let us return briefly to *A Theory of Justice*. In that work, Rawls sought to preserve a sharp distinction between individual agents and the circumstances within which they are required to act. He explicitly denied that his conception of justice rested on an ideal conception of the person, and he "avoided attributing to the parties [in the original position] any ethical motivation." Instead, he depicted them as the rational prudential agents of neoclassical economics or social-choice theory. The original position, on the other hand, incorporated morally nonneutral constraints on rational agents in the form of conditions that express the "moral point of view" or are "widely recognized as fitting to impose on the adoption of moral principles" (*A Theory of Justice*, hereafter *TJ*, pp. 584–585). In *A Theory of Justice*, then, an ideal of the person enjoys at most derivative status. Choices in the original position generate principles of justice, which may in turn be employed to define a "partial ideal of the person." The ideal of the person is not the foundation, but rather the outcome, of the theory of justice.

In the Dewey Lectures (hereafter DL), the ideal of the person plays a direct rather than derivative role. First, as we shall see, Rawls now depicts individuals in the original position as moral agents, in the sense that their choices are seen as pursuing, or expressing, basic features of moral personality. Second, the elements of the original position lose their previous character as reasonable moral constraints on individual choice, and become instead representations of the moral personality of the individuals themselves.

Moral persons are, Rawls tells us,

> characterized by two moral powers and by two corresponding highest-order interests in realizing and exercising these powers. The first power is the capacity for an effective sense of justice, that is, the capacity to understand, to apply and to act from (and not merely in accordance with) the principles of justice. The second moral power is the capacity to form, to revise, and rationally to pursue a conception of the good. (DL, p. 525)

Moral persons, so characterized, are said to be *free*, in two senses: They are thought of as "self-originating sources of valid claims [that] carry weight on their own without being derived from prior duties or obligations owed to society or to other persons" (DL, p. 543). They are regarded as free, second, because they "do not view themselves as inevitably tied to the pursuit of the particular conception of the good and its final ends which they espouse at any given time" (DL, p. 544). And moral persons are said to be *equal* because each is equally capable of "understanding and complying with the public conception of justice... and of being full participants in social cooperation throughout their lives" (DL, p. 546).

This new conception of moral personality leads directly to a drastically revised account of primary goods. In *A Theory of Justice*, we recall, these goods are defined relative to the objectives of prudential calculators. They were, Rawls specified, a class of goods "that are normally wanted as parts of rational plans of life which may include the most varied sorts of ends." The account of these goods depends on "psychological premises" (*TJ*, p. 260). In the Dewey Lectures, on the other hand:

> Primary goods are singled out by asking which things are generally necessary as social conditions and all-purpose means to enable human beings to realize and exercise their moral powers [and] the conception of moral persons as having certain specified highest-order interests selects what is to count as primary goods. . . . Thus these goods are not to be understood as general means essential for achieving whatever final ends a comprehensive empirical or historical survey might show people usually or normally have in common under all social conditions. (DL, pp. 526–527)[4]

The account of moral personality in the Dewey Lectures alters not only the understanding of primary goods but also the character of Rawls's theory taken as a whole. *A Theory of Justice* rejected "perfectionism" as both improper and superfluous. Perfectionism, Rawls alleged, violates our considered judgments about human liberty and equality. Moreover, "to find an Archimedean point [for appraising institutions] it is not necessary to appeal to . . . perfectionist principles" (*TJ*, p. 263).

But the revised theory of the Dewey Lectures verges on perfectionism. The ideal of the person functions as a moral goal, in two respects. Individuals choosing principles of justice seek, first and foremost, to create circumstances in which they can realize and express their moral powers. Second, we as observers appraise social institutions in light of their propensity to promote the realization and facilitate the expression of these powers, and this standard takes priority over our other concerns.

In what sense is this theory distinguishable from the perfectionism Rawls continues to reject? There are, it seems, two major distinctions. First, perfectionism as Rawls describes it takes as its goal nonmoral excellence, whereas his own theory focuses on the development of moral powers. Second, perfectionism focuses on the excellence achievable only by the few, whose claims are given disproportionate (if not absolute) weight relative to those of ordinary individuals, whereas the moral powers Rawls emphasizes are, he supposes, within the capacity of every normal person to develop and to exercise, at least in favorable circumstances.

Now (to take the first point) it would appear that Rawls's new theory and perfectionism differ, not generically, but rather as species within a single genus. In each case, philosophical reflection must somehow pick out normatively favored individual ends and interests. Rawls would perhaps argue that although individuals may differ on criteria for nonmoral excellence, they are in substantial agreement about at least the main features of moral excellence. Thus, for both theoretical and practical reasons, it makes sense to set controverted ideals to one side and to build social institutions on a more solid normative foundation.

There are two difficulties with this contention. First, it is by no means obvious that we are in hopeless disagreement about the components of nonmoral excellence. Clearly we have a pluralistic conception. There are many dimensions of excellence, not one of which enjoys clear priority. But to admit this is not to deny that we have a criterion sufficiently determinate for purposes of social judgment and public policy. Second, even if we restrict our attention to moral excellence, matters are more complex than Rawls suggests. Some might wish to argue that the ideal of the moral person should incorporate a wider range of virtues (e.g., those sketched in Aristotle's *Ethics*). It is by no means clear why a sense of justice should be emphasized whereas courage and a variety of social virtues are altogether excluded from Rawls's model conception. In this respect, at least, it is not self-evident that moral excellence is simpler or less open to reasonable disagreement than is nonmoral excellence.

Rawls believes he has answered this kind of objection in the Dewey Lectures by grounding his view of moral personality in the conception "implicitly affirmed in . . . the public culture of a democratic society" (DL, p. 518). As I later argue, this defense of a Kantian view of moral personality is doubly questionable: It misrepresents what is in fact our shared cultural understanding of personality, and it entails the abandonment of the fundamental aims of Kantian moral philosophy.

Let us now turn to the second point of difference, between perfectionism as a hierarchical doctrine and Rawls's theory as egalitarian. It cannot be denied that some perfectionist thinkers have given something approaching absolute priority to the sorts of excellence achievable only by the few. But this is *not* a defining characteristic of perfectionism. Many perfectionists have believed that unusual development along a particular dimension of excellence differs quantitatively, not qualitatively, from ordinary competence. The rare genius raises to a higher power traits characteristic of normal human beings. Thus, in cases where societies face a stark choice between the normal development of the many and the extraordinary development of the few, perfectionism as an ideal-teleological theory is likely to give more weight to the aggregate good of the many, unless it can be shown that favoring the few here and now will eventually produce a greater social good.

Of course, it is possible to construct a quantitative measure that gives rare excellence many times the weight of normal development. But it is as least as plausible to argue for the diminishing marginal weight of incremental individual development. Suppose that a society must choose between two policies. Under A, all available resources are devoted to the full development of X (a potential genius), while Y (a potentially normal individual) is wholly ignored and allowed to remain illiterate, unskilled, and brutish. Under B, the same resources are used to develop both X and Y up to the point of normality. Naturally, egalitarians and contractarians will select B over A. But so will ideal-utilitarian perfectionists who believe that the gain to Y under B exceeds the loss to X – who believe, that is, that to deprive an individual of the chance to achieve normal development and to lead a normal life is to subject that individual to the greatest conceivable harm.

II

As a point of departure for social theory, the Rawlsian view of moral personality is remarkable at least as much for what it *excludes* as for what it *affirms*. In *A Theory of Justice*, Rawls had excluded knowledge of individual conceptions of the good from the original position. Pressed to defend this exclusion, he subsequently argued that

> our final ends . . . depend on our abilities and opportunities, on the numerous contingencies that have shaped our attachments and affections. That we have one conception of the good rather than another is not relevant from a moral standpoint. In acquiring it we are influenced by the same sort of contingencies that lead us to rule out a knowledge of our sex and class.[5]

But in light of the revised account in the Dewey Lectures, this thesis is no longer tenable. The power to form a conception of the good, Rawls now argues, is a core aspect of developed moral personality, a manifestation not of heteronomous contingency but, rather, of autonomous reflection and choice. There is no longer any basis to argue that the specific exercise of this power is arbitrary from a moral point of view.

Not surprisingly, the Dewey Lectures offer a different argument for excluding conceptions of the good. By assumption, Rawls contends,

> in a well-ordered democratic society under modern conditions, there is no settled and enduring agreement on [conceptions of the good. This disagreement seems] bound to obtain in the absence of a sustained and coercive use of state power that aims to enforce the requisite unanimity. . . . Because [the principles of justice] are to serve as a shared point of view among

citizens with opposing ... conceptions of the good, [the veil of ignorance] needs to be appropriately impartial among these differences. (DL, pp. 542–43)

Strikingly, Rawls does not argue that rational judgment about the worth of different conceptions of the good is impossible. Rather, he emphasizes the practical difficulties of institutionalizing a specific conception. The implicit argument is that even if a conception is valid, the evil of the coercion that would be required to give it public effect would outweigh the benefits of inculcating general belief in its validity.

This is, of course, a classical premise of liberalism. It originated in the seventeenth-century wars of religion and in the determined efforts of Locke and others to shape a doctrine of toleration that could serve as a basis of peace and mutual accommodation. But to arrive at his doctrine, Locke went a long way toward denying the truth claims of the sectarian combatants. If he had accepted the view of any party that its beliefs and practices were required for eternal salvation, the relative evils of coercion and toleration would have appeared in a very different light. Similarly, Rawls's admission that some contending conceptions of the good may be superior to others makes it difficult to maintain without further ado that coercion is *always* inferior to impartiality among these conceptions. (This point is perfectly consistent with the existence of sound prima facie reasons for avoiding coercion, and for placing a heavy burden of proof on those who advocate it.)[6]

The continued exclusion of conceptions of the good seems arbitrary from another standpoint as well. Rawls insists that the original position must be impartial among opposed conceptions. But there is no reason to believe that impartiality requires ignorance. Presumably, impartiality will prevail if every conception of the good may be freely expressed and each is given equal weight in the determination of social outcomes. That is, impartiality requires only that no conception of the good be accorded an initially privileged position.

Rawls's remaining objections to what we may call full-information impartiality reduce to two: that no agreement will be possible in such circumstances, or that any agreement reflecting knowledge of the good will somehow be biased. Neither objection seems tenable. Suppose, to begin with, that individuals are asked to agree on principles governing the relation between church and state. Rawls grants to them the knowledge that they differ profoundly in religious belief. But how will the situation differ if, instead of this general knowledge, each individual knows what his or her beliefs are? For as long as unanimity is required, each individual can block an outcome adverse to his or her convictions. Quickly the group will realize that its alternatives reduce to no agreement and some form of toleration for all religions. Indeed, history presented precisely this choice to the religious combatants of the early modern period. Some decades of no agreement, replete with civil conflict, international convulsions, and unspeakable brutalities on all sides, sufficed to bring home the lesson that the consequences of a moderation of claims all around are preferable to those of futilely pressing one's maximal demands.

Nor is it clear why agreements made in full awareness of differing conceptions of the good will necessarily be "biased." Of course, individual A's conception may require considerable resources while B's can be realized much more simply. To be sure, the more expensive one's conception of the good, the more dependent one is likely to be on the advantages of social cooperation. Those with cheaper conceptions lose less from no agreement, and they may therefore be able to exploit their stronger bargaining position to achieve a greater than proportionate share of the advantages of cooperation. But this possibility does not militate decisively against full-information bargaining, for two reasons: First, as we have seen, conceptions of the good are *not* like race and sex. They are (or so Rawls now insists) within our power to choose and to alter. If so, it is not unreasonable to expect individuals selecting expensive conceptions to take into account the risk that the resources they require will not be (wholly) available. Second, Rawls's index of primary goods takes no notice whatever of differences in cost among conceptions of the good. It is thus far *more* biased against expensive conceptions than any full-information agreement is likely to be.[7]

III

Bernard Williams has argued that if, as Rawls contends, utilitarianism fails to take seriously the *separateness* of persons, Kantianism gives insufficient weight to their *distinctiveness*. Kantian theories ask us to arrive at principles valid for all human beings (or, in Kant's own view, all rational beings) without taking into consideration the specific features that distinguish us one from another. Our obligations are independent of our identity or character. This abstraction from character is, Williams contends, a fundamental mistake. My character – my predilections, projects, and conceptions of the good – are conditions of my taking any interest in the world at all, either on my own account or on anyone else's. By detaching us not just from our social circumstances but also from our selves, Kantian impartiality makes it impossible for us to take any interest in, or to regard as binding, the conclusions to which it gives rise.[8]

In the Dewey Lectures, Rawls attempts without notable success to respond to this charge. He distinguishes between the conceptions of the person appropriate to the public world and to "personal affairs." In the latter, something like Williams's view prevails: Individuals cannot regard themselves as detached from their specific ends and beliefs. In the former, they must adopt the Kantian perspective. This dualism, Rawls adds, is in no way vicious: "Within different contexts we can assume diverse points of view toward our person without contradiction so long as these points of view cohere together when circumstances require" (DL, p. 545).

But Williams's point is that they do *not* cohere. Kantian impartiality requires us to nullify core aspects of our character, not only in original position reflection but also in concrete moral conduct. As Rawls himself says, our ends *must*

127

be revised whenever they conflict with principles of justice – principles constructed without concrete reference to these ends (DL, p. 544).

To clarify this issue, we may distinguish four different interpretations of the relation between justice and character:

1. *The neutral interpretation:* Principles of justice are defined without reference to conceptions of the good actually held by individuals, and these principles override conceptions of the good in cases of conflict.

2. *The full-information interpretation:* Principles of justice are defined in a manner sensitive to actually held conceptions of the good but, as in the neutral interpretation, justice overrides these conceptions.

3. *The personal-identity interpretation:* Principles of justice are defined in a manner sensitive to actually held conceptions of the good, but in case of conflict, justice has no clear (lexical) priority over individual projects and attachments.

4. *The perfectionist interpretation:* Principles of justice are defined relative to ideal standards of the good; in cases of conflict, justice has no clear priority over individual excellence conforming to that ideal.[9]

Williams's critique of the neutral interpretation is directed both at the manner in which it defines principles of justice and at the lexical priority it accords them. But the latter point seems contingent on the former. If, as in the full-information interpretation, principles of justice are sensitive to actually held conceptions of the good, the case for according priority to those principles is considerably strengthened. After all, individual identity has *already* been given fair weight. For a particular individual to demand exemption from the requirements of justice, so defined, is a form of excessive self-regard. Thus, persons who refuse to fight for their country during wartime on the ground that their characters would be degraded by brutality would hardly be entitled to our respect, for they ignore the harm to others their refusal may engender. In particular, they ask someone else to do their dirty work and to risk undergoing the same fundamental transformations of attitude and character.

Thus, Williams's critique of Rawls rests on the tacit assumption that there is no alternative lying between the personal-identity interpretation and the neutral interpretation. But there *is* an alternative – what I have called the full-information interpretation – and it is hardly implausible on its face. Rawls's insistence on the priority of justice is not (as he supposes) undermined, but rather supported, by the full-information interpretation. And, as we have seen, there are a number of other reasons to prefer it to the neutral interpretation.

It is not clear, however, that Rawls continues to espouse the neutral interpretation. To the extent that my earlier argument is correct, the reconstructed theory of the Dewey Lectures is a kind of perfectionism. If so, Williams's critique must be recast. The problem with Rawls's revised Kantian doctrine is not that it abstracts completely from conceptions of character but, rather, that it prescribes, as valid for all, a single, substantive, eminently debatable ideal of moral personality that gives pride of place to the capacity for just action.[10]

To the extent that justice as fairness rests on a moral ideal applicable to every member of the democratic community and regulative of every desire, Rawls must defend this theory both against its competitors and against the sorts of objections he elsewhere raises against notions of rationally justified final aims. That is, he must enter into precisely that arena of conflicting perfectionist claims that the formal structure of justice as fairness was designed to sidestep. And he must answer more fully the contentions of those who, with Williams, see in Rawls's Kantian universalism a systematic violation of the individual particularity that characterizes the human good.

Of the many difficulties this raises for Rawls, let me cite just two at this juncture. First, he asserts that for an ideal conception of personality to be acceptable, "it must be possible for people to honor it sufficiently closely." Hence, "the feasible ideals of the person are limited by the capacities of human nature" (DL, p. 534). In his view, nothing we now know, or are likely to learn, about human nature suggests that his own conception is beyond our capacities (DL, p. 566). But that view is at least controversial. One may wonder, for example, whether the men who drafted the U.S. Constitution would have embraced it. There is much evidence to suggest that they did not, that in their view the dominance of both passion and interest was such as to make an effective sense of justice the exception rather than the rule. While they did not wholly denigrate the social role of individual virtue, they felt compelled to rely heavily on what James Madison called "auxiliary precautions," that is, on institutions whose workings did not depend on the just motivations of office-holders or of ordinary citizens. At the very least, I would suggest, the question of the feasibility of Rawls's ideal deserves more than the cursory, almost dismissive treatment he provides.

Second, while Rawls's conception of moral personality may strike some as unattainble, it may strike others as unacceptable. Rawls say that he hopes to "invoke a conception of the person implicitly affirmed in [our] culture, or else one that would prove acceptable to citizens once it was properly presented and explained" (DL, p. 518). But I wonder whether (for example) religious fundamentalists would regard the capacity to form and revise a conception of the good as a good at all, let alone a highest-order interest of human beings. They might well declare that the best human life requires the submissive capacity to receive an external good (God's truth) rather than actively to form a conception of the good for oneself, and to hold fast to that truth once received rather than to revise it. Rawls's Kantian conception would strike them as a sophisticated, and therefore dangerous, brand of secular humanism. Nor (as we saw at the end of Chapter 5) would they be impressed with the suggestion that whatever may be true of their nonpublic identity, their public personality should be understood in Rawls's fashion. From their perspective, the disjunction between the public and nonpublic realms represents an injunction to set aside God's word, the only source of salvation, in determining the principles of our public order. I would argue, in short, that Rawls's conception of moral personality will appeal only to those who have accepted a particular understanding of liberal political community, and that our public culture is at present characterized not by consensus on, but rather by acute conflict over, the adequacy of liberalism so understood.

IV

So far we have discussed the implications of excluding individual character and conceptions of the good from free and equal moral personality. We now reach the most controversial exclusion: differences of natural endowment, that is, of skills and talents and of the propensity to develop and exercise them. Rawls's argument, familiar since *A Theory of Justice* and reinforced in the Dewey Lectures, is that natural differences are as much the product of accident and chance as are differences of family background and social circumstance. Because natural differences, like those of family and social class, are arbitrary from a moral point of view, they are in principle unsuited to serve as the bases of distributive outcomes.

To this argument several critics have offered a powerful retort. Rawls's rejection of the moral force of natural assets rests on the proposition that desert claims cannot be based on something undeserved. But this proposition is questionable, perhaps incoherent. To begin with, there is nothing self-contradictory about basing a claim on some undeserved feature of yourself, as long as you did not come to possess it by arbitrarily depriving someone else of his or her legitimate possession.[11] Second, the demand that desert bases be deserved amounts to a nullification of the entire procedure of claiming: We "either have an infinite regress of bases of desert or arrive at some basis, some beginning point, which the individual cannot claim to have deserved or to be responsible for."[12] Moral personality is no exception, for one's existence as a moral person is every bit as accidental and undeserved as any special abilities and traits of character.

131

Now, one can imagine Rawls replying to this by dismissing altogether the relevance of desert for distributive justice. There is no dilemma: Desert *is* an incoherent concept; however, a properly constructed theory of justice can get along perfectly well without it. Indeed, justice as fairness is the theory that results from denying the existence of any "prior and independent notion of desert, perfectionist or intuitionist, that could override or restrict the agreement of the parties" (DL, pp. 551–52).

But matters are not so simple, for you can get to be a party to the agreement only if you are a *moral person*. If you are not (if you are, say, a chimpanzee), then your interests are of no weight in determining acceptable principles of justice. Or, to put it the other way around, moral personality is the basis of your claim to be taken into account. As Rawls himself puts it, all moral people (and, he might have added, *only* moral people) think of themselves and of one another as "self-originating sources of claims," which they are not required to justify further (DL, p. 548). And thus, if by desert we mean "the possession of some attribute in light of which an individual's claims are accorded moral weight," then Rawls does not (as he seems to believe) dispense with desert altogether. Rather, he establishes, as the sole relevant desert basis, a feature of our lives (moral personality) that equally characterizes nearly all of us. But, to repeat, he cannot employ the distinction between the arbitrary and the nonarbitrary to do this, because moral personality is every bit as contingent as any other feature of our existence. The exclusion of natural endowments from Rawls's theory of valid claims represents a *choice* of equal over unequal claims.[13]

Rawls is hardly unaware that he has made this choice. He attempts to justify it in the Dewey Lectures by appealing to the formal features of a theory of justice. In constructing such a theory, we are not really interested in individual cases. Rather, "we seek principles to regulate the basic structure into which we are born to live a complete life. The thesis is that the only relevant feature in connection with these principles is the capacity for moral personality" (DL, p. 551). The question then becomes, Why is the principle of "fair equality of opportunity" – expectations of success based on effort and ability, without regard to background or social class – unsuited to govern the basic structure of society? As far as I can tell, Rawls gives only one answer: As long as the institution of the family is allowed to exist, fair equality can be only imperfectly realized (*TJ*, p. 74).

This is of course true. But it hardly constitutes a decisive argument against fair equality of opportunity. *If* effort and ability ought to be reflected in distributive outcomes, then the pattern that emerges when natural endowments are filtered through the family may be the best we can attain, even though there will be significant deviations from pure equality of opportunity. From the fact that there will be deviations, it does *not* follow that the second-best solution is a basic structure that ignores effort and ability altogether.

Besides, few proponents of fair equality of opportunity insist that it must be the sole principle governing the basic structure of society. Most recognize that other principles and institutions must be given due weight. Typically, fair equality of opportunity is only part (albeit an important part) of a broader conception of an ideal society in which opportunities for development of individual talents are maximized. Taken as a whole, the evidence suggests, the institution of the family plays a key role in individual development. Thus, proponents of the thesis that natural endowments have moral weight will be willing to balance pure fairness against, say, the average level of individual development. Pure fairness at a lower level (*ex hypothesi*, without the family) may reasonably be regarded as inferior to a measure of unfairness at a higher level. And this is especially likely to be true if social institutions other than the family – property, education, compensatory programs – are arranged so as to mitigate unfairness.[14]

The issue between Rawls and proponents of fair equality of opportunity, then, turns on differing conceptions of what political society is *for*. Rawls looks to the development and exercise of moral personality; his opponents emphasize a fuller range of human powers. Rawls cannot legitimately criticize proponents of fair equality of opportunity as teleologists, for his own theory is teleological in exactly the same sense: "Free persons," as Rawls conceives of them, "have a regulative and effective desire to be a certain kind of person" (DL, p. 548). Nor can Rawls simply appeal to the greater parsimony of his conception, for, as Bernard Williams has forcefully reminded us, parsimony in moral theory is hardly a neutral or formal criterion. It entails, rather, an abstraction from concrete individual moral life, which ought to enjoy a natural primacy in our moral reflection, at least as a point of departure. It is therefore the movement toward, *not* away from, a narrower conception of personality that requires special justification.

Rawls's most powerful objection to the "full development" theory underlying fair equality of opportunity is that it presupposes, as a ground of agreement on principles of justice, knowledge of a specific conception of the good. But this is precisely the sort of knowledge that should be excluded "in order to have a lucid representation of the notion of freedom that characterizes a Kantian view" (DL, p. 550). But it is at this point that Rawls *diverges* from the Kantian view. In *The Doctrine of Virtue*, Kant argues that "it is a command of morally practical reason and a duty of man to himself to cultivate his powers . . . and to be, from a pragmatic point of view, a man equal to the end of his existence."[15]

As Patrick Riley has argued, it is hardly possible to make sense of Kant's moral philosophy unless this teleological component is given due weight. To treat "rational nature" as an "end in itself" is to treat the development of human powers, *broadly* conceived, as a duty.[16] Without this premise, Kant's treatment of the South Sea Islands example in the *Foundations of the Metaphysics of Morals* is unintelligible. Because Kant sees this teleology of natural powers as *contained* in the conception of the person, he does not regard it as conflicting in any way with his understanding of moral freedom. Thus, Rawls is quite correct to identify Kantian "autonomy" with whatever is contained in Kant's concept of moral personality and to stress that "in a Kantian doctrine a relatively complex conception of the person plays a central role" (DL, pp. 559–60). But, ironically, Rawls departs from Kant's understanding of freedom because his conception of the person is *less* complex than Kant's. And it is only this deviation that permits Rawls to rule out – as a breach of freedom – the view of individual personality and development that underlies the doctrine of fair equality of opportunity.

V

The conceptual arguments supporting Rawls's view of personality as the appropriate point of departure for social theory are, we have seen, far from persuasive. But his view cannot be adequately understood on this plane alone, for it is embedded in a broader vision of the nature and purpose of political philosophy.

In the Dewey Lectures, Rawls develops a distinction between two types of ethical theory. *Rational intuitionism* asserts that the first principles of morality are "fixed by a moral order that is prior to and independent of our conception of the person and the social role of morality. This order is given by the nature of things and is known . . . by rational intuition" (DL, p. 557). *Kantian constructivism*, by contrast, specifies a "particular conception of the person" and a "reasonable procedure of construction" (DL, p. 516). Principles of justice are constructed by persons, so conceived, through that procedure, without appealing to any prior moral facts. In Rawls's view, the very possibility of Kantian constructivism blunts the strongest argument in favor of intuitionism: that some form of intuitionist theory is necessary if objectivity is to be achieved (DL, p. 570).

If the only issue between intuitionism and constructivism were the *location* of key premises (the natural order and the person, respectively), Rawls's point would be well taken. The difficulty, of course, is that constructivists must offer some support for the specific conception of the person they choose to employ. Here they encounter a dilemma. If they appeal to something external to the person to justify their choice, they return to intuitionism through the back door. If they do not, they must concede that the formal *concept* of personality is compatible with a wide variety of *conceptions*, each of which leads to somewhat different moral conclusions through the procedure of construction.

As we have seen, Rawls constrains this choice by looking for conceptions appropriate to democratic culture. But unless one has some prior reason for preferring democratic to nondemocratic culture, this either pushes the problem of justification back one step, without resolving it, or changes the question entirely. Objectivity within a culture is *not* what intuitionists mean by objectivity. The moral order on which they rest their case is (or so they think) accessible to all human beings as such, not just to Europeans and Americans. Thus, Rawls defends constructivism against the charge of relativism only by altering the very conception of objectivity, in a manner that has the effect of conceding the substance, if not the letter, of the intuitionist critique.[17]

Rawls's reconstructed theory is divided against itself. It is explicitly Kantian, but implicitly Hegelian. It avoids formalism only at the cost of abandoning the Kantian standpoint above history and culture. Instead, the content of its principles is provided by the shared beliefs of the democratic community. The new task of political philosophy is to develop these implicit principles into a coherent structure, that is, to display the community to itself by bringing it to full consciousness of itself.[18]

Rawls deviates even farther from Kant by stressing the "practical" task of political philosophy. We are to look for principles that can achieve a "public and workable agreement on matters of social justice which suffices for effective and fair social cooperation" (DL, p. 560). We must thus set to one side the difficult issues raised by relations between societies and between the human species and other living things (DL, p. 524). We must accept, as fixed constraints, the basic features of modern democratic society. We must

136

discard "first principles" that cannot be generally understood and easily applied. We must rule out certain moral considerations as irrelevant because eliminating them increases the capacity of the remaining considerations to fulfill their social role. We must lay aside inconvenient facts about unfortunate human beings – congenitally inadequate mental powers, unusual and costly needs – with which social theory and practice must eventually come to grips (DL, p. 546). And we must employ concepts that, to the extent possible, are publicly verifiable and "less open to dispute" (DL, p. 563). If the publicity condition is to be satisfied, therefore, we must sacrifice some portion of what we believe to be morally relevant, making do instead with rough-and-ready approximations. It is in this light, Rawls explains, that features of his theory such as the basic structure, priority rules, and primary goods are to be understood (DL, pp. 561–63). Rawls sums up this strategy of argument as follows:

> We are accustomed to the idea that secondary norms and working criteria, by which our views are applied, must be adjusted to the normal requirements of social life as well as to the limited capacities of human reasoning. . . . But we tend to regard these adjustments as made in the light of various first principles, or a single principle. First principles themselves are not widely regarded as affected by practical limitations and social requirements. [But in Kantian constructivism, the] very content of the first principles of justice . . . is determined in part by the practical task of political philosophy. (DL, p. 543)

The contrast with Kant's own views could not be starker. For Kant, first principles lose all their moral force if they are shaped by the requirements of social practice. Kant concedes (as any theorist must) that "ought implies can." But Kant defines "possibility" relative not to the social world as we know it but, rather, to conceivable transformations of that world. And he places the burden of proof on the proponents of impossibility. Unless it can be *shown* that an otherwise compelling moral proposition rests on an assumption that cannot ever be realized, the proposition must be accorded full normative weight, even though it cuts radically against the grain of prevailing beliefs and practices, even though it makes the most stringent demands on our powers of moral reflection and action. For Kant, it is *reason* – not the need for agreement, not the circumstances of agreement – that determines the content of our appropriate social undertakings.

Rawls has an answer to this: His deviation from Kant in the name of social practice is necessary and proper because it helps to overcome the "dualisms" that disfigure Kant's doctrine (DL, p. 516). But matters are not so simple. From Aristotle to the present day, the point of ideal theory has been to elucidate the first principles that would be fully actualized in the most favorable circumstances conceivable, as a guide for action in the much less hospitable circumstances of ordinary political life. To build the circumstances of ordinary life into our first principles is of course to reduce the gap between theory and practice. But it is also to forget the point of having first principles, to judge our institutions and practices, not merely to codify them.[19]

Moreover, the "practical" conception of first principles opens the door to the arbitrary selection of practical constraints. For example, Rawls refuses to rest the content of first principles on highly developed powers of reflection, because such powers cannot be regarded as widely shared. But he does not hesitate to presuppose (against all evidence) that a sense of justice (or at least a capacity for it) *is* widely shared. I confess that I do not see the ground for distinguishing these two cases. If we are allowed to take our bearings from fully developed moral powers, even though most individuals do not possess them, then why cannot the content of first principles reflect fully developed intellectual powers, rather than the average powers of the individuals we encounter in daily life? Why is Rawls willing to be so noumenal, so counterfactual in the one case, so phenomenal and practical in the other?

I suspect that in this case (as in so many others), the conclusions Rawls wishes to reach dictate the premises he chooses to employ. It is at least possible to conjecture that under the most favorable circumstances, all or nearly all individuals will develop roughly equal capabilities for moral conduct. This conjecture becomes especially plausible if we focus, in good Kantian fashion, on intention rather than performance. But the parallel conjecture in the case of intellectual powers would be wholly incredible. Under the most favorable circumstances, the undeniable inequalities of natural intellectual endowment would necessarily be reflected in inequalities of intellectual performance. To incorporate fully developed moral powers into our first principles of justice is to support the moral legitimacy of equality. To incorporate fully developed intellectual powers would be to open the door to, if not to legitimate, various forms of social hierarchy. For if principles of social organization are complex and difficult to apply, then the cause of justice itself may require a ruling class selected (in part) on the basis of superior intellectual competence. Rawls's practical *conception* of political philosophy is, I suspect, governed by his overall practical *intention:* to uphold the understanding of equality that stands at the heart of his conception of democratic public culture.

Chapter 7

Pluralism and social unity

In Chapter 6, I explored the expanded notion of "moral personality" Rawls has placed at the center of his revised argument. But this is not the only change he has offered in the course of constructing a moral but minimal political liberalism. Three other shifts strike me as being of particular importance. First, he has fleshed out his views on the good and on the role that a conception of the good can play within the priority of the right. Second, he now explicitly characterizes the overall theory as "political," that is, as drawn in part from basic political facts that constitute practical constraints *and* as detached from broader philosophical or metaphysical considerations. Finally, he has more explicitly come to view his theory of justice not as developed *sub specie aeternitatis* but, rather, as drawn from (and addressed to) the public culture of democratic societies. It is to these three new strands of political liberalism that this chapter is devoted.

I

Underlying the various shifts toward political liberalism, I believe, is a core concern that has become increasingly prominent in Rawls's thought. Modern liberal-democratic societies are characterized by an irreversible pluralism, that is, by conflicting and incommensurable conceptions of the human good (and, Rawls now stresses, of metaphysical and religious conceptions as well).[1] The grounds of social unity are not hard to specify in homogeneous communities. But where are they to be found in societies whose members disagree so fundamentally? The answer, Rawls believes, lies in the lessons liberal-democratic societies have slowly learned in the modern era. Alongside the "fact of pluralism" is a kind of rough agreement on certain basics: the treatment of all individuals as free and equal, the understanding of society as a system of uncoerced cooperation, the right of each individual to a fair share of the fruits of that cooperation, and the duty of all citizens to support and uphold institutions that embody a shared conception of fair principles. Once we devise a strategy for excluding from public discourse the matters on which we fundamentally disagree and for reflecting collectively on the beliefs we share, we can be led to workable agreements on the content of just principles and institutions.

This new emphasis on pluralism can be understood, I believe, in the context of the political and cultural history of the United States over the past generation. Most readers of *A Theory of Justice* came away with the sense that the central issue for modern liberalism is distributive, that is, the manner in which rights, resources, and opportunities should be divided among the members of liberal societies. To the extent that scholarly debate focused on the substance of Rawls's case rather than its metatheoretical complications, it emphasized the Difference Principle and its implications for social policy.

In so doing, Rawls and his interpreters reflected the 1960s' preoccupation with the intertwined issues of race and class and with the role that activist government could play in redressing historic inequities through redistributive programs. They also reflected the broader temper of the times: a widespread disposition to believe that public activities directed toward narrowing income disparities do not infringe on (the core requirements of) liberal freedom but, rather, represent the most appropriate expression of our shared commitment to equality.

Since the 1970s, however, there has been a shift of emphasis. The civil rights movement unleashed a torrent of new demands on the part of previously marginized groups, defined by gender, sexual orientation, race and ethnicity, national origin, class, age, physical status, conscientious moral conviction, and religion. A central focus of social policy became the legitimation of difference.

This movement toward diversity sparked a concerned reaction: Diversity was a fine thing, to be sure, but what then was the glue that held us together as a society? On the political plane, this concern engendered a turn toward "traditional values" and contributed to the triumph of Reaganism. In neoconservative social criticism, it generated worried examinations of liberalism's alleged drift toward a morally incapacitating relativism and of the resulting need to counteract this liberal self-immolation with external sources of authority – religious, moral, or historical. And in liberal social philosophy, it produced a renewed emphasis on the task of forging a meaningful and usable political unity in the midst of (some would say, in the teeth of) ever increasing social diversity.

Rawls's recent writings, it seems to me, exemplify this shift. The concern for distributional issues engendered by moderate scarcity has not wholly disappeared, but it has been displaced by a new focus on questions raised by the facts of social diversity. The guiding metaphor for his revised argument was furnished by the early modern wars of religion and by the doctrine of toleration that eventually flowed from them. Rawls seeks to widen the sphere of toleration to include the fullest possible range of practice and belief. For liberal political purposes, the principle of toleration is extended even to philosophy itself: The "comprehensive" claims about the good life and the good society to which philosophy characteristically gives rise are not to serve as the basis for liberal institutions, and are to be excluded, to the extent possible, from liberal public discourse.

Yet in spite of this emphasis on tolerance for diversity – in more current terms, on the widest possible state neutrality concerning conceptions of the good life – Rawls is in basic accord with a tradition stretching back to Aristotle. No political community can exist simply on the basis of diversity or of natural harmony; every community must rest on – indeed, is constituted by – some agreement on what is just. Rawls's famous principles represent his proposal for an agreement consistent with the basic features and commitments of liberal societies. As such, they express his understanding of how the fact of pluralism is best reconciled with the need for social unity.

I believe that in focusing his recent thought on the problem of forging unity amidst diversity, Rawls has posed exactly the right question. I am less sure that he has arrived at the right answer. In addressing the fact of pluralism, I would argue, Rawls goes both too far and not far enough: too far, because in trying to avoid all deep differences of metaphysics and religion and to set questions of truth to one side, he deprives social philosophy (including his own) of resources essential to its success; not far enough, because the grounds of agreement he professes to find latent in our public culture would be rejected by many individuals and groups who form important elements of that culture. The alternative, I suggest, is to recognize that social philosophy, liberalism included, cannot wholly let its case rest on social agreement and must ultimately resort to truth claims that are bound to prove controversial. This is a problem for liberalism only if the concept of individual freedom central to liberalism is constructed so broadly as to trump the force of such truth claims. But there are no sufficient reasons to understand liberal freedom so expansively, and many compelling reasons not to.

II

Let me continue my examination of Rawls's political liberalism by taking up the expanded account of the good and its enhanced role in his overall theory.

In 1982, I published an article in which I argued that every contemporary liberal theory relies, explicitly or tacitly, on the same triadic theory of the good, which asserts the worth of human existence, the value of the fulfillment of human purposes, and the commitment to rationality as the chief guide to both individual purposiveness and collective undertakings. This is, to be sure, a restricted theory of the good, but it is by no means a trivial one, for it is possible to identify approaches to social morality that deny one or more of its elements.[2]

In a 1988 paper, in part an explicit rejoinder to my argument, Rawls acknowledges the presence of these elements of the good in his theory. He writes that any workable conception of justice

> must count human life and the fulfillment of basic human needs and purposes as in general good, and endorse rationality as a basic principle of political and social organization. A political doctrine for a democratic society may safely assume, then, that all participants in political discussions of right and justice accept these values, when understood in a suitably general way. Indeed, if the members of society did not do so, the problems of political justice, in the form with which we are familiar with them, would seem not to arise.[3]

Nor is this the totality of the liberal theory of the good as Rawls now understands it. In another paper, he develops the notion of a workable political conception of justice for a modern democratic society as resting on the fact of pluralism, that is, on the existence of diverse and irreconcilable conceptions of the good. This "fact" does not, however, have the status of an unchangeable law of nature but, rather, is relative to specific institutions and policies. Rawls acknowledges that a public agreement on a single conception of the good can indeed be established and maintained, but "only by the oppressive use of state power."[4] The empirical fact of pluralism, then, rests on the normative commitment to noncoercion and to the achievement of "free and willing agreement."[5]

This commitment to noncoercion goes very deep. It might be thought, for example, that pluralism makes sense only if no conception of the good can be known to be rationally preferable to any other. Rawls denies this: "The view that philosophy in the classical sense as the search for truth about a prior and independent moral order cannot provide the shared basis for a political conception of justice ... does not presuppose the controversial metaphysical claim that there is no such order."[6] Even if there were such an order and it could be rationally specified, it could not properly serve as the basis for a political order unless it happened to be generally accepted by the citizenry, which would be highly unlikely in the absence of a coercive or at least tutelary state. In short, the claims of noncoercion – of individual freedom – trump even those claims based on comprehensive philosophical truths. The freedom to choose one's own conception of the good is among the highest-order goods.

Finally, Rawls's expanded conception of the human good offers an account of justice itself as a key element of that good. Citizens of a just society "share one very basic political end, and one that has high priority: namely, the end of supporting just institutions and of giving one another justice accordingly." This is the case in large measure because "the exercise of the two moral powers [the basic elements of moral personality] is experienced as good."[7] Not only, then, is justice a highest-order moral power and interest, but also there is an intrinsic impulse to develop and employ it in society.

Yet Rawls hesitates to embrace this argument in its full rigor. In the very article in which he most decisively links justice to moral personality, as an end in itself, he also asserts that justice must be compatible with the comprehensive conceptions of the good held by individuals:

> Just institutions and the political virtues expected of citizens would serve no purpose – would have no point – unless those institutions and virtues not only permitted but also sustained ways of life that citizens can affirm as worthy of their full allegiance. A conception of political justice must contain within itself sufficient space, as it were, for ways of life that can gain devoted support. In a phrase: justice draws the limit, the good shows the point.[8]

This assertion raises two very different kinds of issues. The first is conceptual: If doing justice is truly one of the two

145

highest-order interests of moral personality, an end in itself, then why does it need a "point" outside itself? If individuals genuinely accept that justice is "supremely regulative as well as effective"[9] and that citizens' desires to pursue ends that transgress the limits of justice "have no weight,"[10] then, surely, adequate space for conceptions of the good lends added support for just institutions, but it cannot be vital to their acceptability. Conversely, if space for ways of life is indeed critical, then a purportedly just regime that is systematically biased against certain kinds of lives cannot expect wholehearted support from individuals who cherish those lives.

This brings me to the second issue raised by Rawls's revised account of the relation between just institutions and individual ways of life. In his earlier account (as we have seen), Rawls had already conceded that certain ways of life are systematically likely to lose out in liberal society. But that does not imply (so he then argued) that this bias in any sense represents a morally relevant loss. Indeed, the sorts of lives it tends to screen out are in themselves questionable from the standpoint of justice.

In Rawls's more recent account, however, the bias of liberalism becomes much more problematic. He now repudiates the view that only unworthy ways of life lose out in a just constitutional regime. "That optimistic view," he states flatly, "is mistaken." In its place, he endorses the view of Isaiah Berlin that "there is no social world without loss – that is, no social world that does not exclude some ways of life that realize in special ways certain fundamental values."[11] In particular, a society constructed in accordance with the conception of justice as fairness will ask certain individuals and groups to give up for themselves their ways of life or to surrender any real chance of passing their most cherished values on to their children. Moreover, what Rawls calls "the facts of common-sense political sociology" tell us which ways of life are most likely to lose out – to wit, those that presuppose more control over the immediate cultural environment than is generally feasible within liberal societies.

This new position, it seems to me, poses a deep difficulty for justice as fairness. If I know that the principles adopted in the original position may impair my ability to exercise, or even require me altogether to surrender, the values that give my life its core meaning and purpose, then how could I agree in advance to accept those principles as binding – any more than I could subscribe to a procedure that might result in my enslavement as the outcome of a utilitarian calculus? Freedom is a great good, but is one's moral identity a lesser good? If it is unimaginable to risk losing the former, how can it make sense to embrace a decision procedure that risks losing the latter?

Rawls's answer is that there is no alternative, once the justice is cast as a fair system of cooperation among free and equal persons within the fact of pluralism: If the oppressive use of state power is ruled out, justice as fairness – with its characteristic bias – is the necessary outcome. It is not adequate, however, to depict adherents of endangered ways of life as facing a choice between becoming victims or oppressors. There is a third alternative: retreat or exit from pluralistic societies into communities marked by a greater degree of moral, religious, or cultural homogeneity. And this is likely to be the preferred option for groups that see themselves as the probable victims of liberal bias.

This line of argument amounts to the proposition that for some, the costs of treating pluralism as a "fact" are prohibitive, for it is a pluralism that excludes them. We reach a similar conclusion, starting with the observation that Rawls takes for granted the existence of a demarcated society whose members already accept the necessity of living together under common rules. From his perspective, the question is not *whether* I shall seek grounds of cooperation with the other members of my society but, rather, *what form* that cooperation will take. But it is perfectly possible to treat as problematic precisely what Rawls takes for granted. The costs of cooperation under common rules with individuals who differ radically from me may appear prohibitive, especially if those rules are to be drafted under procedures that require free and willing consent. It might well be rational for me to prefer a multiplicity of separate homogeneous communities, one of which is my natural home, to a single pluralistic community in which I fear I may have no real place.

A similar difficulty may be reached via another line of argument. In his recent work, Rawls has focused increasingly on the possibility of conflict between individual conceptions of the good, on the one hand, and the demands of social cooperation, on the other. He has sought to reduce the probability – and severity – of this conflict in two ways: by emphasizing the respects in which justice as fairness simultaneously promotes its own political vision of the good and allows for the pursuit of many (though not all) individual conceptions of the good; and by indicating how justice as fairness can be seen as the focus of an "overlapping consensus" among differing religious and comprehensive philosophical views.

As the role of the political good in Rawls's theory has expanded, the theory has become noticeably more teleological. Not only have existence, purposiveness, and social rationality received explicit recognition as intrinsic goods, but also the account of moral personality has provided the foundation for the recognition of freedom and justice as ends in themselves – that is, as essential aspects of our human good. In the process, justice as fairness has verged on a kind of democratic perfectionism.

We may then ask, If the teleological component of Rawls's theory is so enhanced, then what of the much discussed priority of the right over the good? The answer, I think, is that the priority of the right is subtly reinterpreted as the priority of the public over the nonpublic. That is, permissible conceptions of the good are delimited by the determination to give priority to social cooperation. Over and over again in his recent writings, Rawls repeats his hope that, taking as his point of departure the core concept of a fair system of cooperation, he can arrive at an expression of political values that "normally outweigh whatever other values may oppose them."[12]

Yet matters are not so simple. Rawls never really addresses the charge, leveled by Bernard Williams among others, that the public understanding of moral personality comports poorly with our nonpublic aims and attachments and that no basis for the unification of these two dimensions of our character is laid in the revised account of justice as fairness. The possibility therefore looms that giving priority to the requirements of social cooperation will compel individuals to make sacrifices of their core commitments and of aspects of their character that they regard as basic to their identity and integrity.[13]

In the end, Rawls recognizes this. He concedes that the priority of the public is always provisional, always threatened: "Political good, no matter how important, can never in general outweigh the transcendent values – certain religious, philosophical, and moral values – that may possibly come into conflict with it."[14] And because a liberal society cannot be equally hospitable to all conceptions of the good, the social basis for such conflict is always likely to exist. From the standpoint of social stability, the best that can be hoped for is that the overwhelming majority of individuals and groups will find sufficient space within liberal society for the expression of their distinctive conceptions of the good. But for those who are left out, it is hard to see how liberalism can be experienced as anything other than an assault. Resistance is therefore to be expected, and it is far from clear on what basis it is to be condemned.

III

Of all the distinctive claims in Rawls's more recent work, the one he presses most forcefully and develops most fully is the assertion that justice as fairness is a *political* conception. In Rawls's usage, this adjective takes on manifold meanings. A political conception of justice is directed toward the basic structure of society rather than toward the full range of moral conduct, and it is therefore prepared to accept sharp differences between public and nonpublic principles. It is nevertheless a moral notion in the sense that, as we have noted repeatedly, it rests on the possibility of conscientious public action from, and not merely in accordance with, principles of public right; that is, it rejects as inadequate the purely "Hobbesian" appeal to rational self-interest. A political conception is based on the facts of political history and sociology. It is constrained by the requirements of practicality; indeed, these requirements are said to enter into the construction of first principles and not merely their application. It must meet the criterion of publicity; no principles that depend on secrecy or misrepresentation can be deemed acceptable. A political conception is both drawn from and addressed to a specific public culture, and its justification lies in its fidelity to the shared understandings of that culture rather than its correspondence to some universe of moral facts. Finally, it is (as far as possible) detached from, independent of, and neutral with respect to broader and inherently controversial philosophical, metaphysical, and religious commitments.

The final section of this chapter examines the notion of political philosophy as cultural interpretation. In the present section, I focus on what I take to be Rawls's key, and highly controversial, contention that principles of justice can be independent of broader commitments.

Contemporary communitarians offer a searching critique of what they take to be the metaphysical conception of individuality, which is peculiar, and necessary, to Rawlsian liberalism: a conception of the self as freely chosen and self-created; as separable from its aims and attachments; as detached from, critical of, unencumbered by, its history and circumstances. This critique is most closely identified with Michael Sandel, and I cannot improve on his summary:

> Can we view ourselves as independent selves, independent in the sense that our identity is never attached to our aims and attachments? I do not think we can, at least not without cost to those loyalties and convictions whose moral force consists partly in the fact that living by them is inseparable from understanding ourselves as the particular persons we are – as

150

members of this family or community or nation or people, as bearers of that history, as citizens of this republic. . . . To imagine a person incapable of constitutive attachments such as these is not to conceive an ideally free and rational agent, but to imagine a person wholly without character, without moral depth. For to have character is to know that I move in a history I neither summon nor command, which carries consequences nonetheless for my choices and conduct.[15]

Any sensible response to this argument must begin by accepting one of its essential premises. There *are* aims and allegiances that are not in the first instance chosen, that arise out of our history and circumstances, and that to some considerable extent constitute our individual identities. No one chooses to be the child of *these particular* parents, a relationship that nonetheless creates not only special duties to those parents but also the special identity of that child. Analogous relationships exist between citizens and the communities into which they are born. To reject these facts would not only impoverish individual identity but also deny the obvious.

Once this point is granted, defenders of liberalism must choose between two strategies. The first, espoused most directly by Rawls, is to draw a sharp line between these constitutive relations and the conception of the person required by the political conception of liberal justice – that is, to deny that liberalism rests on any specific conception of individuality. Properly understood, liberalism is "political not metaphysical." The original position within which the various alternative principles of social cooperation are to be examined is simply a "device of representation." That is, it embodies the distinction between considerations that are held to be relevant in choosing principles of justice and those thought not to be relevant, or to bias the deliberative results. The veil of ignorance, therefore, has "no metaphysical implications concerning the nature of the self; it does not imply that the self is ontologically prior to the facts about persons that the parties are excluded form knowing." We enter the original position not by denying our unique selfhood but, rather, by screening out, for purposes of moral justification, knowledge of social position and other individual contingencies held to be morally arbitrary.[16]

Rawls's argument is exposed to several objections. To begin with, as Amy Gutmann has argued, it is one thing to say that liberalism does not presuppose a single metaphysical view of the individual, but quite another to say that liberalism is compatible with all such views. Rawls depends on the latter – stronger – claim, which cannot be sustained. There are some conceptions of the individual (understood, for example, as "radically situated") that liberalism simply cannot accommodate.[17]

The second objection to Rawls's argument is that conflict within liberal societies may force metaphysical issues onto the public agenda. Consider abortion: Many individuals who share an understanding of moral personality disagree fundamentally on who is to be considered a moral person, so understood. Opponents of abortion insist that fetuses must be taken to be persons; proponents of unrestricted abortion must at a minimum deny this proposition. Each position raises deep metaphysical issues, and the fact that the contending parties must live together under common rules means that tacitly, if not in its declaratory doctrine, the state must incline toward one or the other metaphysical view.[18]

Rawls eventually acknowledges the force of this objection. In affirming a political conception of justice, he concedes,

> we may eventually have to assert at least certain aspects of our own comprehensive . . . religious or philosophical doctrine. This happens whenever someone insists, for example, that certain questions are so fundamental that to ensure their being rightly settled justifies civil strife. . . . At this point we may have no alternative but to deny this, and to assert the kind of thing we had hoped to avoid.[19]

I should note that although Rawls speaks only of rejecting the necessity of strife, the example of pre–Civil War slavery suggests that we may sometimes be compelled to accept it.

There is yet a third objection to the sharp separation between the political conception of justice and broader commitments. It is that Rawls's argument manifestly depends on
a specific affirmative conception of individuality. Persons
must be emotionally, intellectually, and ontologically capable
of drawing an effective line between their public and nonpublic identities and of setting aside their particular commitments, at least to the extent needed to enter the original
position and to reason in a manner consistent with its
constraints.

A number of contemporary liberals, in fact, have been
drawn toward such a conception of individuality: not the
unencumbered self (which Sandel rightly criticizes) but,
rather, the *divided* self. On the one side stands the individual's personal and social history, with all the aims and attachments they may imply. On the other side stands the
possibility of critical reflection on – even revolt against – these
very commitments. The self most at home in liberal society,
so understood, contains the potentiality for such critical distance from one's inheritance and accepts the possibility that
the exercise of critical faculties may in important respects
modify that inheritance.[20]

This is in many ways an attractive view, with links to both
the Socratic ideal of the examined life and the Enlightenment
ideal of the rational society. Moreover, it draws support from
the liberal conviction that individuality is not only shaped
but also threatened by community, that concentrations of
social and political power can serve as vehicles for repressing
as well as expressing individual identity.

My objection to this version of liberalism is not that it rests
on an affirmative conception of individuality; that is inevitable. The objection (raised in Chapter 5 and spelled out more
fully in Chapters 10 and 11) is rather that this conception is
unnecessarily partial and partisan, that it tends to exclude
individuals and groups that do not place a high value on
personal autonomy and revisable plans of life. There is, I
believe, an understanding of individuality that is both more
inclusive in practice and more consistent at the theoretical

level with core liberal principles. This understanding focuses on the ability of diverse individuals within liberal societies to agree on the virtues needed to sustain such societies and to make the practice of these virtues effective in their lives.

Of course, liberal virtues lack appeal for those individuals who do not feel advantaged by liberal society and who do not wish to sustain it. But, as I argue in Chapter 8, the human goods available in, or promoted by, liberal polities are capacious enough to evoke wide support from groups who otherwise agree on little else. The accommodation of diversity within a determinate but limited conception of liberal public purposes is a better foundation for liberal philosophy than is the promotion of rational reflection or personal autonomy – however attractive these values may be to important professions and social classes within liberal societies.

IV

I turn, finally to Rawls's new conception of political philosophy as both drawn from and addressed to a specific public culture.

Liberalism in its classic form saw itself as the product of a decisive break with opinion, tradition, and myth. It claimed for its key premises the status of universal knowledge, independent of time and place, and it maintained that these premises could be used to judge all existing regimes.

In this self-understanding, at least, liberalism was simply a continuation of the tradition of political philosophy pioneered by Plato and Aristotle and taken over by medieval thinkers of different faiths. The highest task of political philosophy, so understood, was the comparative evaluation of regimes. To this end, philosophers developed idealized accounts of desirable political orders, in the form either of discursive principles or of concrete utopias. On this account, it should be noted, the discovery of truth is an activity quite distinct from argument within a public consensus. The former is the task of political philosophy, whereas the latter is the province of rhetoric.

154

The "death" of political philosophy proclaimed a generation ago was the loss of confidence in the possibility of transcultural, truth-based political evaluation. *A Theory of Justice* was greeted with excitement in part because it was seen as restoring the legitimacy of political evaluation so conceived. Rawls's "ideal theory," abstracted from the empirical contingencies that differentiate existing political orders, was designed to judge and (when possible) to improve them. And, he contended, his theory was neither produced by specific historical and social circumstances nor intended to defend any existing order. The theory was rather "impartial," for it was constructed *sub specie aeternitatis*, regarding the human situation "not only from all social but also from all temporal points of view."[21]

In the Dewey Lectures and subsequently, however, Rawls abandons this effort. Political philosophy, he now contends, is always addressed to a specific "public culture." It either appeals to the principle latent in the common sense of that culture or proposes principles "congenial to its most essential convictions and historical traditions." In particular, justice as fairness addresses the public culture of a democratic society. It tries "to draw solely upon basic intuitive ideas that are embedded in the political institutions of a constitutional democratic regime and the public traditions of their interpretation." Justice as fairness "starts from within a certain political tradition," and (I may add) it remains there.[22] The question of truth or falsity is thus irrelevant. Justice as fairness presents itself "not as a conception of justice that is true, but [as] one that can serve as a basis of informed and willing political agreement. . . . Philosophy as the search for truth about an independent metaphysical and moral order cannot, I believe, provide a workable and shared basis for a political conception of justice in a democratic society."[23] As a consequence, the classic distinction between political philosophy and rhetoric collapses:

On this view, justification is not regarded simply as valid argument from listed premises, even should these premises be

155

true. Rather justification is addressed to others who disagree with us, and therefore it must always proceed from some consensus, that is, from premises that we and others publicly recognize as true; or better, publicly recognize as acceptable to us for the purpose of establishing a working agreement on the fundamental questions of political justice.[24]

In the Dewey Lectures and subsequently, Rawls sets aside the central concern of traditional political philosophy and puts in its place a new set of questions, to which justice as fairness purports to provide the answer. How are "we" – reflective citizens of a liberal democracy – to understand freedom and equality, the ideals to which we are (or so we say) individually and collectively committed? How are we to resolve the recurrent conflict between these ideals? Which principles of justice are most consistent with them, and how are we to transform these principles into workable institutions?

These questions are well worth asking. But they raise three difficulties that Rawls does not appear to me to have adequately addressed.

To begin with, Rawls's account of political philosophy leaves no obvious basis for the comparative assessment of regimes. When we are faced with evils like Hitlerism, Stalinism, and apartheid, it is not enough to say that these practices violate *our* shared understandings. The point is that we insist on the right to apply our principles to communities that reject them, that is, communities that deny the premises on the basis of which our principles could be "justified" (in Rawls's sense) to them. Indeed, systematic public evils challenge the very validity of our principles, which therefore require a defense that transcends interpretation.

If principles of political right do not apply across the boundaries of public cultures, then many practices we take for granted would have to be abandoned. No American president could have gone to Moscow in 1988 and criticized Soviet restraints on freedom of speech and expression – restraints that reflected, at least as much as they repudiated, the tradition of Russia's public culture. Organizations such as Amnesty International could not rightly apply a common standard of decency to all nations. And forceful, even coercive efforts to foster liberal democracy would be ruled out. In the wake of World War II, for example, the United States undertook to reconstruct not just the political institutions but also the public culture of its defeated enemies. Authoritarian social and economic groupings were dismantled; textbooks were purged; democratic doctrines were aggressively purveyed to bolster the viability of the democratic practices we had imposed. In virtually every respect, the United States overrode the preferred self-understandings of its adversaries. It was a perfect example of what political theory, understood solely as cultural interpretation, would preclude. But it was not wrong.

Now it is open to Rawls to reply (as, indeed, he does) that he does not wish to deny the possibility of applying certain normative principles across cultural boundaries. Rather, he begins from the special case of the closed, self-sufficient community. The extent to which conclusions reached within this domain may be extended farther "cannot be foreseen." Moreover, methods of moral argument, such as the appeal to independent and preexisting moral facts, ruled out in the construction of principles of justice for a single society, may conceivably be used for the elucidation of principles governing relations among societies.[25]

Indeed, it may be argued that Rawls's entire argument tacitly proceeds in two steps. The first is the premise, supported perhaps by moral philosophy, that liberal democracy in its broad outlines is clearly superior to alternative forms of political organization; the second step is the effort, to which Rawls devotes nearly all his attention, to arrive at the most plausible interpretation of what the core commitments of liberal democracy entail. The former step employs strategies of moral validation that cannot be reduced to (deep) consensus, whereas the latter can appeal only to what we believe, or can be led to believe on due reflection.[26]

This reply raises, in turn, the following question: If there can be public principles whose validity rests on truth rather than agreement, then why can't such principles apply *within* liberal-democratic communities? Rawls's answer is that within such communities, the freedom of moral persons is not to be violated, not even in the name of truth. But is the absolute priority of freedom over truth really the polestar of liberal-democratic public culture? And how is that alleged priority to be squared with a public culture whose independent history begins with the declaration that "We hold these truths to be self-evident"?

This question leads to the second objection to Rawls's account of political philosophy: By asking us to separate general truth claims from the elucidation of our shared understandings, it distorts the deepest meaning of those understandings. When Americans say that all human beings are created equal and endowed with certain unalienable rights, they intend this not as a description of their own convictions but, rather, as universal truths, valid everywhere and binding on all. Indeed, that claim is at the heart of their normative force. If our principles are valid for us only because we (happen to) believe them, then they are not binding even for us.[27]

The reason is straightforward. If someone argues that we ought to do something because it corresponds to the best interpretation of the shared understandings that constitute our culture, it is always open to me to ask why I should consider myself bound by those understandings. That simple question launches the philosophical quest for grounds of action and belief beyond the sheer factuality of culture – a quest that cannot be set aside without doing violence to the profoundest of all human longings. There may in the end be no viable grounds for transcultural justification, in which case we shall be faced after all with Nietzsche's choice between life-denying openness and life-affirming horizons. But to set aside *in advance* the quest for truth, to insist as Rawls does that the principle of religious toleration must for political purposes be extended to philosophy itself, is to demand something that no self-respecting individual or public culture can reasonably grant.

The final (and most immediately practical) difficulty with

Rawls's conception of political philosophy is this: His theory, now allegedly derived from an interpretation of the public beliefs of America's democratic culture, seems at critical junctures contestable and even arbitrary as cultural interpretation. Thus, for example, Rawls's core notion of free and equal moral personality, which excludes knowledge of differing conceptions of the good from the original position and rules out individual desert as a core element of America's collective self-understanding that should shape the principles of justice we adopt, does violence not only to a reasonable account of the "moral point of view" but even to the most plausible description of the shared understanding of America's public culture.

For there is (at least in broad outline) a contemporary American consensus concerning just principles and institutions. Every citizen is entitled to at least a minimally decent existence. Those who are able to work receive the wherewithal to live decently in the form of wages (supplemented by public subsidies in the case of low wages). Those who cannot work – either because they are incapable of working or because they cannot find work to do – are to be compensated by the community. Those who can work but choose not to have no valid claims against other individuals or against the community. Above the level of minimal decency defined by the minimum wage, tax credits, the welfare system, unemployment insurance, and social security, individuals are permitted to achieve unequal rewards by developing their natural talents and persuading others to employ and remunerate them. The community supervises this domain of competitive inequality by equalizing opportunities to develop talents and by ensuring that the distribution of rewards is governed by task-related factors rather than irrelevant characteristics such as race, sex, and family background. But it is recognized that this supervision will necessarily remain imperfect, because fair equality of opportunity could be fully achieved only through a system of total regulation that would gravely impede the ability of individuals to lead their lives as they see fit.

Underlying this broad consensus about justice are general conceptions of equality and freedom. Individuals are held to be morally equal, in the sense that membership in the human species suffices to engender certain minimal claims that other members are obliged to honor. At the same time, individuals are naturally unequal, in ways that both generate and legitimate differences of occupation, income, and status. Individuals are held to be morally free in several respects. They enjoy a sphere of privacy within which coercive interference by other individuals or by the state is thought to be illegitimate. They may select and pursue their own plans of life. And they are free, finally, because they are considered – and consider themselves to be – responsible for the choices they make. But individual freedom is far from unlimited. It is circumscribed by duties both to ourselves and to others. We owe it to ourselves to develop our gifts so that we may lead lives of independence and self-respect. We owe it to others to honor the valid claims they have against us, claims that precede (and to some extent govern) our collective choice of social principles and institutions.

Rawls's conception of free and equal moral personality diverges radically from this American understanding of freedom and equality and leads to principles of justice significantly different from those most Americans embrace. At least for political purposes, Rawlsian moral freedom liberates us from all antecedent principles – all duties and obligations, all intrinsic values other than freedom itself. Rawlsian moral equality reduces to moral nullity the respects in which we are naturally unequal. And Rawlsian justice severs the link between what we *do* and what we *deserve*. The valid claims we address to one another are posed on the basis of being rather than doing, of bare abstract existence, shorn of any of the features that distinguish us from one another.

Rawls is well aware of the extent of his divergence from prevailing beliefs. In a telling sentence he declares that "the way in which we think about fairness in everyday life ill prepares us for the great shift in perspective required for considering the justice of the basic structure itself."[28] But it is *Rawls* who ill prepares us for this shift. The conceptual foundation of the basic structure – free and equal moral personality – is supposedly addressed to the citizens of our society. But Rawls's reconstruction of justice as fairness does *not* invoke – indeed, it flatly rejects – the conception of the person underlying our beliefs and practices. There is little evidence to support – and much to refute – Rawls's hope that his conception of personality will prove acceptable to us once its implications are fully grasped. Yet his "constructivist" metatheory leaves him no other grounds of persuasion or verification.

What has led Rawls to this impasse? I conclude with two hypotheses, one rooted in the itinerary of modern social philosophy, the other in the vagaries of contemporary politics.

Rawls is of course a leading figure in the revival of normative social philosophy. In crucial respects, however (as we have seen), this revival remains rooted in the climate of moral skepticism that it has supplanted. Few contemporary theorists (and Rawls is surely no exception) are more willing than were their overtly skeptical predecessors to entertain perfectionist, intuitionist, or naturalist theses. But modern liberal-democratic culture contains many elements of this sort. Thus, any philosophic attempt to reconstruct this culture on quasi-skeptical foundations is bound to do violence to the beliefs of its members. As we have seen, Rawls's proposed reconstruction, carried out in Kant's name, goes so far as to reject perfectionist principles that Kant found it necessary to affirm as elements of both his moral and his political philosophy, principles that we continue to embrace.

It is, in the second place, not accidental that Rawls's thought came to fruition and burst into prominence at the very moment when "advanced" liberal politics, preoccupied with the plight of the worst-off groups in our society, severed its bonds with the moral convictions of the working class. For it is the American working class that clings most fervently to the principle of fair equality of opportunity, to desert as the basis of distribution, to ability, effort, and self-denial as the bases of desert. In their zeal to right the wrongs inflicted on the least advantaged, liberal politicians employed rhetoric and adopted programs that, in effect if not in intention, rejected the beliefs and undercut the interests of the working class.

What these politicians initiated in practice, Rawls brought to completion in theory. For justice as fairness was a systematic effort to discard, as morally arbitrary or irrelevant, precisely those features of human life on which the claims, and the self-respect, of the working class rested. Rawls severed the connection between the willingness to produce and the right to consume; he replaced claims based on achievement with those based on bare existence; he dismissed, as unrelated or even hostile to the conduct of our public life, the claims of particularity and of religion.

Rawls offers us, in short, a dangerously one-sided reconstruction of the liberal tradition, the inadequacies of which are mirrored in the national electoral disasters of contemporary liberalism. In Parts III and IV of this book, I try to show how those elements of this tradition that he so unwisely repudiated may be restored to their rightful place.

Part III

Liberalism without neutrality

Chapter 8

Liberal goods

If the arguments offered in Part II are correct, liberalism cannot do without, and presupposes, a nonneutral account of the human good. That this is so is apparent on three different levels: theory, individual moral judgment, and liberal social practices. As we saw in Chapter 4, even the most ardently neutralist liberal theorists end by relying on a triadic account of the human good as existence, fulfillment of purposes, and practical rationality. With regard to individual judgment (as T. M. Scanlon has argued persuasively), we assess human well-being and the claims it may entail by employing criteria of importance and urgency distinct from, and to a large extent independent of, individually defined tastes and interests.[1] On the level of social practice, our most basic agencies and programs take for granted certain core human purposes: the protection of life against external aggression, internal disorder, and disease; the relief of abject misery; the development of essential human capacities in children; and so forth. As Michael Ignatieff puts it: "For all the apparent relativism of liberal society – our interminable debate about what the good in politics consists in – in practice a shared good is administered in our name by the welfare bureaucracies of the modern state."[2]

Section I of this chapter elaborates some of the principal background conditions that an acceptable liberal account of the human good must satisfy; Section II sketches the main substantive elements of such an account; and Sections III through VI explore its significance for liberal social theory.

Throughout, my purpose is not to break any new analytical ground but, rather, to assemble what I take to be the most fruitful insights of the moral and political theory of the 1970s and 1980s.

I

The following points seem to me to represent the principal background conditions for a liberal account of the human *good* (or *well-being*; I use these terms interchangeably). To avoid any misunderstanding, I state at the outset that not all of these conditions are distinctively liberal; some form part of *any* acceptable account of well-being.

1. The elements of individual well-being do not constitute the totality of morally basic considerations either for individual action or for social policy. As A. K. Sen has argued, it is reasonable to believe that at least two other kinds of considerations are equally basic: notions such as desert and equality, which can serve as the basis of claims and which cannot plausibly be viewed simply as instrumental to individual well-being; and individual agency, the value of which cannot altogether be understood in light of well-being.[3]

2. As Judith Shklar has reminded us, the liberal understanding of well-being is in key respects deeply secular, or (to put it as narrowly as possible) stands in tension with the characteristic outlook of much moral theology. The liberal attitude toward pain, suffering, and death, the liberal antipathy to all cruelty (even, or especially, pious cruelty) is fundamentally this-worldly:

> To put cruelty first is to disregard the idea of sin as it is understood by revealed religion. . . . By putting it unconditionally first, with nothing above us to excuse or to forgive acts of cruelty, one closes off any appeal to any order other than that of actuality.[4]

This does not mean, of course, that liberal societies rule out otherworldly conduct on the part of individuals or voluntary communities. But it does mean that for purposes of liberal public policy, the human good is understood as of this world, an understanding that (as I argued in Part II) is bound to have an effect on nonsecular conduct within societies.

3. While a liberal theory of the human good must achieve at least minimal unity and objectivity, it must also leave very substantial room for individual choice and diversity. For example, James Griffin has proposed an account of certain human goods that are prudential values for any life. But these values do not go so far as to constitute, or define, a single preferred way of life. Not only do they leave untouched substantial areas of human possibility, but also among the core prudential values there is no single balance that is right for everyone.[5] As Stuart Hampshire has argued, the very idea of the human good as a balance among competing considerations is a partisan and eminently contestable ideal.[6]

On the social level, a liberal account of well-being must simultaneously provide a basis for scrutiny and criticism across cultures and allow for a significant realm of legitimate cultural differences.[7] One widely shared conjecture is that the liberal account represents something like the minimal conditions for, or ingredients of, a human life that can be regarded as normal, tolerable, or worthwhile. As Hampshire puts it, "The common needs . . . may be characterized as constituting the minimum common basis for a tolerable human life. They are in this respect comparable with the biological needs. They could be called the conditions of mere decency in human lives."[8]

One way of understanding these commonalities is to observe the deep implausibility of Kant's demand for a moral understanding that is freed from propositions about "the nature of man or . . . the circumstances in which he is placed."[9] While it is posible to sympathize with the considerations that brought Kant to this point, the underlying conception seems unsustainable. If the human species had basic characteristics very different from the ones it now possesses, or had to deal with challenges very different from the ones it now confronts, the nature of our good, and of the virtues and duties corresponding to it, would surely shift dramatically. As Aristotle suggests, our understanding of the human good reflects the contingent but pervasive and enduring features of our bodily constitution, our emotions, our need for society, and our rationality.[10] As Martha Nussbaum, interpreting and developing Aristotle's conception, puts it, "The idea is to begin by considering certain perfectly general conditions of human life that appear to be common to all human societies."[11] This procedure, she argues, offers real promise of achieving the requisite balance between generality and local-temporal particularity.[12]

Another way of moving toward the limited but nonetheless objective account of well-being required for liberal theory is to note that the liberal theory of the good arises in large measure from a deep common experience of the bad. (This is the point of Shklar's insistence that we focus on the vices and give injustice its due.)[13] We can agree that death, wanton cruelty, slavery, poverty, malnutrition, vulnerability, and humiliation are bad without having a fully articulated unitary account of the good. We can, as Hobbes suggested, recognize a *summum malum* without embracing a *summum bonum*. To quote Hampshire once again:

> Moral relativism has always rested on an underestimate of universal human needs, and therefore of the negative aspects of morality – as opposed to diversity in ideals and interests, diversity in conceptions of the good, which are the positive aspects of morality. There is nothing mysterious or "subjective" or culture-bound in the great evils of human experience, re-affirmed in every age and in every written history and in every tragedy and fiction. . . . That these great evils are to be averted is the constant presupposition of moral arguments at all times and in all places, and particularly when the costs involved in pursuing different conceptions of the good are being counted. . . . All ways of life require protection against the great evils, even though different conceptions of the good may rank their prevention in very different orders of priority.[14]

It is notorious, of course, that all statements that begin with the phrase "all ways of life" are vulnerable to objection

168

in the form of sociological or historical counterexample. This fact was already known to Aristotle, who responded by offering a distinction between the degrees of precision and universality to be expected in political and moral (as opposed to mathematical and logical) discourse. Even the best account of political philosophy, he insisted, would be true only for the most part, and approximately.[15] In the course of formulating a theory of liberal freedom, Richard Flathman provides a useful, and broadly applicable, gloss on this ancient theme:

> If such arguments are to be based in part on facts about human beings, they will have to rest upon generalizations, not upon universal truths. The significant question . . . is not whether we can identify exceptions . . . ; rather the question is whether exceptions occur so frequently as to make it clumsy and distracting to rely on the generalizations in forming a general orientation.[16]

I suggest that these broad generalizations – propositions rooted in basic commonalities of human nature, experience, and circumstance – come as close as possible to fulfilling the requirement, advanced by Scanlon and others, that normative social philosophy must simultaneously achieve a measure of distance from subjective sentiments and appeal to widely shared premises. If criteria of well-being are to serve as a basis for criticism and justification of institutions, they must, Scanlon suggests, "represent a kind of consensus, at least among those to whom this criticism or justification is addressed."[17] But, to repeat, this kind of consensus will almost certainly fall short of unanimity, and do so without losing its normative force. While there is, of course, no algorithm that neatly distinguishes between adequately and inadequately general propositions, the difference emerges with at least tolerable distinctness when we inspect the actual role different propositions play in the judgments we typically make.

4. A viable account of the good must be a theory of ends,

not means. In this regard, Sen's critique of the account of primary goods offered in *A Theory of Justice* is decisive. First, the primary-goods approach cannot take special needs into account – cannot, that is, officially recognize the special claims generated by defects and disabilities that interfere with normal human functioning and render a formally fair share of means less valuable. Second, and more pervasively, the primary goods approach is systematically blind to the sorts of human differences that exist within the normal range of functioning. What these two errors have in common, Sen suggests, is a kind of fetishism: Primary goods are taken as the index of advantage, when the real locus of advantage is rather a relationship between persons and goods. Primary goods (more generally, all means) are good insofar as they contribute to an independently defined set of ends.[18]

5. An account of the human good must be a theory of conditions, capacities, or functionings, not just internal states of feeling. This point has been the focus of much recent moral philosophy. John Rawls has argued that hedonic or preference-satisfaction accounts of welfare are vulnerable to two objections: They do not discriminate between legitimate and morally offensive tastes, and they give excessive weight to desires whose satisfaction requires a far larger than normal share of scarce means.[19] Scanlon has shown that our ordinary moral judgments presuppose distinctions among interests as more and less important, central and peripheral, optional and necessary, all of which depend on a sense of a "range of variation of normal lives" that cannot be derived from differences of intensity among preferences.[20] Sen and Nussbaum have fleshed out a quasi-Aristotelian understanding of well-being that takes as its primary feature the ability of individuals to achieve valuable functionings.[21] In a wide-ranging survey of contemporary debates on the appropriate baseline measure for equality, G. A. Cohen proposes a blanket concept of "advantage" and insists that "in deciding both what qualifies as an advantage and the relative sizes of advantages, it is necessary to engage in objective assessment" that goes well beyond subjective desires and preferences.[22]

The inescapability of at least a portion of this thesis is acknowledged by theorists who attempt to remain within a desire- or preference-based understanding of the good. James Griffin, for example, writes:

> Our desires are shaped by our expectations, which are shaped by our circumstances. Any injustice in the last infects the first. There is no doubt that some accounts of well-being will, therefore, distort moral thought in this way....A moral theory should not use as its base persons' actual expectations. It has to get behind them to what are in some sense legitimate expectations.[23]

Similarly, although Richard Arneson expresses deep skepticism about whether the objective value of a person's capabilities can be judged apart from his or her considered preferences regarding them, he goes on to note that

> filling out a preference-satisfaction approach...would seem to require a normative account of healthy preference formation that is not itself preference-based.... The development and exercise of various capacities might be an important aspect of healthy preference formation, and have value in this way even though this value does not register at all in the person's preference satisfaction prospects.[24]

None of this is to say that the human good excludes preference satisfaction, at least of a certain kind. Indeed, I argue in Section II for a particular understanding of inner satisfaction (pleasure or gratification) as an ineliminable element of our good. As Sen puts it, in criticizing what he takes to be Rawls's effort to exclude subjective satisfaction altogether as morally irrelevant, "That a person's interest should have nothing directly to do with his happiness or desire-fulfilment seems difficult to justify."[25]

6. Any account of the good – the liberal theory is no exception – has two features that may be called ultimacy and contestability. On the one hand, the elements of well-being are not themselves to be justified in light of still "higher"

principles: They are the termination of argument as well as the ends of striving. (This ultimacy is, however, compatible with the view that an account of well-being is embedded in, and gains added credibility from, a network of propositions about our species, its circumstances, and its relations with other species as well as with the world as a whole.)

On the other hand, it would not be self-contradictory to reject any account (or all accounts) of human well-being by spurning as valueless the entire human horizon. As Hampshire notes in response to Hume, ordinary moral and social reasoning presupposes some constancy of normal human feelings. If a national leader admitted that his or her policies increased the likelihood of nuclear holocaust but insisted that this was of no account, we would not know how to continue the discussion.[26] Or, as Nussbaum argues, any viable understanding of the human good is "nondetached." That is, it should not (and cannot be) discovered "by looking at human lives and actions from a totally alien point of view, outside of the conditions and experiences of those lives."[27] It is of course possible to adopt such a standpoint – extreme skepticism or nihilism is always a possibility – but doing so consistently is harder than one might suppose. At any rate, like all other social philosophy, liberal theory presupposes the moral significance of basic human action and sentiment.

7. The last background feature of the human good that I wish to stress is its pluralism. Well-being is composed of a number of heterogeneous elements that cannot be reduced to a single common measure. Nor is there a simple and unique hierarchy among these elements. Nor, finally, is there a lexical ordering among them. As Griffin, Nagel, Scanlon, Flathman, and Sen (among others) have argued, it runs contrary to the most basic facts and judgments of our experience to assert that there is a good such that even the slightest loss cannot be counterbalanced by even tremendous gains along other dimensions. Amounts matter. Nor is the good wholly "innumerate." It makes a moral difference whether an evil befalls one individual, or rather many. Numbers matter.[28]

The radical heterogeneity of the human good easily gives

rise to the suspicion that its specification is at best of little use in moral reasoning. For reasons that I elaborate and illustrate in Section II, this view is too pessimistic. Even if an account of the human good were nothing more than an unorganizable list of particularly weighty and fundamental interests, it would help identify and resolve clashes between one or more of these interests and others characterized by implication as less fundamental. And we can go farther. It may well prove possible to arrive at shared judgments about the relative weights to be attached to increments of two or more goods that cannot be reduced to a single substantive value. As Griffin has argued, pluralism does not imply incommensurability. So, for example, a chronically depressed person may have to choose between suicide and a life of accomplishment perennially accompanied by psychic pain: "If the pain is great enough and the accomplishment slight enough, we should not consider the accomplishment worth the pain." Similarly, we may well believe that it takes a large amount of prosperity to outrank a small amount of liberty. But, he insists, we cannot defend liberalism by giving any one element of the human good absolute pride of place, "by denying the possibility of trade-offs between values, even of trade-offs between liberty itself and other values."[29]

II

Having identified a set of background conditions, let me briefly sketch the key dimensions of what I take to be a liberal conception of the individual human good. I should say at the outset that there is nothing hard and fast about the enumeration that follows. Others have proposed comparable lists with somewhat different components, and I have no way of demonstrating the correctness or completeness of my own.[30] My account seems to me to capture best the intuitions about well-being that underlie liberal social orders. I do not expect it to be accepted without further ado; I shall be satisfied if it promotes discussion leading to a more nearly adequate view. My point is only that (as I have argued throughout this book) liberalism cannot do without some account of human well-being, and that it is therefore the responsibility of dissatisfied critics to propose something better.

1. Life: We believe that life itself is good and that the taking or premature cessation of life is bad. This does not mean that preserving life has an absolute value, for three reasons: First, because life is only one dimension of the good, severe deprivations along other dimensions may reduce its value as perceived by the individual to zero or less. An individual permanently racked by excruciating pain may come to welcome death as a release. Second, person A may act in such a manner that, while A's life continues to be of value to him or her, it ceases to be so to others. (Ted Bundy continued to cherish his existence long after many of us concluded that terminating it would be a blessing.) Third, there are circumstances in which the preservation of life cannot be fully realized – for example, in war and in self-defense against violent criminals. There may sometimes be a flat conflict between B's life and C's.

2. Normal development of basic capacities: Normal members of the human species are endowed with certain basic capacities: the senses, various kinds of physical motion, speech, reason, and sociability, among others. We regard it as good to be born with normal basic capacities, and we regard it as a serious misfortune when infants are born with defective capacities relative to that norm. We regard it as bad for children to grow up in circumstances that prevent them from adequately developing normal capacities and for adults to be placed in circumstances inimical to the maintenance of normal capacities. And we look with special horror on practices that contribute to defective capacities. In the early 1970s, the suppression of information about thalidomide was an international scandal; today, thousands of pregnant women are addicted to crack, and (if recent newspaper stories are to be believed) some of them are using it in an effort to induce premature labor.

3. Fulfillment of interests and purposes: It is an observation common, I suspect, to most societies that human beings are, as Richard Flathman has put it, "desiring, interest-pursuing, end-seeking, purposive creatures." But societies differ in the weight and value attached to this fact. Some regard desires as positive only when consistent with divine law; others regard the desires of certain groups as moral nullities; still others understand desires as hindrances to be overcome rather than opportunities to be fulfilled. Our society, by contrast, embraces what Flathman calls the "Liberal Principle": it is "prima facie a good thing for individuals to form, to act upon, and more or less regularly to satisfy (their) interests and desires, their ends and purposes."[31]

Note the "prima facie." It is there to mark the fact that we recognize significant exceptions to the reach of the principle. Two are of particular importance. First, the realization of A's desires may collide with morally significant phenomena external to A: with B's desires (or legitimate claims), for example, or with general principles of justice. Second, the realization of A's desires may conflict with some other feature of A's good.

4. *Freedom:* We believe freedom to be an indispensable element of each individual's good. There seem to be at least three reasons for this. The first is Flathman's: We value freedom instrumentally, as a means to the realization of our interests. In this sense, freedom equals the absence of a range of impediments to action. Second, quite apart from promoting specific interests, we value the general opportunity for self-assertion or self-determination. (This may be understood as the liberal version of Platonic *thumos.*) Third, we see freedom, understood as noncoercion, as key to integrity, that is, to the individual's ability to act in accord with his or her beliefs and thus to identify with, and take responsibility for, his or her deeds.

5. *Rationality:* Liberal society is very far from giving philosophic reason the privileged status it enjoyed for Plato and Aristotle as the peak of the human good. Indeed, we see our society as providing space for ways of life that emphasize desire, passion, aesthetic apprehension, and faith. Never-

theless, there are elements of rationality that enter into our conception of the human good. Among them are (1) an understanding of means–ends relations sufficient to play an active, independent role in the economy and society; (2) each individual's understanding of himself or herself as similar to others for certain purposes, that is, as properly governed by general social rules; (3) the ability to respond to rational persuasion (as opposed simply to force and threats); and (4) when deliberating publicly in matters requiring collective action, the disposition to employ public reasons, open to inspection by others, whenever possible.

6. *Society:* An important element of our intrinsic good is the network of significant relations we establish with others. The ingredients are familiar: family, friends, social and work acquaintances, associates in voluntary organizations, fellow participants in intense collective endeavors such as politics and military combat, among others. No two individuals, of course, attach exactly the same weight to these various kinds of human relations. But most of us would regard their absence as a severe deprivation. Prolonged imprisonment interrupts many human relations, and solitary confinement is an especially feared punishment because it severs all of them. Individuals suffering under oppressive regimes report that the government's calculated disruption of ordinary human relations is among the least bearable features of tyranny. And an accumulating mass of evidence suggests that the inability to form and maintain significant relations is closely linked to the incapacity either to pursue and savor one's own good or to refrain from harming others.

7. *Subjective satisfaction:* We regard an individual's subjective experience (pleasure versus pain, fear versus security, and so forth) as an important element of his or her good. This does not mean that we are prepared to endorse the experience machines Nozick properly rejects, for the simple reason that subjective states are only one element of our good. Nor does it mean that we regard pleasure accompanying acts of harm done to others or oneself as good. (Indeed, taking pleasure in harmful acts only makes them worse.) It

does mean that we regard a person's inability to take satisfaction in a life marked by real personal accomplishments and positive relations with others as a serious incapacity and severe deprivation of the good, and we may well be prepared to invest in spiritual or psychological counseling, for ourselves or for others, in order to reduce the burden of inner distress. While it is better to be Socrates dissatisfied than a pig satisfied, it is also better, ceteris paribus, to be Socrates satisfied than Socrates dissatisfied.

III

Two opposing sets of objections are typically raised against accounts of the human good along the lines just sketched. It may be argued that such accounts are so "thin" as to be vacuous for purposes of either moral theory or social policy, or alternatively, that they are so "thick" as to be unduly restrictive and inadequately responsive to liberty and diversity. Let me address these objections seriatim.

The liberal account of the good, to begin with, is deliberately thin. (It is certainly more open-ended than, e.g., Platonic or Aristotelian perfectionism, and that is part of its point.) It constitutes, intentionally, a kind of minimal perfectionism that both defines a range of normal, decent human functioning and falls short of defining a full way of life. This incompleteness is not, however, equivalent to vacuousness or useless abstraction. The liberal theory of the plural good is thick enough to rule out (1) secular nihilism – the belief that human life and purposiveness are without moral significance; (2) theological withdrawalism – the belief that what happens here on earth doesn't matter because the real action is in the afterlife; (3) moral monism – "one size fits all" accounts of the good; (4) Nietzschean irrationalism; (5) barbarism – deliberate or heedless deprivations of minimal goods.

Note that when I say these beliefs are "ruled out," I do not mean that they cannot be held (and to some extent acted upon) within our society. I mean, rather, that they cannot be used as the basis of public action. For example, an individual may believe that the Second Coming is close at hand, but as a public official he or she is obligated to carry out policy based on the premise that our ordinary existence will continue indefinitely.

This raises a broader point. The liberal theory of the human good is intended to provide a shared basis for public policy. For example, the commitment to life and normal physical functioning is translated into public efforts to protect individuals against violence, to ward off disease, to fight epidemics, to provide nutritionally safe and adequate food supplies, and so forth. The liberal account of the good can also serve as the basis for public education and persuasion: for example, antismoking campaigns by government agencies and in public schools. And it helps define the sphere within which public authorities may insist, at least in the form of taxation, that individuals contribute to the support of public endeavors.

This account of the good does not, however, legitimate public coercion that seeks to make individuals embrace the good, so understood, in their own lives. As citizens, we may be asked to contribute to public purposes that we reject for ourselves, and a liberal understanding of the good allows us to act out that rejection. For example, I may be required to contribute to a public health system that prolongs life for elderly citizens even though I do not want my own life to be prolonged and would refuse to make use of the medical procedures and technology developed for that purpose.

A generalization of this point has been widely discussed in the recent literature. As Arneson, Cohen, Nussbaum, and Sen have argued (in the works already cited and discussed in this chapter), the appropriate measure of liberal social policy is not the extent to which the human good is realized but, rather, the opportunity it affords individuals to strive for and exercise that good. (Sen labels this concept "capability"; Cohen, "access.") As Nussbaum argues, capability is a complex function: It includes basic genetic endowment, education and training, and a range of external conditions,

institutional and political as well as material. The actual measurement of capability is itself complex and (to some extent)
uncertain. Still, if the liberal polity has treated each individual
fairly with respect to his or her capabilities, it has done all
that is required – and permitted. If adults fail to avail themselves of fair opportunities for development, or if they know-
ingly choose to forgo some aspect of their publicly defined
good, that does not constitute evidence that the state has
failed to discharge its responsibilities. Nor does it warrant
public interference in the lives of such individuals. So, for
example, if an individual with ample access to nutrition decides to starve because of his or her religious beliefs, the
liberal state has not overlooked any duty and should not
intervene to thwart the consequences of that person's choice.

The distinction between public policy directed toward capabilities and opportunities, on the one hand, and the conduct of individual life-plans, on the other, reflects the fact
that liberalism embodies a respect for individual agency as
well as a conception of the good. (To some extent, via the
elements of individual freedom and rationality, respect for
agency is built into the liberal account of the good, but it
would appear, as Sen and others have suggested, that there
are independent aspects of that respect as well.)

Two other – classic – liberal propositions figure as well in
the distinction between opportunity-oriented and conduct-
oriented public policy. As Locke argued, there are aspects of
individual existence that simply do not respond to coercion:
If true religious faith is an inner persuasion of the mind, then
it is a futile (and dangerous) category mistake to attempt to
engender such faith, or to infuse it with a specific content,
through acts of public authority. Second, even if public coercion is effective in specific cases, the overall system of coercion required for regular effectiveness in its exercise may well
prove so intrusive and potentially tyrannical as to be, on
balance, destructive rather than productive of the human
good. (For further discussion, see Chapter 12.)

The outcome of these reflections is so vital to the understanding of liberalism as to deserve special emphasis. It is

this: It is not the absence of an account of the good that distinguishes liberalism from other forms of political theory and practice. It is rather a special set of reasons for restricting the movement from the good to public coercion. These reasons give liberals grounds for refraining from coercion altogether in some circumstances, for limiting coercion to the collective provision of capabilities or opportunities in others, and for substituting respectful persuasion for coercion wherever possible. In this, it is possible to bring our commonsense understanding of the individual good, and of the public role in promoting it, into harmony with the liberal commitment to diversity and resistance to tyranny.

Another version of the claim that my account of the good is too thin has been advanced by David Mapel. In an acute critique of the thesis I offered in *Justice and the Human Good*, Mapel contends that the heterogeneity of the good renders it all but useless for either political theory or public decision. How are we to aggregate well-being (for one individual, let alone a multiplicity of individuals) across qualitatively different categories of the good? If there is no underlying metric, no common scale, we cannot. Individuals who agree on the general elements of the good may disagree vigorously about their relative weight and importance in specific circumstances. There is no philosophical alternative to "commonsense pluralism" and no political substitute for deliberative opportunities to express and to harmonize (to the extent possible) the different emphases that are bound to emerge among individuals in free societies.[32]

There are three different sorts of responses to this argument. First, as I suggested above, even an irremediably pluralist conception of the human good may help eliminate certain possibilities and guide deliberation among those that remain – to say nothing of the fact that such pluralism may represent a not unhealthy balance between moral generality, on the one hand, and individual, social, cultural, and historical differences, on the other.

Second, as Sen has argued, there is an outcome that stands between full pluralism, on the one hand, and a complete ordering and ranking, on the other: namely, a partial, incomplete order. It would, he remarks, "be just as extraordinary if every possible pair of functioning vectors could be compared in terms of overall well-being, as it would be if none of them could be."[33]

And finally, it is possible to talk of an intelligible structure of trade-offs among heterogeneous elements of the good even if no abstract principle can be stated that "explains" that structure. Moral deliberation in particular cases can yield shared judgments that quantity X of good A is more important than quantity Y of good B; that is, reasons for this conclusion capable of determining the intellect can be advanced, and the deliberators will come to see the matter in their light. (I frequently have had deliberative experiences of this sort in committee meetings, and I suspect the reader has as well.) Of course, the question of what background consensus is needed to make deliberative convergence possible remains an open one.

Thus far I have responded to the charge that my account of the human good is too thin to do the work required of it. It is also exposed to the opposite objection that taken together, its elements are in fact excessively restrictive and demanding; in particular, that it exacerbates, to the point of outright conflict, the tension between wide diversity, to which liberal society must be committed, and any more-than-minimal shared conception of the good. I would hope that some of the arguments advanced above – especially the limits on coercive public promotion or enforcement of the good – would provide some reassurance. To mitigate further (if not wholly dispel) this fear, let me offer three additional considerations.

First, the judgment that liberal societies allow the greatest possible scope for diversity is compatible with some limitations on individual choice. Pluralism implies neither complete openness nor the absence of all restraints.

Second, my proposed account of our shared understanding of the good is compatible with human diversity in two key respects. What is good for A need not be good for B.

Indeed, no plausible theory of the human good suggests that there is a single way of life valid for all (there may, however, be a common core). Capacities (physical, social, intellectual, moral) differ, and any conception of the good must take this fact into account. Moreover, tastes and desires differ and are translated into differences of purpose. Within a very broad range, the Liberal Principle accommodates these differences.

Finally, because the liberal theory of the good arises, at least in part, in response to a common experience of the bad, it constitutes a less than full account of the good life. To repeat: We can agree that death, wanton cruelty, malnutrition, slavery, poverty, vulnerability are bad without having a fully articulated, unitary account of the good. The resulting scope for diversity and disagreement is considerable indeed.

For the most part, a liberal society will understand the good as opportunity rather than coercive command. It will try to see to it that every adult has fair access to the good (or to the means to it), including the developed inner capacities needed to define and pursue a decent life, but will typically not try to enforce its conception on resisters. It will, however, try to impart its conception of the good to children and to protect them from violations of it. For example, Douglas Besharov has advocated the revision of federal law to facilitate the removal of infants from the care of crack-addicted parents – a proposal I endorse.[34]

IV

Social theory needs some way of moving from the good of individuals to collective determinations. Within a liberal society, I suggest, a key mediating principle is *liberal equality* – the commitment to give each individual's good equal weight in the determination of social policy. This does not (necessarily) mean that policy should be determined by aggregating (let alone maximizing) the good of all affected individuals. The point is negative, not positive: It is that no social policy can be sustained if its justification gives unequal weight to the good of different individuals within a society. One example of what would be excluded is the Hindu caste belief that the well-being of each Brahmin is thirty times as important as that of each Untouchable. The limit case of the forbidden is a policy that simply ignores – gives zero weight to – the good of some clearly affected individuals. (For further discussion of liberal equality, see Chapter 9.)

V

The liberal account of the human good provides the basis for two core elements of liberal political philosophy: a theory of public purposes and a theory of public claims. Let me touch briefly on purposes, which were discussed in Section III, before moving on to the more complex issue of claims.

A liberal polity may be viewed as a cooperative endeavor to create and sustain circumstances within which individuals may pursue – and to the greatest possible extent achieve – their good. This view does *not* deny the fact of social conflict. It implies, however, that this conflict takes place within a framework of partial agreement and potential mutual advantage. The partial agreement is provided by the liberal accounts of the good and of equality. The potential mutual advantage consists in the obvious fact that in many circumstances collaborative activities can be so arranged as to enable each individual to achieve more good than would be possible through uncoordinated endeavors. The preambular references in the U.S. Constitution to the "common defense" and the "general welfare" embody, it seems to me, both the collaborative nature of the liberal polity and its directedness toward certain specific goods for individuals.

To say that individuals are joined in a collaborative endeavor is to suggest that they may make special claims on one another. Within a liberal framework, three kinds of claims are of particular importance: those arising from the bare fact of membership in the community (need); those arising from contribution to the community (desert); and those arising from the voluntary individual disposition of resources in areas left undetermined by the legitimate claims of others (choice). I have discussed these claims at length in *Justice and the Human Good* (though I would no longer subscribe to every detail of my presentation there), and I offer only a brief summary here.

1. *Need:* As Michael Walzer has suggested, needs are the claims we can make on one another simply by virtue of fellow membership in a political community.[35] Within a liberal polity, these claims are defined relative to the basic elements of the liberal good. And because all individuals are equally members, need claims are imperative demands for equal access to the liberal good, or to the means to it.

So needs constitute a sphere of equality; but how extensive is that sphere? I think Walzer is right to stress the ineliminable element of local-historical particularity that enters into its specification. Even within a single community, there may be deep differences about the proper weights to be attached to the various elements of the (shared conception of the) good. Still, political processes of deliberation and negotiation tend to produce a certain consensus: within the United States, for example, that no one should starve for lack of food, or suffer for lack of primary medical attention, or go without the basic education needed to function as a competent citizen and contributory worker. Public policy does not always fully reflect these shared moral understandings, but when it does not, as in the case of U.S. medical care, other institutions and processes tend to take up much of the slack.

Because the principle of need is defined in relation to the good as a set of end states, it generates valid claims to widely varying levels of resources for different individuals. For example, resources required to preserve the lives of premature babies or to give handicapped people an equal chance to develop their capacities are typically significantly greater than for individuals born without such impediments. This differential ratio of resources to the good of diverse individuals means that conceptions of means (e.g., Ackerman's "manna," Dworkin's "equality of resources") cannot possibly be an adequate benchmark for egalitarian (and more broadly, distributive) social policies.

To define the satisfaction of need claims as *access* to the good, or to the means to it, implies a social principle of respect for individual responsibility. In cases of normally responsible adults, societal obligation to meet needs is fulfilled by providing individuals access either to adequately remunerative occupations or directly to adequate levels of resources. The use individuals make of this access is not a matter of further collective concern: The refusal to accept a decent job, or the propensity to squander resources on drugs or drink, does not generate any additional need claims that society is obliged to honor.[36]

2. *Desert:* Desert, in the liberal understanding, is based not on personal virtue but, rather, on individual contribution to the cooperative endeavor to create opportunities for the good life. The concept of contribution means that working versus shirking is a great moral divide in a liberal society. It implies, that is, a thoroughgoing critique of individuals who are physically and mentally able to make a contribution but nonetheless fail to do so.

The flip side is that the application of this principle is subject to the condition that opportunities to contribute are in fact available. It is clearly inappropriate to apply it to individuals who do not have equal opportunity to make a contribution. It is just as clearly inappropriate for a liberal society to deprive some of its members of that opportunity. This conception of contribution opportunity applies not only to the availability of jobs for adults but also to the availability of adequate opportunities for children and youth to develop their capacities to contribute.

The contribution-based desert principle implies that differences of natural endowments are not irrelevant and are not required to be nullified through social policy, as long as need claims are satisfied. To put it another way: Equal attention to needs reflects our understanding of the extent to which we are morally required to treat differences of natural endowments as a shared fate. (As a matter of deep description of what "we" believe, Rawls's total rejection of desert and its replacement with the idea of natural endowments as collective assets is simply mistaken. Nor for that matter does his position fare well under tests of wide justification.)[37]

Contribution has both quantitative and qualitative dimensions. Key quantitative variables include sacrifice, effort, duration, and productivity. The key qualitative variable is the importance of different functions, as defined either by the community as a whole or (more typically) by some socioeconomic entity within the community.[38]

Two sorts of objections have been raised against the appropriateness, or possibility, of contribution-based desert claims. The first, by Rawls, is that the notion of an individual's contribution to society as a whole has no meaning, because

> there is no set of agreed ends by reference to which the potential social contribution of an individual could be assessed. Associations and individuals have such ends, but not a well-ordered society ... Contributions can only be locally defined as contributions to this or that association in this or that situation. Such contributions reflect an individual's worth (marginal usefulness) to some particular group. These contributions are not to be mistaken for contributions to society itself, or for the worth to society of its members as citizens.[39]

If my account of liberalism has even the most rough and approximate validity, Rawls's thesis is mistaken. Because, as members of the liberal community, we share a conception of the good (limited and partial, but still significant), the liberal polity as a whole pursues certain ends defined by that good, and individual contributions to those ends can be assessed. Consider, for example, individuals who defend the community against external aggression, or against internal breach of law. They contribute to the community's ends, and they serve the legitimate interests of all members of the community. That, in part, is why veterans are thought to have some special claims on the community after their term of military service, and why they receive special access to housing, education, health care, and even employment ("veterans' preference"). Conversely, there are individuals whose lives detract from the shared purposes of the community: mentally and physically able individuals who could work but choose instead to be burdens on society, or individuals whose repeated breach of law jeopardizes the life and property of others and compels the polity to expend scarce resources on systems of law enforcement and incarceration.

Another criticism of contribution-based desert has been advanced by David Mapel. There does not, he says, appear to be "any standard measure for directly determining the relative value of all the diverse sorts of tasks performed across the society as a whole. Instead, we must rely on markets to indicate, through wages, the relative worth of various economic activities."[40] This argument, it seems to me, proceeds too briskly. As an empirical matter, a very high percentage of the U.S. population works within large institutions, public and private, whose internal wage structures are guided substantially by nonmarket criteria. This phenomenon is far broader than the movement for "comparable worth": Many public institutions and corporations have developed elaborate nonmarket formulas for determining the worth of qualitatively different tasks, and there appears to be a significant degree of convergence not only on the key variables but also on the relative weights to be attached to them.[41]

More generally, U.S. wages tend to be a function of both market and nonmarket considerations, and even wages that are in fact market-generated are subject to nonmarket moral critiques. (See Section VI.)

3. *Choice:* Liberal societies are inclined to accept as legitimate the outcomes of the individual use of resources and opportunities legitimately held in accordance with need and desert claims. The liberal embrace of choice rests, as we have seen, on core aspects of the liberal conception of the good: on individual freedom, on the satisfaction of legitimate interests, and on the broader view that this conception is partial and limited, and allows for a very significant range of legitimate diversity.

Choice enters into the liberal conception of voluntary social groups, and it also helps define the extent to which liberals allow market determinations in the economic sphere. It means that the liberal conception of distributive justice is in part path-dependent: Certain inequalities are acceptable if they come about through the differential employment of legitimate holdings. So, for example, it is acceptable if different individual savings/consumption preferences at t_0 yield different holdings at t_1.

VI

The identification of these three basic liberal claims – need, desert, choice – does not resolve, but instead sets the stage for, distributive debate. Indeed, many disputes revolve around their rank order, or relative weight. There is rough agreement that decency is offended by just ignoring basic needs of our fellow citizens, and that the urgency of these needs gives them a priority claim on the community's resources. (Although there is some disagreement about definitions of need and about the actual extent of deprivation, "welfare" programs are morally controversial only to the extent that they are seen as allowing capable adults to avoid providing for themselves and their families or as undermining their psychological ability to do so.)

The tension between desert and the market is one of the staples of contemporary social commentary. Many Americans are disturbed by the spectacle of (arguably) noncontributing paper entrepreneurs – hostile takeover artists, merger and acquisitions sharpies – reaping huge windfalls while ordinary wages and salaries stagnate. There is a vague but pervasive sense that the social contribution of the "helping professions" is not adequately compensated. Routine production workers are deeply ambivalent about salary differentials for managers and supervisors. Experimentation continues with comparable-worth schemes that try to make nonmarket assessments of individual tasks within organizational structures. At the same time, the public tends not, in principle, to disapprove of huge market rewards garnered by rock musicians, movie stars, and professional athletes. (Audiences do feel entitled to value for dollar, however, and pop culture icons reap a rich harvest of moral disapproval if they shirk on the job or display contempt for their fans.)

Need, desert, and choice stand in complex tension not only in liberal conceptions but also in the institutions characteristic of contemporary liberal societies. The polity plays a significant role as the guarantor of basic needs; the market is the locus of choice; and conceptions of desert are embodied in the task and salary structures of large, complex, bureaucratic organizations, public as well as private. Debates among principles frequently take the form of struggles among institutions. To what extent, for example, should the polity enforce a public conception of need on employers through minimum wage laws? To what extent should notions of contribution be publicly enforced through comparable-worth standards and limits on compensation for corporate CEOs? To what extent, conversely, should the realm of market choice be expanded by privatizing public functions, weakening the geographical basis of public school selection, or providing alternatives to Social Security? I doubt that liberal philosophy can resolve these disputes, but it can certainly help us understand why they arise, and the significance of the concepts with which they are characteristically conducted.

Although the specifics of the discussion in this chapter have been drawn from the social and economic sphere, I believe that structurally parallel convictions apply in the political sphere as well. The principle of equality is satisfied by equal voting rights (as well as a range of other rights and protections); that of need, by fair opportunities to develop capacities for the exercise of citizenship; that of desert, by shared understandings of political excellence – distinctive capacities to contribute to the fulfillment of shared purposes (election campaigns serve in part to test the relative capacities of competing candidates); and that of choice, by the belief that when fair procedures govern a sphere in which public authority may legitimately act, the outcome is to be respected. The next chapter is more specific about the ways in which liberal political institutions reflect these distinctively liberal conceptions.

Chapter 9

Liberal justice

I

Every society embodies a conception of justice. As I suggested in Chapter 8, the modern liberal society is no exception. In addition to individual choice, which enjoys a special status within liberal communities, two principles are of particular importance. First, goods and services that serve human interests defined as essential are to be distributed on the basis of need, and the needs of all individuals are to be regarded as equally important. Second, many opportunities outside the sphere of need are to be allocated to individuals through a desert-based competition in which all have a fair chance to participate.[1]

The latter principle entered American political thought under the rubric "equality of opportunity." Much of American social history can be interpreted as a struggle between those who wished to widen the scope of its application and those who sought to restrict it. Typically, its proponents have promoted *formal* equality of opportunity by attacking religious, racial, sexual, and other barriers to open competition among individuals. And they have promoted *substantive* equality of opportunity by broadening access to the institutions that develop socially valued talents.

In this chapter, I sketch the grounds on which I believe equality of opportunity can be defended. In the course of doing so, I revise the generally accepted understanding of this principle in several respects. As I interpret it, equality of opportunity is less juridical and more teleological than is commonly supposed. It rests on an understanding of human equality more substantive than "equality of concern and respect."[2] It is broader than the traditional concept of meritocracy. And it is embedded in a larger vision of a good society.

My argument proceeds in four steps. First, I examine in summary fashion some propositions that provide the philosophical foundation for equality of opportunity. Next I explore the strengths and limits of four kinds of arguments commonly offered in defense of this principle. Third, I discuss some difficulties that attend the translation of the abstract principle into concrete social practices. Finally, I briefly respond to some recent critics of equality of opportunity.[3]

II

In Chapter 8, I sketched a liberal theory of the good, one element of which is the development of basic capacities, and I suggested that a liberal conception of equality is needed to move from the individual good to public institutions and policies. In an effort to bring together these ideas and develop them further, I begin with the notion of the good life.

Every human being is born with a wide range of potential talents. Some ought not to be encouraged – a capacity for ingenious and guiltless cruelty, for example. Among the capacities of an individual that are in some sense worth developing, a small subset are comprehensive enough to serve as organizing principles for an entire life. The fullest possible development of one or more of these capacities is an important element of the good life for that individual.

Corresponding to this developmental aspect of the human good is a principle of liberal equality: In spite of profound differences among individuals, the full development of each individual – however great or limited his or her natural capacities – is equal in moral weight to that of every other. For any individuals A and B, a policy that leads to the full development of A and partial development of B is, ceteris paribus, equal in value to a policy that fully develops B while restricting A's development to the same degree. Thus a policy that neglects the educable retarded so that they do not learn how to care for themselves and must be institutionalized is, considered in itself, as bad as one that deprives extraordinary gifts of their chance to flower.

On one level, this proposal runs counter to our moral intuitions. It seems hard to deny that the full realization of high capacities is preferable to the full development of lower, more limited capacities. But this consideration is not decisive.

We would of course prefer a world in which everyone's innate capacities were more extensive than they are at present, and we would choose to be, say, mathematically talented rather than congenitally retarded. Accordingly, we would prefer *for ourselves* the full development of more extensive capacities to the full development of lesser ones. But it does not follow that whenever the developmental interests of different individuals come into conflict, the development of higher or more extensive capacities is to be given priority.

It may be argued, nonetheless, that there is something more horrible about the incomplete development of great capacities than about the waste of lesser gifts. Perhaps so. But one might say with equal justice that it is more horrible for someone who can be taught to speak to be condemned to a life of inarticulate quasi-animality than it is for someone who could have been a great mathematician to lead an ordinary life. Our intuitions about the relative desirability of the best cases are more or less counterbalanced by the relative unacceptability of the worst.[4]

This understanding of full, diverse, and equal development leads in turn to the idea of the good society. In such a society, the range of social possibilities comes as close as is feasible to equaling the range of human possibilities. Many worthy capacities, that is, find a place within it. Few are compelled to flee elsewhere in search of opportunities for development, the way ambitious young people had to flee farms and small towns in nineteenth-century societies. Further, worthy capacities are treated fairly in the allocation of resources available for individual development within that society.

These criteria, I suggest, are more fully satisfied in liberal societies than in any others. While (as we have seen) liberalism tends to favor – and to screen out – certain ways of life, liberal societies historically have come closest to achieving the universality that excludes no talent or virtue. The development of great gifts encounters few material or political impediments. The development of ordinary gifts is spurred by education and training open to all. The fundamental argument for a diverse society is not, as some believe, that our reason is incompetent to judge among possible ways of life. It is, rather, that the human good is not one thing but many things. And it is equality of opportunity, understood substantively as well as formally, that mediates between the diversity of individual endowments and the relative openness of liberal societies.

Although the principle of equality of opportunity is embedded in this kind of society, the concept is nonetheless commonly thought to presuppose a sharp distinction between the natural endowments of individuals and their social environment. The life chances of individuals, it is argued, should not be determined by such factors as race, economic class, and family background. To the extent that these factors do tend to affect the development and exercise of individual talents, it is the task of social policy to alleviate their force. If malnutrition stunts mental and physical development, then poor children must be fed by the community. If social deprivation leaves some children irreparably behind before they start first grade, then compensatory preschool programs are essential.

The proposition that natural but not social differences should affect individual life chances raises a number of difficult problems. To begin with, natural differences are usually viewed as genetic endowments not subject to external intervention. But increasingly, natural endowments are viewed as malleable, and the time may not be far off when they can be more predictably altered than can social circumstances. This eventuality will transform not only the distinction between the natural and the social but also its normative consequences. To the extent that, for example, modern techniques can overcome genetic defects or even determine genetic endowments, disputes will arise among families over access to these scarce and expensive techniques. Before the opportunity to develop one's capacities will come the opportunity to have certain capacities to develop. At this point – as Bernard Williams rightly suggests – equality of opportunity will merge into broader issues of absolute equality and the morality of genetic intervention.[5]

James Fishkin has reminded us of another crucial difficulty. In an argument that can be traced back to Plato's *Republic*, he shows that the family is a prime – perhaps *the* prime – source of inequalities that affect the development of natural talents and the ability to compete. Full equality of opportunity would therefore require, at a minimum, very substantial invasions of the family autonomy cherished as a basic freedom in a liberal society. Liberalism is a basket of ideals that inevitably come into conflict with one another if a serious effort is made to realize any one of them fully, let alone all of them simultaneously. It follows that our commitment to equality of opportunity – that is, to reducing to a minimum the impact of background social conditions on individual life chances – must be tempered by a sober assessment of the costs, at the margin, of such a reduction.[6]

Assuming that neither natural nor social differences are likely to be expunged, we can still ask why they are regarded so differently, that is, why differences of social background are thought to be impermissible determinants of social outcomes and, conversely, why natural differences are thought to be appropriate determinants.

Why shouldn't the chief's eldest child be the next chief? This question is seldom asked because it seems absurd to us. We take it for granted that a competitive system ought to winnow out the candidate "best qualified" and that family membership is utterly irrelevant to this selection. But of course it need not be. If the tribe is held together by shared loyalty based in part on family sentiments, the chief's child may be uniquely qualified. Descent may be an important ingredient of social legitimacy and therefore an important claim to rule, especially when other sources of legitimacy have been weakened. Contemporary Lebanon, where sons gain power from fathers and assume their murdered brothers' burdens, typifies this sort of society. India and Pakistan offer other instructive examples.

Underlying the usual distinction between social and natural differences is the moral intuition that social outcomes should be determined by factors over which individuals have control. But the wealth and social standing of one's family are facts over which individuals cannot exercise control, and therefore, they should not matter.

The difficulty with this argument is that individuals do not control their natural endowments any more than they do their ancestry. The requirement that the basis on which we make claims must somehow be generated through our own efforts amounts to a nullification of the very procedure of claiming *anything*.[7]

The costs of this conclusion are high. Every conception of justice presupposes the distinction between valid and invalid claims, which in turn rests on some facts about individuals. There can be no theory of justice without some notion of individual desert, and no notion of individual desert that does not eventually come to rest on some "undeserved" characteristic of individuals.

It is perfectly true, as Rawls has urged, that from the "moral point of view" (as distinguished, say, from a theological point of view) the distribution of natural talents must be regarded as arbitrary. But this consideration is hardly decisive, for three reasons: From the moral point of view, the bare fact of our individual existence is just as arbitrary. So if undeserved talents cannot give rise to valid claims, undeserved existence cannot either.[8] In addition, our unearned characteristics are deeply woven into the fabric of our individual identity. As I argued in Chapter 6, Rawls's quasi-

Kantian account of moral personality is just too parsimonious to do justice to the intuitive understanding of identity that we (properly) bring to social theory.[9] And finally, the proposition that natural talents are not to be regarded as "ours" for purposes of social justice violates what G. A. Cohen has called the principle of self-ownership, the intuitive force of which must (he argues) be acknowledged even by left-wing critics of liberalism.[10]

For all these reasons, the contention that we must somehow be responsible for the aspects of ourselves on the basis of which we make claims is less than compelling. The world's fastest sprinter doesn't "deserve" his natural endowment of speed, but surely he deserves to win the race established to measure and honor this excellence. There is nothing in principle wrong with a conception of individual desert that rests on the possession of natural gifts.

This does not mean that we are wholly unencumbered in the translation of natural gifts into social and material advantages. As I argued in the previous chapter, desert claims are significantly constrained by claims based on need: Equal attention to needs reflects the liberal understanding of the extent to which we are morally required to treat differences of natural endowments as a shared fate.

The complex interplay of need and desert is more than an ad hoc compromise. It also reflects a deep duality in the human condition and in our response to it. As Anthony Kronman puts it, we must retain simultaneously a lively sense of moral arbitrariness and an understanding of the seamlessness of personal identity. The ambivalence we feel "reflects a general tension inherent in the moral point of view: although morality requires us to look at human affairs from the timeless standpoint of reason itself, its prescriptions must somehow be accommodated to the contingent and irrational features of the human condition."[11] I would suggest that the normative distinction between social facts and natural endowments is not so sharp as many interpretations of equality of opportunity presuppose.[12] This distinction provided the historical impetus for the development of the principle: The triumph of meritocratic over patriarchal and hereditary norms is an oft-told tale. But philosophically, the distinction between nature and society (or, for that matter, between what we have earned and what befalls us) must be reinterpreted as the distinction between relevant and irrelevant reasons for treating individuals in certain ways.

To push this reinterpretation forward, I examine in the following section four ways in which equality of opportunity can be defended.

III

First, and most obviously, equality of opportunity can be justified as a principle of *efficiency*. Whatever the goals of a community may be, they are most likely to be achieved when the individuals most capable of performing the tasks that promote those goals are allowed to do so. Such efficiency, it may be argued, requires a system that allows individuals to declare their candidacy for positions they prefer, and then selects the ablest. From this standpoint, equality of opportunity is a dictate of instrumental rationality, a measure of collective devotion to social goals.

But a complication arises immediately. Competition among individuals to fill social roles may not produce aggregate efficiency, even if the most talented is chosen to fill each individual role.

To see why, consider a two-person society with two tasks. Suppose that person A can perform both tasks better than person B and is by an absolute measure better at the first task than at the second. If A is only slightly better than B at the first but much better at the second, it may be more productive for the society as a whole to allocate the first task to B, even though A will then not be doing what he or she does best.

In actual societies, the differential rewards attached to tasks can produce comparable distortions. If (say) lawyers are paid much more than teachers, the talent pool from which lawyers are selected is likely to be better stocked. Teachers will then tend to be mediocre, even if the best are selected from among the candidates who present themselves. This circumstance may well impose aggregate costs on society, at least in the long run.[13]

These difficulties arise for two reasons. First, applying equality of opportunity to a society characterized by division of labor produces a set of individual competitions whose aggregate results will fall short of the best that society could achieve through more centralized coordination among these contests. Second, equality of opportunity embodies an element of individual liberty. Individuals can choose neither the rules of various competitions nor their outcomes. But they can choose which game to play. The fact that society as a whole will benefit if I perform a certain task does not mean that I can be coerced to perform it. Within limits, I can choose which talents to develop and exercise, and I can refuse to enter specific competitions, even if I would surely emerge victorious. "From each according to his ability" is not the principle of a liberal society, for the simple reason that the individual is regarded (for most purposes, anyway) as the owner of his or her capacities. Equality of opportunity is a meritocratic principle, but it is applied to competitions among self-selected individuals.

I do not wish to suggest that this liberty is anywhere near absolute. Duties to other individuals, particularly family members who have made sacrifices on my behalf, may require me to develop and exercise certain abilities. Similarly, duties to my country may require me to become a first-rate general or a physicist, if I am capable of doing so. But after all such duties are taken into account, there will still be a range of choices into which a liberal society should not intrude. This will always be a barrier to the single-minded pursuit of efficiency, and to the use of coercive meritocracy to achieve it.

A second justification of equality of opportunity focuses on the notion of *desert*. For each social position, it is argued, a certain range of personal qualities may be considered relevant. Individuals who possess these qualities to an outstanding degree deserve those positions. A fair competition guided by equality of opportunity will allow exemplary individuals to be identified and rewarded.

Many critics have objected to this line of reasoning. It is a mistake they argue, to regard social positions as prizes. In athletic competition, first prize goes to the one who has performed best. It would be inappropriate to take future performance into account or to regard present performance in the context of future possibilities. The award of the prize represents a recognition only of what has already happened. The prizewinner has established desert through completed performance. In the case of social positions, on the other hand, the past is of interest primarily as an index of future performance. The alleged criterion of desert is thus reducible to considerations of efficiency.

This critique contains elements of truth, but I believe that the sharp contrast it suggests is overdrawn. After all, societies do not just declare the existence of certain tasks to be performed. They also make known, at least in general terms, the kinds of abilities that will count as qualifications to perform these tasks. Relying on this shared public understanding, young people strive to acquire and display these abilities. If they succeed in doing so, they have earned the right to occupy the corresponding positions. They deserve them. It would therefore be wrong to breach these legitimate expectations, just as it would be wrong to tell the victorious runner, "Sorry. We know you crossed the finish line first, but we've decided to give the prize to the runner who stopped to help a fallen teammate."

To be sure, circumstances may prevent society from honoring legitimate desert claims. Individuals may spend years preparing themselves for certain occupations, only to find that economic or demographic changes have rendered their skills outmoded. Socially established expectations cannot be risk-free – a fact that security-seeking young people are not always quick to grasp. But this fact does not distinguish social competition from athletic competition. The Americans who worked so hard for the 1980 Olympic Games, only to be denied the right to compete, were deeply disappointed, but they could not maintain that they had been treated unjustly. In short, no clear line can be drawn between tasks and prizes. Many tasks *are* prizes; opportunities to perform activities are intrinsically or socially valuable. These prizes are of a special character – forward looking rather than complete in themselves – which gives rise to legitimate disagreement about the criteria that should govern their distribution. There is no science that permits completely reliable inferences from past to future performance in any occupation.[14] But once criteria, however flawed, have been laid down, they create a context within which claims of desert can be established and must be honored if possible. Performance criteria may be altered, but only after existing claims have been discharged, and only in a manner that gives all individuals the fairest possible chance to redirect their efforts.

A third kind of justification of equality of opportunity focuses on *personal development*. When a society devotes resources to education and training, when it encourages individuals to believe that their life chances will be significantly related to their accomplishments, and when it provides an attractive array of choices, there is good reason to believe that individuals will be moved to develop some portion of their innate capacities. Thus, it may be argued, equality of opportunity is the principle of task allocation most conducive to a crucial element of the human good.

I accept this argument. But it has significant limitations. It ignores, for example, ways in which individuals may benefit from performing certain tasks even if they are less competent to do so than others. If apprentices are not permitted to perform the activities of their craft, they cannot increase their competence. In this process of apprenticeship, the master craftsman must be willing to accept errors and inefficiencies. This is true even if the learner can never achieve the full competence of the best practitioner. Even individuals of mediocre talents can increase their knowledge, skill, and self-confidence when they are allowed to discharge demanding responsibilities. Thus developmental considerations may suggest rotating some tasks fairly widely rather than restricting them to the most able.

In addition, most individuals can achieve excellence in specific demanding tasks only when they concentrate on mastering that task to the exclusion of all others. Equality of opportunity is thus linked to the division of labor, to specialization, and to the principle of "one person, one job." An argument of considerable antiquity questions the human consequences of this principle. Perhaps it is better for individuals to be developed in many areas rather than allowing most of their capacities to lie fallow. Perhaps a system of task assignment that deemphasizes competence in favor of variety is preferable.

These considerations raise a broader issue. Human activities have both external and internal dimensions. On the one hand, they effect changes in the natural world and in the lives of others. On the other hand, they alter – develop, stunt, pervert – the character and talent of those who perform them. Neither dimension can be given pride of place; neither can be ignored.

Without a measure of physical security and material well-being, no society can afford to devote resources to individual development or to exempt individuals from material production for any portion of their lives. In societies living at the margin, child labor is a necessity, and scholarly leisure is an unaffordable luxury. But structuring a social and economic system to promote productive efficiency is justified only by physical needs and by the material preconditions of development itself. Thus a fundamental perversion occurs when the subordination of development to production continues beyond that point. A wealthy community that determines the worth of all activities by the extent to which they add to its wealth has forgotten what wealth is for. A system of training, education, and culture wholly subservient to the system of production denies the fuller humanity of its participants.[15]

For these reasons, I suggest, a prosperous society must

carefully consider not only how it allocates its tasks but also how it defines and organizes the tasks it allocates. The very concern for individual development that makes equality of opportunity so attractive leads beyond that principle to basic questions of social structure.

Finally, equality of opportunity may be defended on the grounds that it is conducive to *personal satisfaction*. Within the limits of competence, individuals are permitted to choose their lives' central activity, and they are likely to spend much of their time in occupations they are competent to perform. No system can guarantee satisfaction, of course. But one that reduces to a minimum the compulsory elements of labor and allows individuals to feel competent in the course of their labor will come closer than any alternative.

Although this argument is probably correct, it is important to keep its limits in mind. To begin with, the satisfaction derived from an activity is not always proportional to our ability to perform it. We may want to do what we cannot do very well, and we may secure more pleasure from doing what we regard as a higher task in a mediocre manner than from doing a lower task very well. In addition, in a system fully governed by equality of opportunity, there would be no external causes of failure and no alternative to self-reproach for the inability to achieve personal ambitions.

An equal opportunity system stimulates many to strive for what they cannot attain. By broadening horizons, it may well increase frustration. Of course, this is not necessarily a bad thing. Such a system does induce many who can excel to develop themselves more fully. It is not clear that a system that increases both achievement and frustration is inferior to one that increases the subjective satisfaction of the less talented only by decreasing the motivation of the more talented to realize their abilities. And many people not capable of the highest accomplishments nevertheless develop and achieve more in a context that infuses them with a desire to excel. A permanent gap between what we are and what we want to be need not be debilitating. On the contrary, it can be a barrier to complacency, a source of modesty, an incentive for self-discipline, and a ground for a genuine respect for excellence.

IV

I remarked at the outset that the principle of equality of opportunity gains both content and justification from the society in which it is embedded. There are, I believe, four major dimensions along which this abstract principle is rendered socially concrete; first, the range of possibilities available within a society; second, the manner in which these activities are defined and organized; third, the criteria governing the assignment of individuals to particular activities; and finally, the manner in which activities are connected to external goods such as money, power, and status.

I need not add much to the previous discussion of possibilities. A good society is maximally inclusive, allowing the greatest possible scope for the development and exercise of worthy talents.

Opportunities for development are affected not just by the kinds of activities that take place within a society but also by their manner of organization. Consider the provision of health care. At present in the United States, doctors, nurses, orderlies, and administrators perform specific ranges of activities, linked to one another by rigid lines of authority. It is possible, and probably desirable, to redraw these boundaries of specialization. Nurses, for example, could well be given more responsibility for tasks now performed by doctors, particularly in some areas where judgment, experience, and sensitivity to the needs of specific individuals are critical. Similarly, it is possible to reorganize the process of production. At some plants, small groups of workers collectively produce entire automobiles, performing the required operations sequentially in the group's own area rather than along an assembly line. Proposals to expand managerial decision making to include production workers have been tried out in a number of European countries.

Behind all such suggestions lies the belief that the existing organization of social tasks rests more on habit and special privilege than on an impartial analysis of social or individual benefit. Occupational hierarchies in which all creativity and authority are confined to a few tasks while all the rest enforce routine drudgery are typically justified on the grounds of efficiency. Maintaining a certain quality and quantity of goods and services is said to demand this kind of hierarchy. In general, there is little evidence to support this proposition and much to question it. Besides, as we have seen, there are other things to consider – in particular, the effect of tasks on the development and satisfaction of the individuals who perform them. Equal opportunity requires an appropriate balance between the preconditions of productive efficiency and the internal consequences of tasks – a balance that may well depend on a far-reaching reorganization of social tasks.

Let me assume that a society has actually reached agreement on such a balance. The assignment of individuals to the tasks embodied in that agreement will remain controversial, because criteria of assignments are open to reasonable dispute. Some considerations are clearly irrelevant. Barring aberrant background circumstances, such factors as the color of one's hair or eyes should have no bearing on one's chances of becoming a doctor, because they have no bearing on one's capacity to practice the medical art. But beyond such obvious cases, there is disagreement – for example, about the nature of the good doctor. In the prevailing view, the good doctor is one who is capable of mastering a wide variety of techniques and employing them appropriately. But dissenters suggest that moral criteria should be given equal weight: The good doctor cares more about patients' welfare than about his or her own material advancement, gives great weight to need in distributing medical services, never loses sight of the humanity of his or her patients. Still others believe that the willingness to practice where medical needs are the greatest is crucial. They urge that great weight be given to the likelihood, or the promise, that a prospective doctor will provide health care to rural areas, small towns, urban ghettos, or other localities lacking adequate care. From this standpoint, otherwise dubious criteria such as geographical origin or even race might become very important.

This dispute cannot be resolved in the abstract. The relative weight accorded the technical, moral, and personal dimensions will vary with the needs and circumstances of particular societies. It will also vary among specialties within professions. In the selection of brain surgeons, technical mastery is probably paramount. For pediatricians, human understanding is far more important. Whatever the criteria, they must be made as explicit as possible, so that individuals can make informed commitments to courses of training and preparation. Those who control the selection are not free to vary publicly declared criteria once they have engendered legitimate expectations.

I turn now to the connection between activities and external goods. Here my point is simple. A fair competition may demonstrate my qualification for a particular occupation. But the talents that so qualify me do not entitle me to whatever external rewards happen to be attached to that occupation. I may nevertheless be entitled to them, but an independent line of argument is needed to establish that fact. So, for example, in accordance with public criteria, my technical competence may entitle me to a position as a brain surgeon. It does not follow that I am entitled to half a million dollars a year. Even if we grant what is patently counterfactual in the case of doctors – that compensation is determined by the market – the principle of task assignment in accordance with talents does not commit us to respect market outcomes. Indeed, the kind of competition inherent in a system of equal opportunity bears no clear relation to the competition characteristic of the market.

This distinction has an important consequence. Many thinkers oppose meritocratic systems on the ground that there is no reason why differences of talent should generate or legitimate vast differences in material rewards. They are quite right. But this is not an objection to meritocracy as such.

It is an objection to the way *rewards,* not *individuals,* are assigned to tasks.

Indeed, one could argue that current salary inequalities should be reversed. Most highly paid jobs in our society are regarded as intrinsically desirable by the people who perform them. In moments of candor, most business executives, doctors, lawyers, generals, and college professors admit that they would want to continue in their professions even at considerably lower income levels. The incomes generally associated with such occupations cannot then be justified as socially necessary incentives.

There are, however, some rewards that are intrinsically related to tasks themselves. The most obvious is the gratification obtained from performing them. Another is status. Although I cannot prove it, it seems likely that there is a hierarchy of respect and prestige independent of income, correlated with what is regarded as the intrinsic worth of activities. Tasks involving extraordinary traits of mind and character or the ability to direct the activities of others are widely prized.

Finally, certain activities may entail legitimate claims to some measure of power and authority. As Aristotle pointed out, there are inherent hierarchical relations among specialized functions. The architect guides the work of the bricklayer and the plasterer. Moreover, if members of a community have agreed on a goal, knowledge that conduces to the achievement of that goal provides a rational basis for authority. If everyone wishes to cross the ocean and arrive at a common destination, then the skilled navigator has a rational claim to the right to give orders. But the navigator's proper authority is limited in both extent and time. It does not regulate the community's nonnavigational activities, and it vanishes when all reach their destination.

v

To conclude this analysis of equal opportunity, I want to touch on four arguments that are frequently brought against it. The first objection is the *libertarian*, raised in its purest form by Robert Nozick. According to Nozick, equality of opportunity understates the individualistic character of human existence. Life is not a race with a starting line, a finish line, a clearly designated judge, and a complex of attributes to be measured. Rather there are only individuals, agreeing to give to and receive from each other.[16]

I believe that this contention overlooks important social facts. Within every community, certain kinds of abilities are generally prized. Being excluded from an equal chance to develop them means that one is unlikely to have much of value to exchange with others: Consider the problem of hard-core unemployment when the demand for unskilled labor is declining. To be sure, there is more than one social contest, but the number is limited. In a society in which more and more educational credentials are demanded for even routine tasks, exclusion from the competition for education and training – or inclusion on terms that amount to a handicap – makes it difficult to enter the system of exchange. Equality of opportunity acknowledges these prerequisites to full participation in social competition, and it therefore legitimates at least some of the social interventions needed to make full participation possible.

The second objection is the *communitarian*. According to this view, advanced by John Schaar among others, even the most perfect competition is insufficient, because competition is a defective mode of existence. It sets human beings apart from each other and pits them against one another, in an essentially destructive struggle.[17]

Certainly an equal opportunity system contains some competitive elements. But not all forms of competition are bad. Some competition brings human beings closer together, into communities of shared endeavor and mutual respect. (Consider the embrace of two exhausted boxers at the end of a match.) Moreover, competition can be mutually beneficial. Scientific competition may produce simultaneous discoveries, neither of which would have occurred without the presence of the competitor; gymnastic competition may inspire

two perfect performances. And finally, the traditional antithesis between competition and community is too simple.
Community rests on some agreement. A competitive system
can be a form of community if most participants are willing
to accept the principle of competition.

The third objection to equality of opportunity is the *democratic*. According to this objection, articulated by Michael
Walzer among others, equality of opportunity is at best a
limited principle because it cannot apply to the sphere of
politics. Technical expertise may confer a limited authority.
But because there is no rationally binding conception of the
good, there is no technique for selecting the ends of political
life. Political power does not look *up* to Platonic ideas, but
rather *around* to prevailing opinions – that is, to the citizens'
shared civic consciousness.[18]

I do not believe that any contemporary political thinker
has adequately defended the crucial premise of this argument: that no rational theory of political ends is available.
But let me set this question to one side and focus briefly on
the qualities needed to direct a community in accordance
with its own self-understanding.

I would argue that there are distinctive political excellences
and virtues; they are necessary for the success of all political
orders, including democracies; and they do constitute one
valid claim to political authority, because they contribute to
needed cooperation and to the achievement of shared purposes. Without them, a political community will lose its bearings and its self-confidence. It would be very fortunate if
these virtues were widely distributed. But experience suggests that the percentage of individuals who possess them
to any significant degree within a given community is small.
This does not necessarily mean that democracy is based on
a mistake. As Jefferson saw, the main problem of democracy
is to achieve some convergence of participation, consent, and
excellence. He believed that this problem is soluble, in part
through social and political institutions that single out the
natural *aristoi*, develop their special gifts, and reliably promote them to high office. From this standpoint, the purpose

of elections is not just to register opinion but also to identify excellence. Indeed, the test of an electoral system is its propensity to confer the mantle of leadership on those most worthy to lead. Properly understood, the distribution of power in democracies is not wholly distinct from, but rather partly governed by, the merit-based principle of equal opportunity.[19]

The final, and surely the most ironic, objection to equality of opportunity is the *liberal*. (I say "most ironic" because equality of opportunity has fair claims to be regarded as the core principle of liberal society.) We have already encountered and addressed a version of the liberal critique, in James Fishkin's warnings against pressing equality of opportunity so far as to erode other liberal values. Another set of liberal objections is offered by Judith Shklar. There are, she argues, at least three problems with a social system based on equality of opportunity. It requires a powerful, and therefore dangerous, central authority to regulate its operation. It presupposes a measure of social agreement about goals, tasks, and qualifications that is most unlikely to be forthcoming. And to the extent that agreement does not exist, it invites public authority to behave paternalistically, "dispensing shares in accordance with his intuitions about the local meanings of the fair and the just."[20]

There can be no decisive response to these objections. But two considerations seem to me to diminish their force. To begin with, it is important not to overstate the role of central authority in administering a system of equal opportunity. Public authority will, up to a point, endeavor to establish fair background conditions within which individuals may strive to develop and exercise their talents. To the extent that some tasks are considered to be public offices, public authority will have to take responsibility for defining their qualifications. But beyond that, there will be a multiplicity of local and private competitions, each with its own definition of tasks and associated capabilities. Here, government will have a role only at the margin – to weed out patently discriminatory criteria and to ensure that private associations behave fairly (i.e., consistently with their own criteria) in the allocation of tasks and rewards.

Second, a system of equal opportunity does not presuppose any (fictitious) social agreement concerning goals and qualifications. It presupposes rather, as I have said, that there will be a multiplicity of competitive arenas reflecting differing conceptions of what is worthwhile. It also presupposes that in cases where some collectively binding determination must be made, standard liberal democratic decision-making procedures will come into play. A public school system, for example, may propose new criteria for hiring teachers; various individuals and groups will have their say; an elected, accountable school board will make the final determination – subject, of course, to correction at the next election.

I do not mean to suggest that there is no tension whatever between merit-based selections and liberal democracy. The point is, rather, that liberalism is guided not by one monistic or dominant goal but by a number of basic goals that can, when pressed to the hilt, come into conflict with one another. I quite agree that, taken too far, implementing equality of opportunity can pose threats to liberal freedom, diversity, and security. This is a perfectly good argument against losing our balance and mistaking the part for the whole. But it is no objection to equality of opportunity as such.

VI

Suppose that I have succeeded in establishing some version of the theses urged in Chapter 8 and this chapter: first, that there is a distinctive, noninstrumental liberal understanding of the human good; and second, that this understanding figures centrally in the liberal conception of justice. The next challenge is to determine the practical prerequisites for making these propositions effective in the actual life of liberal communities.

The response proceeds in two steps. The first, which is

relatively noncontroversial, is to link liberal principles to specific, historically tested institutions: representative politics, dynamic diverse societies, and suitably tempered but robust market economies. This brings us to the second step: consideration of the political culture needed to sustain liberal institutions. Here consensus gives way to controversy. Many have argued that it is the special genius of liberal institutions to function successfully even in the absence of public-regarding individual motives. Others have contended that liberal orders, like all others, cannot sustain themselves over time without appropriate beliefs and desires among their citizens.

Each of these theses has deep roots in the liberal tradition. In the next chapter, I associate myself with the latter and explore the kinds of convictions and motivations that liberal communities most need. My proposal is that we can empirically define a list of "liberal virtues," each of which is required to sustain some aspect of liberal institutions.

Chapter 10

Liberal virtues

I

For two generations, scholarly inquiry has been dominated by the belief that the liberal polity does not require individual virtue. On the theoretical plane, liberalism has been understood by many as the articles of a peace treaty among individuals with diverse conceptions of the good but common interests in self-preservation and prosperity. On the level of basic institutions, the liberal constitution has been regarded as an artful contrivance of countervailing powers and counterbalancing passions. In the arena of liberal society, individual behavior has been analyzed through the prism, and public policy guided by the precepts, of neoclassical economics.

The conclusion that liberalism could be severed, in theory and in practice, from the concern for virtue was shared by scholars of widely divergent orientations. Although Leo Strauss was on the whole sympathetic and C. B. Macpherson hostile to the liberal polity, they converged on an interpretation of Locke that stressed his effort to liberate individual acquisitiveness from traditional moral constraints.[1] Martin Diamond and Gordon Wood could agree on the essentials of the interest-based "new science of politics" that displaced civic republicanism and undergirded the Constitution.[2] The understanding of modern liberal society as an agglomeration of self-interested individuals and groups formed a common point of departure for defenders of pluralism (such as Robert Dahl in his 1950s incarnation) and its critics (led by Theodore Lowi).[3]

213

Although the various analysts of liberalism were not in agreement on a specific conception of virtue, they united in the belief that liberal theory and practice stood in tension with virtue however conceived. For Strauss and many of his followers, liberalism placed in jeopardy both the restraints on passion that should govern the daily life of the many and the striving for excellence that should guide the activities of the few. For J. G. A. Pocock and his allies, liberalism represented the evisceration of republican virtue, understood as the disposition to subordinate personal interests to the common good.[4] For Charles Taylor and his fellow communitarians, liberalism undercut the very possibility of community and thus the significance of the virtues, understood as the habits needed to sustain a common life.[5] To the extent that virtue could nonetheless be found in the actual practices of liberal society, it was to be understood, argued Irving Kristol and many others, as the residue of an older moral and religious tradition at odds with – and under relentless assault by – liberalism's most fundamental tendencies.[6]

The proposition that liberalism does not rest on virtue is not the arbitrary invention of contemporary scholarship. Albert Hirschman has traced the emergence in seventeenth- and eighteenth-century social thought of the thesis that republican government could best be secured not through civic virtue but, rather, through the liberation of the commercial, acquisitive "interests" of the middle class in opposition to the politically destructive "passions" of the aristocracy.[7] The most famous *Federalist* papers (numbers 10 and 51) contain memorable formulations of the need to counteract interest with interest, and passion with passion. Immanuel Kant, who was at once the profoundest moral philosopher and the most devoted liberal theorist of his age, argued vigorously for the disjunction between individual virtue and republican government:

> The republican constitution is the only one entirely fitting to the rights of man. But it is the most difficult to establish and even harder to preserve, so that many say a republic would

have to be a nation of angels, because men with their selfish inclinations are not capable of a constitution of such sublime form. But [this is an error: republican government] is only a question of a good organization of the state, whereby the powers of each selfish inclination are so arranged in opposition that one moderates or destroys the ruinous effect of the other. The consequence . . . is the same as if none of them existed, and man is forced to be a good citizen even if not a morally good person. The problem of organizing a state, however hard it may seem, can be solved even for a race of devils, if only they are intelligent.[8]

In spite of the considerable evidence for the proposition that the liberal-republican polity requires no more than the proper configuration of rational self-interest, this orthodoxy has in recent years come under attack from scholars who argue that liberal theory, institutions, and society embody – and depend upon – individual virtue. Judith Shklar has traced the emergence of liberalism to a revulsion against the cruelty of religious wars – that is, to a decision to replace military and moral repression with a "self-restraining tolerance" that is "morally more demanding than repression."[9] Rogers Smith has found in Locke a core conception of "rational liberty" on which a distinction between liberty and license and an account of individual excellence are based.[10] Summarizing a painstaking reexamination of the neglected *Thoughts Concerning Education*, Nathan Tarcov concludes that "instead of a narrowly calculating selfishness, Locke teaches a set of moral virtues that make men able to respect themselves and be useful to one another both in private and in public life."[11] Ronald Terchek extends this thesis to Adam Smith and John Stuart Mill, whom he interprets as recommending "the cultivation of those habits which turned us toward the practice of virtue."[12] J. Budziszewski offers a general argument for the proposition that liberalism and the cultivation of the virtues can be logically compatible and even mutually supportive.[13] In Harvey Mansfield, Jr.'s striking rereading of the *Federalist*, the "automatic or mechanical" view of our constitutional arrangements is replaced by a focus on well-ordered souls as the foundation of sustainable republican government: "Not only are the people expected to be virtuous but also those who run for office."[14] James Q. Wilson's survey of contemporary public policy dilemmas concludes that economic diagnoses and prescriptions, which treat individual dispositions as fixed and exogenously determined "tastes," are at best one-sided. The challenge of social policy is not just the manipulation of incentives but also the formation of character: "In almost every area of important public concern, we are seeking to induce persons to act virtuously. . . . In the long run, the public interest depends on private virtue."[15]

If this line of argument is correct, there is a tension at the heart of liberalism. The liberal state must by definition be broadly inclusive of diversity, yet it cannot be wholly indifferent to the character of its citizens. As Thomas Spragens, Jr., has noted, "A citizenry without public spirit, without self-restraint, and without intelligence accords ill with the demands of effective self-governance."[16] To quote Judith Shklar once more: The alternative before us

> is not one between classical virtue and liberal self-indulgence
> . . . Far from being an amoral free-for-all, liberalism is, in fact,
> extremely difficult and constraining, far too much so for those
> who cannot endure . . . the risks of freedom. The habits of freedom are developed, moreover, both in private and in public,
> and a liberal character can readily be imagined.[17]

The challenge, then, is to give an account of individual virtue that supports rather than undermines liberal institutions and the capacious tolerance that gives liberal society its special attraction.

The thesis that liberalism rests in some measure on virtue is not the palpable absurdity that the liberal polity requires an impeccably virtuous citizenry, a "nation of angels." Nor is it incompatible with the mechanical-institutional interpretation of liberalism, for clearly the artful arrangement of "auxiliary precautions" can go some distance toward compensating for the "defect of better motives." Nor, finally, does this thesis maintain that the liberal polity should be understood as a tutelary community dedicated to the inculcation of individual virtue or excellence. The claim is more modest: that the operation of liberal institutions is affected in important ways by the character of citizens (and leaders), and that at some point, the attenuation of individual virtue will create pathologies with which liberal political contrivances, however technically perfect their design, simply cannot cope. To an extent difficult to measure but impossible to ignore, the viability of liberal society depends on its ability to engender a virtuous citizenry.

While this requirement is not unique to liberal societies, it poses special difficulties for them. The liberal way of life frees individuals from traditional restraints and allows them to pursue their own conceptions of happiness. To the extent that the liberal virtues are not simply consistent with individual self-interest, processes of forming and maintaining them will come into conflict with other powerful tendencies in liberal life. The liberal virtues are the traits of character liberalism needs, not necessarily the ones it has. Yet these virtues need not be imported from the outside, for they are immanent in liberal practice and theory. The tension between virtue and self-interest is a tension within liberalism, not between liberalism and other traditions.

II

The classical conception of the relation between virtue and politics was elaborated by Aristotle. Individual virtue (or excellence – the Greek *arete* bears both meanings) is knowable through everyday experience, definable through philosophical inquiry, and always and everywhere the same. For Aristotle, the virtues are not just Greek but, rather, human virtues. Political life must be seen in large measure as a means to the attainment of virtue, understood as an end in itself. Once the threshold conditions of physical and material security are met, the political community should structure its institutions and policies to promote virtue in its citizens, and its worth as a community depends on the extent to which it achieves that goal.

Aristotle was under no illusion that the communities of his day were actually organized in pursuit of virtue. Some, like Sparta, were devoted to military victory; others, to commercial prosperity; most had no single discernible goal. Each nonetheless had a largely tacit, operative conception of the virtuous individual as the good citizen whose character and conduct were most conducive to the preservation of the community and of its way of life. In this understanding, the relation of politics and virtue is reversed: Virtue becomes the means, and the political community provides the end.

This reversal gave rise to the question explored by Aristotle in Book III of the *Politics*: Are the virtues of the good human being and of the good citizen identical or different? It turns out that they are nearly always different, a conclusion that generates a double dilemma. If a community is notably imperfect, citizens who shape themselves in its image and devote themselves to its service will undergo a kind of moral deformation. Conversely, the virtues of good human beings *simpliciter* may not only not promote but may actually impede the activities of the particular communities in which they happen to find themselves.

Liberal theorists were not unaware of this dilemma, and they responded to it in two very different ways. Some, such as John Stuart Mill, retained a place for the Aristotelian conception of virtue as an intrinsic good but argued that the practice of virtue, so understood, would also be supportive of the liberal polity. In a liberal order, the same virtues are both ends and means: The good human being and the good citizen are identical.

The other liberal strategy was to cut the knot by denying the very existence of intrinsic virtue, that is, by reinterpreting virtue as purely instrumental to the nonmoral goods that constitute the true ends of liberal politics. Thus Hobbes:

All men agree on this, that peace is good, and therefore also [that] the way, or means, of peace, which . . . are justice, gratitude, modesty, equity, mercy, and the rest of the laws of nature, are good. . . . But the writers of moral philosophy, though they acknowledge the same virtues and vices, [do not see] wherein consisted their goodness; nor that they come to be praised as the means of peaceable, sociable, and comfortable living.[18]

Since the 1970s, John Rawls has moved between the Hobbesian and Millian strategies. For Rawls, the ultimate justification – and overriding objective – of the liberal polity is the attainment of justice, viewed not as an individual virtue but as a social state of affairs. Rawls rejects "perfectionism" – the thesis that society should be so arranged as to maximize the achievement of individual virtue or excellence. Yet justice as a virtue predicated of individuals does occupy a place within his overall theory. Individuals are presumed to have a capacity for a sense of justice – that is, the ability to accept and to act upon the agreed-on principles of social justice, which in turn supply the substantive content of individual justice. As this conception is developed in *A Theory of Justice*, the engendering of just individuals is not the goal of liberal society but, rather, the means to the preservation of that society. That is why each member of a well-ordered liberal society wants the others to have a developed sense of justice. And more broadly, Rawls declares in a Hobbesian spirit, "A good person has the features of moral character that it is rational [i.e., instrumentally rational] for members of a well-ordered society to want in their associates."[19] In his more recent work, however, he has placed increased emphasis on the development and exercise of "moral personality" as an intrinsic good or end in itself. The very practices that help sustain a just society also express our nature as free and equal rational beings who have realized their innate capacity for justice.[20]

In the liberal tradition, then, we find traces of both sides of the Aristotelian conception – virtue as end and as means.

It would be surprising, however, if on closer inspection the liberal canon of the virtues turned out to mirror the classical enumeration. Indeed, I shall argue (*pace* Hobbes) that it does not. The liberal virtues are not simply the classical virtues justified on a different basis. They are in important respects different virtues.

III

I begin by examining the liberal virtues understood instrumentally, as means to the preservation of liberal societies and institutions. To fix terms, let me characterize the liberal polity as a community possessing to a high degree the following features: popular-constitutional government; a diverse society with a wide range of individual opportunities and choices; a predominantly market economy; and a substantial, strongly protected sphere of privacy and individual rights. And to avoid misunderstanding, let me briefly characterize the status of the propositions I am about to advance.

1. The discussion of the instrumental virtues in this section is a catalog not of logical entailments within liberal theory but, rather, of empirical hypotheses concerning the relation between social institutions and individual character. I offer at most fragmentary evidence in support of these hypotheses, an adequate test of which would require a far more systematic historical and comparative inquiry.

2. When I speak of certain virtues as instrumental to the preservation of liberal communities, I mean not that every citizen must possess these virtues but, rather, that most citizens must. The broad hypothesis is that as the proportion of nonvirtuous citizens increases significantly, the ability of liberal societies to function successfully progressively diminishes.

3. The fact (if it is a fact) that the instrumental virtues are socially functional does not mean that they are individually advantageous. To be sure, there is some overlap between these two objectives. The liberal virtues demand less self-discipline and sacrifice than do the virtues of classical antiq-

uity, of civic republicanism, or of Christianity, and the simultaneous practice of many of these social virtues makes it easier for individuals to succeed within liberal communities. Still, these virtues are not reducible to self-interest, even self-interest "rightly understood." Thus, while the liberal virtues do not presuppose a specific moral psychology, they do at least imply the rejection of any comprehensive egoism.

General virtues

Some of the virtues needed to sustain the liberal state are requisites of every political community. From time to time, each community must call upon its members to risk their lives in its defense. Courage – the willingness to fight and even die on behalf of one's country – is thus very widely honored, even though there may be occasions on which the refusal to fight is fully justified.

In addition, every community creates a complex structure of law and regulations in the expectation that they will be accepted as legitimate, hence binding, without recourse to direct threats or sanctions. The net social value of a law is equal to the social benefits it engenders minus the social costs of enforcing it. As the individual propensity to obey the law diminishes, so does a society's ability to pursue collective goals through the law. Law-abidingness is therefore a core social virtue, in liberal communities and elsewhere. (This does not mean that disobedience is never justified, but only that a heavy burden of proof must be discharged by those who propose to violate the law.)

Finally, every society is constituted by certain core principles and sustained by its members' active belief in them. Conversely, every society is weakened by the diminution of its members' belief in its legitimacy. Loyalty – the developed capacity to understand, to accept, and to act on the core principles of one's society – is thus a fundamental virtue. And it is particularly important in liberal communities, which tend to be organized around abstract principles rather than shared ethnicity, nationality, or history.

Beyond the virtues needed to sustain all political communities are virtues specific to liberal communities – those required by the liberal spheres of society, economy, and polity.

Virtues of liberal society

A liberal society is characterized by two key features: individualism and diversity. To individualism corresponds the liberal virtue of independence – the disposition to care for, and take responsibility for, oneself and to avoid becoming needlessly dependent on others. Human beings are not born independent, nor do they attain independence through biological maturation alone. A growing body of evidence suggests that in a liberal society, the family is the critical arena in which independence and a host of other virtues must be engendered. The weakening of families is thus fraught with danger for liberal societies. In turn, strong families rest on specific virtues. Without fidelity, stable families cannot be maintained. Without a concern for children that extends well beyond the boundaries of adult self-regard, parents cannot effectively discharge their responsibility to help form secure, self-reliant young people. In short, the independence required for liberal social life rests on self-restraint and self-transcendence – the virtues of family solidarity.

I turn now from individualism to diversity, the second defining feature of liberal society. The maintenance of social diversity requires the virtue of tolerance. This virtue is widely thought to rest on the relativistic belief that every personal choice, every "life plan," is equally good, hence beyond rational scrutiny and criticism. Nothing could be further from the truth. Tolerance is fully compatible with the proposition that some ways of life can be known to be superior to others. It rests, rather, on the conviction that the pursuit of the better course should be (and in many cases has to be) a consequence of education or persuasion rather than of coercion. Indeed, tolerance may be defined as the ability to make this conviction effective as a maxim of personal conduct.

Virtues of the liberal economy

The liberal market economy relies on two kinds of virtues: those required by different economic roles and those required by liberal economic life taken as a whole. In a modern market economy, the basic roles are those of the entrepreneur and the organization employee. The entrepreneurial virtues form a familiar litany: imagination, initiative, drive, determination. The organizational virtues are very different from (and in some respects the reverse of) the entrepreneurial. They include such traits as punctuality, reliability, civility toward co-workers, and a willingness to work within established frameworks and tasks. As economic units evolve, one of the great management challenges is to adjust the mix of entrepreneurial and organizational practices. Sometimes this takes the form of an organizational displacement (or routinization) of entrepreneurial charisma, as in the ouster of Steven Jobs as head of Apple Computer. Sometimes it requires just the opposite, as when a large, stodgy organization replaces a centralized structure with semiautonomous units and loosens individual task and role definitions in an effort to encourage more entrepreneurial practices on the part of its employees.

There are three generic (as distinct from role-specific) virtues required by modern market economies. The first is the work ethic, which combines the sense of obligation to support personal independence through gainful effort with the determination to do one's job thoroughly and well. The second is the achievement of a mean between ascetic self-denial and untrammeled self-indulgence; call it a capacity for moderate delay of gratification. For although market economies rely on the liberation and multiplication of consumer desires, they cannot prosper in the long run without a certain level of saving, which rests on the ability to subordinate immediate gratification to longer-run self-interest.

The third generic economic virtue is adaptability. Modern market economies are characterized by rapid, sweeping changes that reconfigure organizations and occupations. Pat-

terns of lifelong employment within a single task or organization, common for much of this century, are being
displaced. Most individuals will change jobs several times
during their working lives, moving into new occupations,
new organizations, and even new sectors of the economy.
To be sure, collective political action can help regulate the
pace of change, ameliorate its consequences, and share its
costs. Still, domestic and international pressures combine to
make the fact and basic direction of economic change irresistible. Thus, the disposition to accept new tasks as challenges rather than threats and the ability to avoid defining
personal identity and worth in reference to specific, fixed
occupations are essential attributes of individuals and economies able to cope successfully with the demands of
change.[21]

Virtues of liberal politics

I come, finally, to the sphere of politics, which calls for virtues
of both citizens and leaders.

1. *Virtues of citizenship:* Some generic citizen virtues have
already been identified: courage, law-abidingness, loyalty.
In addition to these are the citizen virtues specific to the
liberal polity. Because a liberal order rests on individual
rights, the liberal citizen must have the capacity to discern,
and the restraint to respect, the rights of others. (Invasion
of the rights of others is the form of *pleonexia* specific to liberal
political life.) Because liberalism incorporates representative
government, the liberal citizen must have the capacity to
discern the talent and character of candidates vying for office,
and to evaluate the performance of individuals who have
attained office. Liberalism also envisions popular government, responsive to the demands of its citizens. The greatest
vices of popular governments are the propensity to gratify
short-term desires at the expense of long-term interests and
the inability to act on unpleasant truths about what must be
done. To check these vices, liberal citizens must be moderate
in their demands and self-disciplined enough to accept pain-

ful measures when they are necessary. From this standpoint, the willingness of liberal citizens to demand no more public services than their country can afford and to pay for all the benefits they demand is not just a technical economic issue but a moral issue as well. Consistently unbalanced budgets – the systematic displacement of social costs to future generations – are signs of a citizenry unwilling to moderate its desires or to discharge its duties.

The liberal citizen is not the same as the civic-republican citizen. In a liberal polity, there is no duty to participate actively in politics, no requirement to place the public above the private and to systematically subordinate personal interest to the common good, no commitment to accept collective determination of personal choices. But neither is liberal citizenship simply the pursuit of self-interest, individually or in factional collusion with others of like mind. Liberal citizenship has its own distinctive restraints – virtues that circumscribe and check, without wholly nullifying, the promptings of self-aggrandizement.

2. *Virtues of leadership:* The need for virtue and excellence in political leaders is perhaps more immediately evident than is the corresponding requirement in the case of citizens. The U.S. Founding Fathers saw popular elections as the best vehicle for discerning and selecting good leaders. Thomas Jefferson spoke for them when he wrote to John Adams:

> There is a natural aristocracy among men. The grounds of this are virtue and talents. . . . The natural aristocracy I consider as the most precious gift of nature, for the instruction, trusts, and government of society. . . . May we not even say, that that form of government is the best, which provides the most effectively for a pure selection of these natural *aristoi* into the offices of government? . . . I think the best remedy is exactly that provided by all our constitutions, to leave to the citizens the free election and separation of the *aristoi* from the *pseudo-aristoi*.[22]

The leadership virtues specific to liberal polities include patience – the ability to accept, and work within, the constraints on action imposed by social diversity and constitutional institutions. Second, liberal leaders must have the capacity to forge a sense of common purpose against the centrifugal tendencies of an individualistic and fragmented society. Third, liberal leaders must be able to resist the temptation to earn popularity by pandering to immoderate public demands. Against desire liberal leaders must counterpose restraints; against the fantasy of the free lunch they must insist on the reality of the hard choice; against the lure of the immediate they must insist on the requirements of the long term. Finally, while liberal leaders derive authority from popular consent, they cannot derive policy from public opinion. Rather, they must have the capacity to narrow – insofar as public opinion permits – the gap between popular preference and wise action. The liberal leader who disregards public sentiment will quickly come to grief, but so will the leader who simply takes that sentiment as the polestar of public policy. Through persuasion, the liberal leader tries to move the citizenry toward sound views. But the limits of persuasion must constitute the boundaries of public action, or else leadership becomes usurpation.

As the authors of the *Federalist* insisted, and as experience confirms, there are also specific virtues required for the successful conduct of the different offices in a liberal-constitutional order: optimism and energy in the executive, deliberative excellence and civility in the legislator, impartiality and interpretive skill in the judge.[23] And, as Jefferson suggested, the ultimate test of systems of election or appointment is their tendency to select officeholders with the appropriate virtues. For that reason, it is appropriate and necessary to inquire whether particular systems of selection (e.g., presidential nominating primaries) tend on balance to reward the kinds of personal traits that their corresponding offices require.

3. *General political virtues:* There are two other political virtues required of liberal citizens and leaders alike. While not all public policies need be made in the full light of day, liberal politics rests on a presumption of publicity, that is, on a

commitment to resolve disputes through open discussion unless compelling reasons can be adduced for restricting or concealing the policy process. Thus, a general liberal political virtue is the disposition, and the developed capacity, to engage in public discourse. This virtue includes the willingness to listen seriously to a range of views which, given the diversity of liberal societies, will include ideas the listener is bound to find strange and even obnoxious. The virtue of political discourse also includes the willingness to set forth one's own views intelligibly and candidly as the basis of a politics of persuasion rather than manipulation or coercion.

A second general political virtue is the disposition to narrow the gap (insofar as it is in one's power) between principles and practices in liberal society. For leaders, this means admitting and confronting social imperfections through a public appeal to collective convictions. For citizens it can mean either such a public appeal, or quiet acts that reduce the reach of hypocrisy in one's immediate community. For both, it can lead to a tension between social transformation and law-abidingness, which can be resolved prudentially only with reference to the facts of specific cases. (This is a tension rather than a contradiction between these two liberal virtues, because the virtue of law-abidingness embodies not the absolute priority of law but, rather, a presumption in favor of the law that can be rebutted in a narrow range of instances.)

IV

In the preceding section I tried to sketch a catalog of instrumental liberal virtues understood as empirical hypotheses about connections between individual character and social institutions. There is another approach that yields complementary results. The analysis of the liberal theory of the good can enlarge our understanding of the liberal virtues.

Many contemporary liberal theorists have sought to rely on a "thin" account of the good as means to the attainment of whatever objectives individuals may pursue. Critics have wondered whether *any* means can really be equally service-able for each and every goal. But the deeper difficulty lies elsewhere. As we saw in Chapter 4, neutralist liberalism presupposes individuals who value their earthly existence, who give positive weight to the achievement of their pur-poses, and who are prepared to accept rationality as a con-straint on social action and principle. (This presupposition – the minimum content of the liberal good – may be regarded as a subset of the more expansive conception sketched in Chapter 8.)

This liberal theory of the noninstrumental good can serve as an independent basis for a range of instrumental liberal virtues. The worth of existence implies, first, severe strictures against cruelty and brutality as dispositions that tend to the needless destruction of existence; and second, an endorse-ment of the humanitarian disposition to act affirmatively to preserve the existence of others, at least when this can be done without excessive cost to ourselves. The value liberal-ism attaches to the fulfillment of individual purposes rests on a critique both of otherworldliness, which denigrates earthly striving in light of the hereafter, and of nihilism, which in the name of the absurdity of existence withdraws all moral significance from such striving. When combined with the empirical diversity of human purposes, the liberal account of purposiveness leads directly to the vindication of tolerance, interpreted as the settled disposition of each in-dividual to minimize interference with the strivings of others. Finally, the liberal endorsement of social rationality provides a basis for a distinctively liberal account of moderation, that is, a critique of passions and desires insofar as they weaken the disposition to confine the pursuit of individual purposes to the limits set by rational social principle.

v

The thrust of the argument thus far has been to specify the virtues instrumental to the preservation and operation of the liberal polity. I turn now from considering liberal virtues as means to examining them as ends. The question is whether there is a conception of the virtuous or excellent individual linked intrinsically to liberal theory and seen as valuable, not instrumentally, but for its own sake.

It might be thought that the answer must be negative. After all, it is characteristic of both liberal societies and liberal theories to be open to a wide variety of life plans and to their corresponding excellences. Yet the liberal tradition is by no means silent on this question. Indeed, it suggests three conceptions of intrinsic individual excellence, overlapping yet distinct.

The first is the Lockean conception of excellence as rational liberty or self-direction. As persuasively reconstructed by Rogers Smith, rational self-direction includes the capacity to form, pursue, and revise life plans in light of our personal commitments and circumstances. But it is a substantive, not merely instrumental, standard:

> If we value rational self-direction, we must always strive to maintain in ourselves, and to respect in others, these very capacities for deliberative self-guidance and self-control. Correspondingly, we must see the habitual exercise of these capacities as constituting morally worthy character and their enhancement as constituting morally praiseworthy action.[24]

The second noninstrumental liberal conception of individual excellence is the Kantian account of the capacity to act in accordance with the precepts of duty – that is, to make duty the effective principle of personal conduct and to resist the promptings of passion and interest insofar as they are incompatible with this principle. Judith Shklar has offered a fine sketch of Kant's morally excellent individual in action:

> At all times, he must respect humanity, the rational moral element in himself and in *all* other men. For his own sake, he must choose to avoid all self-destructive and gross behavior, and above all else, he must not lie. . . . To other men he owes no liberality or pity or *noblesse oblige* of any kind, because this might humiliate the recipients. What he does have to show

them is a respect for their rights, decent manners, and avoidance of calumny, pride, and malice.... This is a thoroughly democratic liberal character, built to preserve his own self-respect and that of others, neither demanding nor enduring servility.[25]

The third liberal conception of individual excellence has been adapted in different ways from Romanticism by John Stuart Mill, Ralph Waldo Emerson, Henry David Thoreau, and Walt Whitman. It is the understanding of excellence as the full flowering of individuality. As Mill expounded this thesis, the excellence of individuality combines the Greek emphasis on the development, through activity, of human powers with the modern realization that the blend and balance of these powers will differ from individual to individual. Because liberal societies allow maximum scope for diversity, they are the most (though not perfectly) conducive to the development of individuality. And because liberal societies rest on individual freedom, they tend to foster the self-determination that is at the heart of true individuality. As Mill put it, "He who lets the world, or his own portion of it, choose his plan of life for him, has no need of any other faculty than the ape-like one of imitation. He who chooses his plan for himself, employs all his faculties."[26] Or, as George Kateb sums up the parallel argument within the Emersonian tradition:

> One must take responsibility for oneself – one's self must become a project, one must become the architect of one's soul. One's *dignity* resides in being, to some important degree, a person of one's own creating, making, choosing rather than in being merely a creature or a socially manufactured, conditioned, created thing.[27]

Can these three distinct, but recognizably liberal, conceptions of human excellence be made to cohere in a single unified view? Yes, to a point. They have a common core – a vision of individuals who in some manner take responsibility for their own lives. Each links excellence to a kind of activity.

And all lead to a vindication of the dignity of every individual and to the practice of mutual respect. Beyond this common core, however, certain tensions become manifest. The exercise of Lockean rational liberty can lead to a wide range of deliberative outcomes, whereas Kantian duty usually prescribes a single course of conduct as generally binding. The pursuit of Emersonian individuality can tend toward a kind of poetic, even mystical self-transcendence at war with both the rationalism of Kantian morality and the prosaic, orderly self-discipline of Lockean liberty.[28]

It is possible, of course, to resolve these tensions by giving one conception pride of place and requiring the others to maintain consistency with the preferred standard. (This is the course that Rawls, like Kant, follows when he subordinates the rational pursuit of individual life plans to the social requirements of moral right.) But it may be more advisable to accept a range of tension and indeterminacy, that is, to see the liberal polity at its best as a community that encourages all of these overlapping but distinct conceptions of individual excellence and provides an arena within which each may be realized, in part through struggle against the others.

VI

The fact that liberalism has accommodated conceptions of intrinsic as well as instrumental virtue raises the question of whether these broad categories are mutually consistent – whether (in Aristotle's terms) the liberal "good man" is the same as the liberal "good citizen." In important respects, it turns out, they are not. As Kateb observes, the Emersonian individual sees laws and institutions – including liberal-democratic institutions – as constraints on true individuality, even though these very institutions are the practical presuppositions for the emergence of the ideal self. On the Emersonian account, moreover, the virtues required to maintain the liberal polity fall far short of the highest human qualities.[29] Similarly, even though Kant himself prescribed law-abidingness as a moral duty, the possibility of laws that command immoral action and challenge self-respect is ever present. In cases of conflict, the preservation of individual integrity and dignity would seem to require that positive law give way to moral law. Finally, the Lockean doctrine of rational self-direction stands in dual tension with the requirements of liberal citizenship. Self-direction, so understood, does not readily lead to, or easily cohere with, the willingness to die for one's country. And self-direction as a maxim of individual perfection is not obviously or always consistent with a maxim of social action, binding on each individual, that commands the maximization of self-direction for all individuals throughout the community. While optimistic empirical assumptions may narrow the disjunction between the imperatives of personal perfection and social solidarity, this gap cannot be fully bridged. Indeed, it would not be farfetched to interpret some of the deepest tensions within liberal polities as a clash between means and ends – that is, between requirements of liberal citizenship and aspirations toward liberal excellence.

VII

It has been the burden of this chapter to argue that the health of liberal polities is intertwined in complex ways with the practice of what I have called liberal virtues. Now, assuming that these virtues are not innate, by what means are they to be engendered? And are they adequately developed in our own liberal community? A full examination of these issues lies well beyond the scope of the present discussion. But let me conclude with three alternative hypotheses.

The optimistic hypothesis claims that daily life in the liberal polity is a powerful if tacit force for habituation to at least the minimal requirements of liberal virtue. The sorts of things regularly expected of us at home, in school, and on the job shape us in the manner required for the operation of liberal institutions. And while hardly models of moral perfection, citizens of modern liberal communities are at least adequately virtuous – and not demonstrably less so than were citizens in times past.

The neutral hypothesis maintains that tacit socialization is not enough; that authoritative institutions such as families, schools, churches, the legal system, political leaders, and the media must deliberately and cooperatively foster liberal virtues; that these institutions are not now performing this task adequately; but that there is no reason in principle why they cannot do so once they come more fully to understand their responsibility.

Finally, the pessimistic hypothesis, associated with such thinkers as Daniel Bell, suggests that powerful strands of contemporary liberal culture tend to undermine liberal virtues, that in particular the various forms of liberal self-restraint have fallen victim to the imperatives of self-indulgence and self-expression.[30] From this perspective, the task of strengthening and renewing liberal virtues requires more than improving the formal institutions of moral and civic education. It requires as well a sustained effort to reverse corrosive tendencies fundamental to modern culture.

Evidence can be adduced for each of these hypotheses. Optimists can point to the demonstrable fact that our polity has generated, or at least has not thwarted the generation of, the minimal conditions for its survival over the past two centuries. Neutralists can argue that key social indicators – crime, drug abuse, family stability, and others – are headed in alarming directions and that the impact of major forces of socialization – in particular, television and popular culture – is on balance negative. And pessimists can observe that with the important exception of organized religion, most sources of social authority have a diminished confidence in their ability to establish, inculcate, and enforce social norms of conduct and character.

In a perceptive study of contemporary city government, Stephen Elkin has argued that the operation of urban political institutions has a pervasive, and predominantly negative, effect on the character of the citizenry. At the heart of the liberal-democratic citizenry a commercial republic needs if it is to move toward the "commercial public interest" is "a disposition to think of political choice as involving the giving of reasons." Public choice is to involve "justification, not just the aggregation of wants and interests."[31] Unfortunately, modern city governments systematically fail to foster this disposition, for three reasons. These governments are executive-centered and are therefore not geared to eliciting reasoned argument from individual citizens, or to listening attentively if it happens to be forthcoming. They induce citizens to relate to one another as interest bearers and as bargainers rather than as participants in a shared process of justification. And finally, many urban citizens relate to one another as "clients" whose interests are defined and mediated by bureaucratic experts.[32] These negative consequences of urban public life cannot be reversed without systematic reform of the characteristic institutions and procedures of city governments.[33]

Richard Dagger also looks to the city as the locus of citizenship, and he is equally discouraged by what he finds. In his view, three features of contemporary urban life are particularly destructive. The sheer size of most cities militates against individual interest in its affairs, and against the development of mutual trust. The fragmentation of governmental responsibility breeds "confusion, disorientation, and a sense of impotence." Rapid mobility loosens the ties that bind individuals to the community and erodes the disposition to participate and cooperate. Like Elkin, Dagger argues that the negative consequences for citizenship of the modern city cannot be reduced without systematic reforms that ameliorate their causes.[34]

George Kateb takes a more optimistic view. He argues that representative democracy has a tendency to foster the kinds of character traits that liberal societies particularly need: independence of spirit, the democratization of social life, and a "general tolerance of, and even affection for, diversity."[35] Overall, liberal democratic society is taught, or teaches itself, a fundamental lesson about the nature of all authority:

234

a pervasive skepticism . . . ; a reluctance to defer; a conviction that those who wield authority must themselves be skeptical toward their roles and themselves and that necessary authority must be wielded in a way that inflicts minimum damage on the moral authority of all people [and] a tendency to try to do without authority wherever possible or to disperse or disguise it, and thus to soften it.[36]

While not insensitive to the very real difficulties inherent in such dispositions, Kateb is willing to defend them, not just as instrumentally necessary for liberal democracies but also as intrinsically preferable to the sets of dispositions associated with alternative forms of political organization – in particular, direct democracy.[37]

Robert Lane has undertaken what is probably the most thorough and systematic effort to assemble and assess the empirical evidence concerning the effects of liberal-democratic life on character formation. He begins by defining, and defending, a model of "mature and developed personality," which has five components: cognitive capacity; autonomy; sociocentrism – the ability to understand and recognize the thoughts and claims of others as well as oneself; identity – some combination of self-knowledge, self-acceptance, and self-respect; and identification with normal values, as a necessary bulwark against sociopathic behavior.[38] Lane then examines in detail the effects of capitalist markets and democratic politics on the development of such a personality. His conclusion is a nuanced blend of hope and concern:

The market has taught us much, including cognitive complexity, self-reliance, and a version of justice where work or contribution to the economy is rewarded. Through its emphasis on transactions it has eroded some of the sources of sociocentrism. By its destruction of sources of humane values, its instrumentalism, it has made identity hard to achieve and its amoralism has made difficult the identification with moral values. Democracy, too, has made people think; it has offered a promise of fate control which it only partially fulfills. While it embodies a form of sociocentrism, it does not model morality for the public, although its form of justice allows for beneficence, the justice of need. And its complex diversity makes identity hard to achieve, but once achieved, all the more valuable.[39]

In a parallel analysis focusing exclusively on the capitalist market, Lane examines – and largely rejects – recent pessimism about its effects. Consumerism has not perceptibly eroded the work ethic; modern industry requires as much cooperation as competition; individuals continue to have confidence in their efficacy, that is, in some nonrandom relation between the effort, contribution, and skill they display, on the one hand, and the rewards they receive, on the other; the capacity to innovate, and to take the initiative, is higher among workers in market economies than in command economies; and the ability to question authority by adopting a skeptical stance toward authoritarian morality remains high.[40]

These findings help us focus the debate among optimists, pessimists, and neutralists. It is surely important, as the optimists insist, to take a long view – to recall that America has survived social conflict and dislocation as severe as any we are now experiencing, and to recognize that our current civic culture retains many healthy elements that help sustain personal liberty while warding off public oppression. But it is at least as important to give sustained attention to the phenomena on which neutralists dwell: rising rates of drug use, crime, and family breakdown; inadequate levels of public education, public provision, and public involvement; greed and shortsightedness in public and private affairs; and the growing barbarization and tribalization of American life. Nor can we afford to ignore the pessimists' thesis that these problems are structural rather than accidental – for example, that media-driven patterns of consumption and self-involvement are steadily breaking down the habits of restraint and responsibility on which the liberal polity (like any other) inescapably depends.

I for one cannot avoid the conclusion that we have at least as much food for concern as for celebration. It is fashionable, and all too easy, to denigrate this stance by pointing out that cultural pessimism is a pervasive theme of human history in nearly every community and in nearly every generation. But the fact remains that political communities can move, and throughout history have moved, from health to disrepair for reasons linked to moral and cultural decay. In the face of this, I do not believe that contemporary American liberals can afford to be complacent. We cannot simply chant the mantra of diversity and hope that fate will smile upon us. We must try as best we can to repair our tattered social fabric by attending more carefully to the moral requirements of liberal public life and by doing what is possible and proper to reinforce them.

Part IV

From theory to practice in the liberal state

Chapter 11

Civic education

Part III ended with a question: To what extent are the formal institutions and informal processes of American society engendering the virtues a liberal polity requires? This chapter and the next represent a more sustained meditation on this theme. This chapter explores the role, and limits, of civic education in producing virtuous citizens, and Chapter 12 explores the links between public virtue and religion. My overall thesis is that conceptions of civic education and the social role of religion can be defined that are at once faithful to liberal principles and far more hospitable to moral and religious traditionalism than is the understanding that dominates contemporary liberal theory.

I

In most times and places, the necessity and appropriateness of civic education have been accepted without question. It has been taken for granted that young people must be shaped into citizens and that public institutions have both the right and the responsibility to take the lead in shaping them. In the United States over the past generation, however, civic education has become intensely controversial. Some believe that our political and social arrangements can function perfectly well without publicly defined (or directed) civic education. Others doubt that any one specification of civic education can be devised for a liberal polity in which individuals, families, and communities embrace fundamentally

241

differing conceptions of choice-worthy lives. Still others argue that any unitary civic education necessarily violates the autonomy and conscience of many individuals and groups in a diverse society.

I believe that these objections are mistaken, that it is both necessary and possible to carry out civic education in the liberal state. If we are to do so rightly, however, the partial truth of the critics' contentions must be recognized in the content and the conduct of that education.

II

Let me begin with a distinction between two very different kinds of education. Philosophical education has as its basic objectives, first, the disposition to seek truth, and second, the capacity to conduct rational inquiry. The training of scientists, for example, requires the inculcation of both an ethic of inquiry (do not fabricate or distort results; take care to prevent your hypotheses, or desires, from affecting your observations) and the techniques of inquiry appropriate to the discipline.

There are, of course, many different forms of philosophical education, corresponding to the numerous ways in which truth may be pursued. Nevertheless, these forms of education share two key features. First, they are not decisively shaped by the specific social or political circumstances in which they are conducted, or (to put it the other way around) they are perverted when such circumstances come to have a substantive effect. There is no valid distinction between "Jewish" and "Aryan" physics, or between "bourgeois" and "socialist" biology; truth is one and universal. Second, and relatedly, philosophical education can have corrosive consequences for political communities in which it is allowed to take place. The pursuit of truth – scientific, historical, moral, or whatever – can undermine structures of unexamined but socially central belief.

Civic education differs from philosophical education in all these respects. Its purpose is not the pursuit and acquisition of truth but, rather, the formation of individuals who can effectively conduct their lives within, and support, their political community. It is unlikely, to say the least, that truth-seeking activities will be fully consistent with this purpose. Nor is civic education homogeneous and universal. It is by definition education within, and on behalf of, a particular political order. The conduct and content of civic education in a liberal democracy therefore differ significantly from those in other kinds of polities. Nor, finally, does civic education stand in opposition to its political community. On the contrary, it fails – fundamentally – if it does not support and strengthen that community.

Now, it might be argued that this alleged opposition between civic and philosophical education is far too sweeping. Whereas some societies are dependent on myths and lies, others are far more open to truth. In particular, liberal democracies are founded on principles that can survive rational inspection, and their functioning is facilitated (or at least not crucially impaired) by unimpeded inquiry in every domain.

This argument does contain an important element of truth. The understanding of liberal society as an "open" society has important historical roots in early modern struggles against repressive tradition and superstition. It found classic formulation in John Stuart Mill's invocation of Socrates as liberal hero. In principle and in practice, liberal democracy does exhibit a degree of openness to philosophical education, and to its social consequences, that is probably without precedent in human history. Indeed, this fact constitutes one of the most important arguments in favor of liberal democracy.

But it would be rash to conclude that the clash between rational inquiry and civic education in liberal societies has ceased to exist. On the level of theory, liberalism takes sides in a series of disputes about the meaning of equality, freedom, and the human good – disputes that cannot be regarded as definitively settled from a philosophical point of view. On the practical level, few individuals will come to embrace the core commitments of liberal society through a process of rational inquiry. If children are to be brought to accept these commitments as valid and binding, the method must be a pedagogy that is far more rhetorical than rational. For example, rigorous historical research will almost certainly vindicate complex "revisionist" accounts of key figures in American history. Civic education, however, requires a nobler, moralizing history: a pantheon of heroes who confer legitimacy on central institutions and are worthy of emulation.[1] It is unrealistic to believe that more than a few adult citizens of liberal societies will ever move beyond the kind of civic commitment engendered by such a pedagogy.

III

There is a long tradition of Mandevillean argument to the effect that liberal polities do not need – indeed, are distinctive in not needing – civic education directed to the formation of liberal citizens because social processes and political institutions can be arranged so as to render desired collective outcomes independent of individual character and belief. As I argued in Chapter 10, however, the proposition that liberal societies are uniquely able to do without the fruits of civic education is exposed to serious objections. Recent interpretations of the liberal-theoretical tradition have emphasized the copresence of institutional and character-based arguments, as have rereadings of the *Federalist*.[2] Recent explorations of public policy problems – crime, drugs, dependency – have focused on the formation of character and belief as well as on the manipulation of incentives.[3] Historical inquiries into American public education have documented the driving role played by the perceived need for a civic pedagogy that could turn immigrants into citizens.[4] Groups across the political spectrum have reemphasized their belief that a refurbished civic education is an urgent necessity:

> Democracy's survival depends upon our transmitting to each new generation the political vision of liberty and equality that unites us as Americans. . . . Such values are neither revealed truths nor natural habits. There is no evidence that we are

244

born with them. Devotion to human dignity and freedom, to equal rights, to social and economic justice, to the rule of law, to civility and truth, to tolerance of diversity, to mutual assistance, to personal and civic responsibility, to self-restraint and self-respect – all these must be taught and learned.[5]

Common experience buttresses what history and argument suggest: that the operation of liberal institutions and the functioning of liberal society are affected in important ways by the character and belief of individuals (and leaders) within the liberal polity.

IV

Liberal-democratic civic education may be *necessary*, but is it *possible?* In the same way that the religious diversity of liberal society makes it impossible to reach a religious consensus suitable for public endorsement, so too the moral and political diversity of the liberal polity might seem to undermine the possibility of a unitary civic pedagogy acceptable to, and binding on, all groups. Indeed, the movement from the religious neutrality of the liberal state to a wider moral and political neutrality is one of the defining characteristics of liberal theory in our time, a development with roots in the opinions of urban-based social elites.

As I argued in Part II, this generalization of liberal neutrality is neither necessary nor wise. To the extent that we accept a shared citizenship, we have something important in common – a set of political institutions and of principles that underlie them. What we share, beyond all our differences, provides the basis for a civic education valid across the boundaries of our differences. In this connection, let me recapitulate the conclusions reached in the previous chapter.

Some of the virtues needed to sustain the liberal state are requisites of every political community: the willingness to fight on behalf of one's country; the settled disposition to obey the law; and loyalty – the developed capacity to understand, to accept, and to act on the core principles of one's society. Some of the individual traits are specific to liberal society: independence, tolerance, and respect for individual excellences and accomplishments, for example. Still others are entailed by the key features of liberal democratic politics. For citizens, the disposition to respect the rights of others, the capacity to evaluate the talents, character, and performance of public officials, and the ability to moderate public desires in the face of public limits are essential. For leaders, the patience to work within social diversity and the ability to narrow the gap between wise policy and popular consent are fundamental. And the developed capacity to engage in public discourse and to test public policies against our deeper convictions is highly desirable for all members of the liberal community, whatever political station they may occupy.[6]

A leading contemporary theorist of civic education, Amy Gutmann, has reached conclusions parallel to but divergent from the theses just sketched. Her point of departure is democracy, and her argument is that our civic pedagogy should be oriented toward democratic virtue: "the ability to deliberate, and hence to participate in conscious social reproduction."[7] In my view, this is a piece – but only a piece – of the civic education appropriate to our situation, and it becomes a distortion when it is mistaken for the whole.

Let me begin with a methodological point. The adequacy of a conception of civic education cannot be determined in the abstract, but only through its congruence with the basic features of the society it is intended to sustain. To depart significantly from those features is to recommend a conception of civic education suitable for some society other than the one at hand. Differently put, it is to endorse a politics of tranformation based on a general conception of the political good external to the concrete polity in question. I do not wish to deny the possibility or appropriateness of such theoretical practices. But I do want to distinguish between them and the task of fitting pedagogical practices to existing communities.

Now, to move to the case at hand, it is at best a partial truth to characterize the United States as a democracy in

Gutmann's sense. To begin with the obvious: In a liberal democracy, the concern for individual rights and for what is sometimes called the "private sphere" entails limits on the legitimate power of majorities, and it suggests that cultivating the disposition to respect rights and privacies is one of the essential goals of liberal-democratic civic education. In Gutmann's account, the power of the majority is limited by the requirement of "nonrepression" and "nondiscrimination," but these limits are themselves derived from the conception of a democratic society all of whose members are equipped and authorized to share in ruling.[8] These considerations, I suggest, are not robust enough to generate anything like a liberal account of protections for individuals and groups against the possibility of majority usurpation.

A second liberal reservation about Gutmann's democracy is the distinction between momentary public whim and the settled will – that is, the considered judgment – of the community. This distinction is what underlies the liberal effort to construct a framework of relatively stable institutions partially insulated from shifting majorities. It is, in short, one of the motives for constitutions as distinct from acts of legislation as well as for processes that complicate the task of forging legislative majorities, at least for certain purposes. A form of pedagogy more fully appropriate than Gutmann's to a liberal-democratic constitutional order would incorporate an understanding of these limitations on "conscious social reproduction."

Third, in liberal democracies, representative institutions replace direct self-government for many purposes. A civic education congruent with such institutions emphasizes, as I suggested, the virtues and competences needed to select representatives wisely, to relate to them appropriately, and to evaluate their performance in office soberly. These characteristics are related to, but in some respects quite distinct from, the traits needed for direct participation in political affairs.[9] Perhaps it would be fairer to say that the balance between participation and representation is not a settled question for us, in either theory or practice. A civic pedagogy for us may rightly incorporate participatory virtues. It may even accommodate a politics more hospitable to participation than are our current practices. But it is not free to give participatory virtues pride of place or to remain silent about the virtues that correspond to representative institutions.

Finally, in liberal democracies, certain kinds of excellences are acknowledged, at least for certain purposes, to constitute legitimate claims to public authority. That is, in filling offices and setting policy, equalities of will and interest are counterbalanced by inequalities of training and accomplishment. Examples include the technical expertise of the public health official, the interpretative skill of the judge, and even the governance capabilities of political leaders. As paradoxical as it may appear, a tradition of political theory extending back to Aristotle has understood the selection of public officials through popular elections as significantly aristocratic in its effect. In American thought, some of our greatest democrats have embraced this view.[10]

To put this point more broadly, the problem that liberal democracy sets itself is to achieve the greatest possible conjunction between good judgment and virtue, on the one hand, and participation and consent on the other. Democratic processes, suitably refined, may hold out the best prospects for accomplishing this goal. But they are not ends in themselves; they are to be judged by their fruits. Liberal-democratic civic education must therefore aim to engender not only the full range of public excellences but also the widest possible acceptance of the need for such excellences in the conduct of our public life. Populist rancor against the claims of liberal-democratic excellence is understandable, and even at times a useful counterweight to arrogance and usurpation. But it cannot be allowed to obliterate the legitimacy of such claims.

v

Civic education poses a special difficulty for liberal democracy. Most forms of government, classical and contemporary, have tacitly embraced the Aristotelian understanding of politics as the architectonic human association to which all others – family, tribe, economic grouping, even religious denomination – are rightly subordinated. For all such political communities, the government's authority to conduct civic education is unquestioned, because conflicts between political and subpolitical commitments are resolved by the belief that the political enjoys a principled primacy. In liberal societies, by contrast, the resolution of such conflicts is far less clear-cut. Reservations against public authority in the name of individual autonomy, parental rights, and religious conscience are both frequent and respectable. The liberal tradition is animated by the effort to carve out spheres that are substantially impervious to government – an effort set in motion by the historical lesson that the attempt to impose religious uniformity through public fiat undermines civil order as well as individual conscience. Thus, even if liberal theories (or public authorities moved by such theories) succeed in specifying a core of habits and beliefs supportive of the liberal polity, individuals and groups may nonetheless object to civic education that tries to foster these habits and beliefs universally.

Yet while the liberal tradition is sensitive to the claims of individual conscience, early liberal theorists were equally mindful of the dangers and limits of those claims. John Locke, for example, refused to expand his doctrine of religious toleration into an inviolable private sphere of conscience. Indeed, he insisted that in cases of conflict, civil authority takes precedence over conscience or faith, however deeply held. The key criterion is the maintenance of civil order. Opinions that threaten the peace of society may be legitimately opposed or even suppressed. Nor does toleration preclude affirmative public discourse on behalf of those necessary rules. The fact that the sovereign cannot legitimately command adherence to a specific belief does not mean that civil authority cannot offer systematic arguments for, or instruction in, that belief." Thus, although Locke thought that in practice, civic education would occur in families rather than through state mechanisms, his theory leads directly to the legitimation of the conduct of such education through public means, individual conscience to the contrary notwithstanding.

Two other lines of argument bolster this conclusion. In practice, the private sphere within which conscience is exercised can be defended only within civil society. In the classic American formulation, government is instituted "to secure these rights." It follows that individuals must be willing to surrender whatever portion of these rights must be sacrificed to the requirements of public order and institutional perpetuation. Individuals who seek to exercise, without compromise, the totality of their presocial rights will quickly find that conflict with other rights-bearers impedes the attainment of their ends and the security of their liberty. Even if we begin with a robust conception of individual rights defined theoretically rather than historically or politically, we are forced to conclude that public authority may legitimately restrict those rights in the name of maximizing their effective exercise. In particular, government may properly teach those beliefs and habits needed to bolster the institutions that secure liberal rights, and citizens of liberal polities who resist this civic education would be irrationally contradicting their own self-interest, rightly understood.

The second argument follows hard on the heels of the first. If citizenship means anything, it means a package of benefits and burdens shared, and accepted, by all. To be a citizen of a liberal polity is to be required to surrender so much of your own private conscience as is necessary for the secure enjoyment of what remains. To refuse this surrender is in effect to breach the agreement under which you are entitled to full membership in your community.

Now, it is perfectly possible to petition your community for special relief from the burdens accepted by your fellow citizens: "My conscience makes it impossible for me to fight in battle / pledge allegiance to the flag / or whatever." Public authority may then make a prudential determination as to whether granting your request will or won't impose unacceptable costs on public aims and institutions. If you are part of a small minority, and if the grounds on which you

seek exemption from shared burdens are so narrow and idiosyncratic as to suggest that others are unlikely to follow suit,
then it may be possible to grant the exemption. But if the
facts suggest that acceding to you will open the floodgate for
many others, then it will be rational for public authorities to
reject your plea. The issue, to repeat, is one of concrete practice rather than general principle.

A variant of this problem arises when individuals or groups
are willing to take the next step, abjuring the benefits of
citizenship in order to gain release from its burdens. This is,
in effect, to request a kind of resident-alien status within
one's community: You remain subject to basic laws of civil
order, but you are no longer expected to attain the character,
beliefs, and competences needed for effective political membership. Your real desire is simply to withdraw, to be left
alone. Here again, as before, the issue is practical. If there
is reason to believe that granting this request will generate
significant ripple effects, there is a rational basis for public
authority to resist it. Alternatively, it might be argued that
withdrawal is an untenable halfway house between citizenship and actual physical exit. As long as your group remains
located within the domain of wider community, it necessarily
interacts with, and affects, that community in many ways.
Whereas some free-rider problems could be addressed
through taxation, other difficulties would prove far less tract-
able. It is not clear that the political community could afford
to remain indifferent to the example you might set for other
potential withdrawers. (This is not intended as an argument
against the right of physical exit, which rests on quite different foundations and raises different issues. Throughout
most of the postwar period, the Soviets improperly used
arguments parallel to those in this paragraph to thwart the
emigration of disaffected groups.)

VI

Perhaps the most poignant problem raised by liberal civic
education is the clash between the content of that education

and the desire of parents to pass on their way of life to their children. Few parents, I suspect, are unaware of or immune to the force of this desire. What could be more natural? If you believe that you are fit to be a parent, you must also believe that at least some of the choices you have made are worthy of emulation by your children, and the freedom to pass on the fruits of those choices must be highly valued. Conversely, who can contemplate without horror totalitarian societies in which families are compelled to yield all moral authority to the state?

Still, your child is at once a future adult and a future citizen. Your authority as a parent is limited by both these facts. For example, you are not free to treat your child in a manner that impedes normal development. You may not legitimately starve or beat your child or thwart the acquisition of basic linguistic and social skills. The systematic violation of these and related norms suffices to warrant state intervention. Similarly, you are not free to impede the child's acquisition of a basic civic education – the beliefs and habits that support the polity and enable individuals to function competently in public affairs. In particular, you are not free to act in ways that will lead your child to impose significant and avoidable burdens on the community. For example, the liberal state has a right to teach all children respect for the law, and you have no opposing right as a parent to undermine that respect. Similarly, the liberal state has a right to inculcate the expectation that all normal children will become adults capable of caring for themselves and their families.

Thus far, I think, the argument is reasonably strong and uncontroversial. But how much farther may the liberal state go? Gutmann argues that children must be taught both "mutual respect among persons" and "rational deliberation among ways of life," and that parents are unlikely to do this on their own. Indeed, it is precisely because communities such as the Old Order Amish are morally committed to shielding their children from influences that might weaken their faith that the state is compelled to step in:

The same principle that requires a state to grant adults personal and political freedom also commits it to assuring children an education that makes those freedoms both possible and meaningful in the future. A state makes choice possible by teaching its future citizens respect for opposing points of view and ways of life. It makes choice meaningful by equipping children with the intellectual skills necessary to evaluate ways of life different from that of their parents.[12]

I do not believe that this argument can be sustained. In a liberal-democratic polity, to be sure, the fact of social diversity means that the willingness to coexist peacefully with ways of life very different from one's own is essential. Furthermore, the need for public evaluation of leaders and policies means that the state has an interest in developing citizens with at least the minimal conditions of reasonable public judgment. But neither of these civic requirements entails a need for public authority to take an interest in how children think about different ways of life. Civic tolerance of deep differences is perfectly compatible with unswerving belief in the correctness of one's own way of life. It rests on the conviction that the pursuit of the better course should (and in many cases must) result from persuasion rather than coercion – a classic Lockean premise that the liberal state *does* have an interest in articulating. Civic deliberation is also compatible with unshakable personal commitments. It requires only that each citizen accept the minimal civic commitments, sketched above, without which the liberal polity cannot long endure. In short, the civic standpoint does not warrant the conclusion that the state must (or may) structure public education to foster in children skeptical reflection on ways of life inherited from parents or local communities.

It is hardly accidental, however, that Gutmann takes the argument in this direction. At the heart of much modern liberal democratic thought is a (sometimes tacit) commitment to the Socratic proposition that the unexamined life is an unworthy life, that individual freedom is incompatible with ways of life guided by unquestioned authority or unswerving faith. As philosophic conclusions, these commitments have much to recommend them. The question, though, is whether the liberal state is justified in building them into its system of public education. The answer is that it cannot do so without throwing its weight behind a conception of the human good unrelated to the functional needs of its sociopolitical institutions and at odds with the deep beliefs of many of its loyal citizens. As a political matter, liberal freedom entails the right to live unexamined as well as examined lives – a right the effective exercise of which may require parental bulwarks against the corrosive influence of modernist skepticism. I might add that in practice, there is today a widespread perception that our system of public education already embodies a bias against authority and faith. This perception, in large measure, is what underlies the controversy over "secular humanism" that is so incomprehensible to liberal elites.

It is not difficult to anticipate the objections that will be raised against the argument I have just advanced. There are, after all, three parties to the educational transaction: children, their parents, and the state. Perhaps the state has no direct right to shape public education in accordance with the norms of Socratic self-examination. But doesn't liberal freedom mean that children have the right to be exposed to a range of possible ways of life? If parents thwart this right by attempting (as some would say) to "brainwash" their children, doesn't the state have a right – indeed, a duty – to step in?

The answer is no on both counts. Children do have a wide range of rights that parents are bound to respect and that government is bound to enforce against parental violation. As I argued earlier, parents may not rightly impede the normal physical, intellectual, and emotional development of their children. Nor may they impede the acquisition of civic competence and loyalty. The state may act *in loco parentis* to overcome family-based obstacles to normal development. And it may use public instrumentalities, including the system of education, to promote the attainment by all children of the basic requisites of citizenship. These are legitimate intrusive state powers. But they are limited by their own inner logic. In a liberal state, interventions that cannot be justified on this basis cannot be justified at all. That is how liberal democracies must draw the line between parental and public authority over the education of children, or (to put it less conflictually) that is the principle on the basis of which such authority must be shared.[13]

But doesn't this position evade the emotional force of the objection? Doesn't it legitimate parental brainwashing of children, and isn't that a terrible thing? Again, the answer is no, for two reasons. First, the simple fact that authority is divided means that from an early age, every child will see that he or she is answerable to institutions other than the family – institutions whose substantive requirements may well cut across the grain of parental wishes and beliefs. Some measure of reflection, or at least critical distance, is likely to result. Second, the basic features of liberal society make it virtually impossible for parents to seal their children off from knowledge of other ways of life. And as every parent knows, possibilities that are known but forbidden take on an allure out of all proportion to their intrinsic merits.

To these points I would add a basic fact of liberal sociology: The greatest threat to children in modern liberal societies is not that they will believe in something too deeply, but that they will believe in nothing very deeply at all. Even to achieve the kind of free self-reflection that many liberals prize, it is better to begin by believing something. Rational deliberation among ways of life is far more meaningful if (and I am tempted to say *only* if) the stakes are meaningful, that is, if the deliberator has strong convictions against which competing claims can be weighed. The role of parents in fostering such convictions should be welcomed, not feared.[14]

VII

Despite the pluralism of liberal societies, it is perfectly possible to identify a core of civic commitments and competences the broad acceptance of which undergirds a well-ordered liberal polity. The state has a right to ensure that this core is generally and effectively disseminated, either directly, through public civic education, or indirectly, through regulation of private education. In cases of conflict, this civic core takes priority over individual or group commitments (even the demands of conscience), and the state may legitimately use coercive mechanisms to enforce this priority.

But the liberal state must not venture beyond this point. It must not throw its weight behind ideals of personal excellence outside the shared understanding of civic excellence, and it must not give pride of place to understandings of personal freedom outside the shared understanding of civic freedom. For if it does so, the liberal state will prescribe – as valid for, and binding on, all – a single debatable conception of how human beings should lead their lives. In the name of liberalism, it will betray its own deepest and most defensible principles.

Chapter 12

Public virtue and religion

I

Chapter 11 examined the ways in which civic education can appropriately foster the beliefs and character traits that help sustain a liberal community. In this chapter, I broaden the focus by inquiring into features of public culture – particularly, but not exclusively, religion – that many now see as hostile to liberalism, but which many in the past have seen as at least potentially (and in some cases actually) supportive. My thesis is that principled grounds exist for reconciliation between the combatants in the cultural wars of our generation but that if a cease-fire is to be effected, each side will have to moderate its most extreme (and least defensible) claims. Specifically, contemporary liberals who focus on individual rights and moral diversity must come to acknowledge the important respects in which the freedoms they cherish presuppose an underpinning of individual self-discipline and self-restraint. For their part, moral and religious traditionalists must learn to distinguish between the portion of their creed that can play a legitimate role in the public sphere and the portion that must remain within the confines of group practice or individual conscience.

Early liberal theorists worked to disentangle civil society from destructive religious quarrels. But they nevertheless assumed that civil society needed virtue and that publicly effective virtue rested on religion. Juridical liberalism, which focused on the exercise of liberty and the limits of govern-

257

ment, presumed a foundation of individual moral conduct. Although the civil authority in a liberal society need not directly enforce this code in most cases, it should certainly encourage it; at the very least, it should refrain from utterances and policies that undermine it.

This understanding of the proper relation among politics, virtue, and religion dominated the founding of the United States. It suffused Tocqueville's analysis. In clearly recognizable form, it survived well into the twentieth century. In the past generation, however, this understanding came under attack, and the delicate balance between juridical liberalism and its social preconditions was disrupted. As we have seen, influential philosophers argued that the essence of liberalism was public neutrality on the widest possible range of individual choices.[1] Powerful social forces equated liberty with the absence of all restraints. The Supreme Court encouraged this tendency, while reinterpreting the Constitution to require impartiality not just among religious faiths but also between religion and irreligion.

This new dispensation soon encountered difficulties. To begin with, it was not firmly rooted in a popular consensus. The purely juridical understanding of liberalism was accepted by many elites, but by only a relatively small fraction of ordinary citizens. Moreover, actualizing the juridical understanding meant dismantling long-established practices such as school prayer and restraints on pornography, a process that understandably evoked strong passions. A traditionalist counterreaction was not slow to take shape. Much of it is defensive in character, seeking only to halt and reverse what it sees as the excess of the past generation. But important elements of a newly politicized religious fundamentalist movement wish to go well beyond a restoration of the status quo ante, to a commingling of religion and the civil order that threatens the centuries-old doctrine of religious toleration itself.

Neither juridicalism nor fundamentalism can serve as an adequate basis for a liberal society. As I have argued throughout this book, liberalism needs an account of goods and virtues that enable it to oppose the extremes of both unfettered individual choice and unchecked state coercion. I now want to expand this search for a principled middle way by reflecting anew on the cultural preconditions of liberalism and establishing, more precisely than heretofore, how these preconditions can coexist with liberalism's powerful juridical tendencies.

II

The liberal doctrine of religious toleration was expounded in its classic form in John Locke's *Letter Concerning Toleration*.[2] Locke's challenge in the *Letter* was to define the appropriate relation between religion and the civil order. This was not only a theoretical issue. In the wake of the Reformation, Europe had been wracked by a century of religious warfare. All the combatants sought to restore the unity of Christendom by imposing their version of religious truth through the coercive power of the state. In circumstances of deep diversity, these efforts ensured endless strife. Locke's doctrine of toleration was an attempt to reestablish the possibility of decent politics in the context of abiding disagreements about fundamental religious questions.

Locke may be said to make five philosophical arguments in favor of religious toleration, divided into three categories: arguments based on the nature of religious truth, on the nature of coercion, and on the nature of politics. (He also offers a number of arguments based on Scriptural exegesis which, despite their ingenuity, need not detain us here.)

The first of the philosophical arguments may be called *epistemological neutrality*. For a wide range of religious disputes, Locke insists, no rational adjudication is possible among competing claims. This does not (necessarily) mean that there is no religious truth. But it does mean that no judge "on earth" is competent to determine it.[3] Locke's religious epistemology thus denies the basic premise through which public religious coercion is customarily justified.

Locke does not, however, rest his case on the elusiveness

of religious truth. Even if religious truth could be intersubjectively established, he argues, the coercive weapons at the disposal of civil society could not possibly achieve their purported end: the inculcation of true belief or faith. "True and saving religion," Locke observes, "consists in the inward persuasion of the Mind, without which nothing is acceptable to God. And such is the nature of the understanding, that it cannot be compelled to the belief of any thing by outward force."[4] This argument I call *conscience-based neutrality*.

Locke's third argument, *character-based neutrality*, also revolves around the nature of coercion, but from a moral rather than ontological standpoint. Those who use the power of the state to suppress religions invoke regularly as their motives their love of truth and their ardent desire to save souls. In fact, Locke contends, these self-appointed guardians of orthodoxy are typically moved by cruelty and lust for power.[5]

The remaining two arguments focus on the nature of politics. *Rights-based neutrality* rests on Locke's concept of limited government. Human beings enter into civil society to attain and protect nonmoral goods: goods of the body and external possessions. To secure these goods, the civil magistrate is created and invested with coercive power. It follows, Locke insists, that the sovereign's legitimate sway extends no farther than this initial grant: "The whole jurisdiction of the Magistrate reaches only to these Civil Concernments [and] neither can nor ought in any manner to be extended to the salvation of souls."[6]

Even if it were proper for the magistrate to intervene in the religious practices of the citizenry, it would not be wise to do so. Locke's final argument, *prudential neutrality*, draws important conclusions from the fact of religious differences. In circumstances of deep diversity, Locke contends, the consequences of trying to impose uniformity are worse than the consequences of accepting the existence of controversial opinions – even deeply implausible opinions. History shows that religious coercion yields not agreement and civil concord but, rather, discord, destruction, and war. Once invested with power to enforce truth, the sovereign can turn that power against the truth. And finally, the suppression of diversity is in no way necessary to the peace and good order of civil society. Diversity is a threat to peace only if the magistrate is repressive.[7]

Locke's thesis may be summarized in three propositions. Because religious truth cannot be known with certainty, efforts to impose truth through coercion lack rational warrant. Even if religious truth could be established, inward faith cannot be imposed through external coercion. And even if coercion could succeed, it would be wrong to employ it.[8]

Contemporary liberals such as John Rawls have argued that the doctrine of liberal neutrality is a generalization of Locke's doctrine of religious toleration. But in three key respects, Locke's argument is not only less sweeping than, but actually contradicts, the contemporary conception of neutrality.

First, Locke distinguishes between coercion and persuasion. The fact that the sovereign cannot legitimately command a specific religious belief does not mean that civil authority cannot make arguments on behalf of that belief.[9] Tolerance means reliance on speech rather than force; it does not mean that authoritative public discourse should be neutered.

Second, Locke does not extend epistemological neutrality to the moral realm. The fact that doctrinal religious conflicts cannot be rationally resolved does not suggest that moral virtues and rules are equally unknowable. On the contrary, our rational knowledge of morality undergirds both the critique of religious intolerance and the principles governing the relations between religion and the public order.

Finally, Locke refuses to extend the doctrine of religious toleration into a full-blown claim for an inviolable private sphere of conscience or individual liberty. Indeed, he insists that in cases of conflict, civil authority takes precedence over religious faith. The key criterion is the maintenance of civil order. Opinions that threaten the peace of society need not be tolerated. So, for example, Locke declares that "No Opinion contrary to human society, or to those moral Rules which are necessary to the preservation of Civil Society, are to be tolerated by the Magistrate."[10] (Locke has no doubt that such a core morality is politically essential.) Nor would magistrates tolerate religions that diminish their legitimate sovereignty, such as those faiths that preach or imply allegiance to a foreign sovereign. Finally, the magistrate cannot tolerate those "who deny the Being of God" because "Promises, Covenants, and Oaths, which are the bonds of Humane Society, can have no hold upon an Atheist. The taking away of God, tho but even in thought, dissolves all."[11]

The flip side of Locke's strictures against atheism is the remarkable convergence he discerns among all forms of religious faith, not just Christianity or even monotheism: "Neither Pagan, nor Mahumetan, nor Jew, ought to be excluded from the Civil Rights of the Commonwealth, because of his religion. . . . [T]he Commonwealth, which embraces indifferently all Men that are honest, peaceable, and industrious, requires it not."[12] In short, Locke suggests, civil society rests on certain opinions and moral rules, and religion as such tends to be consistent with, and supportive of, these prerequisites for a decent society. (The sole exceptions are those religions whose teachings dilute or divide civil sovereignty.) It follows that the sovereign should encourage all faiths without regard to doctrinal distinction. To be sure, civil authority may legitimately indicate a preference for certain doctrines over others, but not in a manner that prohibits the free exercise of competing doctrines.

Although Locke's characterization of toleration cannot be swallowed whole, it has a number of distinct advantages over its contemporary competitors. The distinction between coercion and persuasion creates space for a legitimate liberal public discourse that can help sustain the liberal polity.[13] The distinction between religious and moral knowledge drives a wedge between theological disputes and the core moral agreement on which the liberal polity depends.[14] The distinction between private conscience and public order provides the liberal polity with principled grounds for self-defense.

It is in this last arena, of course, that a certain amount of social learning has transpired over the three centuries since Locke's *Letter*. It turns out, for example, that public order is compatible with a wider range of religious practices (and nonpractices) than Locke supposed. Arguments for public regulation of conscientious action must therefore be regarded with a higher level of suspicion than Locke evinced. Still, the basic principle remains valid, and it suggests that controversial measures such as restraints on the sacramental use of mind-altering drugs may be justified as serving a legitimate public purpose.

III

This Lockean understanding of the proper relations among morality, religion, and the liberal polity was the orthodox view among the American founders. To be sure, scholars such as Gordon Wood and Martin Diamond have in different ways taught us to interpret the founding of the United States as replacing the reliance on public morality and religion with a "new science of politics" based on self-interest. Bolstering this view is James Madison's classic defense of checks and balances in *Federalist* number 51: "Ambition must be made to counteract ambition. The interest of the man must be connected with the constitutional rights of the place."

Madison's aphoristic summary of his doctrine would seem to clinch the new science thesis. It is, he declared, "a policy of supplying by opposite and rival interests, the defect of better motives."

Yet to stop at this deservedly famous statement would be to offer a decidedly one-sided interpretation of the Founding Fathers' views. It was, after all, the same Madison who argued in *Federalist* number 55:

As there is a degree of depravity in mankind which requires a certain degree of circumspection and distrust, so there are other qualities in human nature which justify a certain portion of esteem and confidence. *Republican government presupposes the existence of these qualities in a higher degree than any other form.* Were the pictures which have been drawn by the political jealousy of some among us faithful likenesses of the human character, the inference would be that there is not sufficient virtue among us for self-government. (Emphasis mine.)

Nor was the invocation of republican virtue confined to the secular plane. Thomas Jefferson is frequently regarded as the American exemplar of Enlightenment-based religious and moral skepticism. In his own time he became famous (in some quarters notorious) for declaring in the *Notes on the State of Virginia* that "it does me no injury for my neighbor to say that there are twenty gods, or no God. It neither picks my pocket nor breaks my leg." But in that same work he asks, "Can the liberties of a nation be thought secure when we have removed their only firm basis, a conviction in the minds of the people that these liberties are of the gift of God?" Five years earlier, Jefferson's Declaration of Independence had traced human equality and human rights to "the Creator." Forty years later, on the threshold of death, Jefferson argued that the beliefs that there is "only one God, and He [is] all perfect" and that there is a "future state of rewards and punishments" would, if generally shared, be conducive to decent politics. Religion, he once wrote, is "a supplement to law in the government of men" and "the alpha and omega of the moral law."[15]

The thesis underlying Jefferson's disparate remarks was perhaps best articulated by George Washington in his Farewell Address:

> Of all the dispositions and habits which lead to political prosperity, religion and morality are indispensable supports. . . . The mere politician, equally with the pious man, ought to respect and cherish them. . . . And let us with caution indulge the supposition that morality can be maintained without religion. Whatever may be conceded to the influence of refined education on minds of peculiar structure, reason and experience both forbid us to expect that national morality can prevail in exclusion of religious principles.

Washington's argument is not that religion provides premises essential to the validity of liberal arguments. It is rather that only a relatively small number of citizens can be expected to understand and embrace liberal principles on the basis of purely philosophic considerations. For most Americans, religion provides both the *reasons* for believing liberal principles to be correct and the *incentives* for honoring them in practice.

Forty years later, Tocqueville provided sociological support for Washington's thesis. America, he observed, is the place where religion has the greatest real power, and it is also the most enlightened and freest country on earth. This conjunction is not accidental: Freedom, unlike despotism, cannot do without faith. While there is "an innumerable multitude of sects in the United States . . . all different in the worship they owe to the Creator," they nevertheless "all agree concerning the duties of man [and] all preach the same morality." In particular, religion places strict limits on the means that can legitimately be employed in pursuit of political ends. It thereby checks the ruthlessness and cruelty that would otherwise characterize a society based on abstract philosophical principles of liberty, individualism, and revolution. "Religion, which never intervenes directly in the government of American society, should therefore be considered as the first of their political institutions, for although it did not give them the taste for liberty, it singularly facilitates their use thereof." Thus, Tocqueville concludes:

> I do not know if all Americans have faith in their religion – for who can read the secrets of the heart? – but I am sure that they think it necessary to the maintenance of republican institutions. That is not the view of one class or party among the citizens, but of the whole nation.[16]

Thus far I have spoken of American religion in the most general of terms. This is consistent with the practices of many of the nation's founders. Washington, for example, employed studiously nondenominational, even non-Christian language when referring to the deity in public utterances. And he argued vigorously that Jews should enjoy full religious freedom and the equal rights of citizenship. Nothing could have been farther from Washington's understanding than the notion of America as a "Christian nation." In general, the founders believed that religion supported secular liberties only up to a point. They were certainly not of the view that politics based on a literal interpretation of the Bible would be supportive of a liberal polity. When they spoke in favor of religion, they had in mind not sectarian particularity but, rather, what all revealed religions were thought to have in common: the concepts of divine creation, order, and judgment; and a compact list of fundamental moral commandments.

Yet matters were not so simple. Against this juridical concept of equal religious liberty was counterposed the sociological fact, noted by Tocqueville, that America was a Christian nation that had informally established an ecumenical dissenting Protestantism. This orientation was only reinforced by the public schools, which from their institution in the mid-nineteenth century until well into the twentieth promulgated a nondenominational Protestantism memorably summarized for generations of schoolchildren in the "Readers" of the Ohio Protestant minister, William McGuffey. Indeed, Catholics established private parochial schools in large measure as a protest against Protestant domination of the public schools.[17]

This Protestantism was, of course, more than a religious orientation. It was the focal point of a set of social practices and understandings that formed the identity of the dominant social group and constituted the standard of conduct and demeanor for all others. I shall henceforth refer to this socioreligious Protestant nexus as "traditional morality."

Recent scholarship has notably enriched our understanding of the American founding. We now know that the founders were aware of, and in some measure drew inspiration from, a range of disparate traditions: Lockean liberalism; English constitutionalism as reinterpreted by Montesquieu; English opposition thought, described most persuasively by

Bernard Bailyn; classical republicanism; dissenting Protestantism; and even Scottish moral philosophy. But we also know that in the half century after the Founding, under the influence of the democratic political order established by the Constitution and of the very special social and geographical conditions that prevailed on our continent, many of these traditions had become attenuated.[18] By Tocqueville's time, a distinctively American political culture had been forged. Its major elements were three: the essentially secular principles of democratic liberalism; the moral maxims derived from Christianity; and the mores of Protestant Americans – in particular, of white Anglo-Saxon males.

This amalgam proved remarkably enduring. At the turn of the century, Lord Bryce nicely captured its delicate balance between liberal and religious tendencies. "It is," he observed, "accepted as an axiom by all Americans that the civil power ought to be not only neutral and impartial as between different forms of faith, but ought to leave these matters entirely on one side." Nevertheless, he continued, "The National government, and the state governments do give Christianity [and by that he meant Protestant Christianity] a species of recognition inconsistent with the view that civil government should be absolutely neutral in religious matters."[19]

IV

This combination of juridical liberalism and moral/religious traditionalism was still intact and clearly recognizable a generation ago. In 1952, Justice William O. Douglas, no foe of civil liberties, was able to begin a Supreme Court decision with the assertion that "the First Amendment does not say that in every and all respects there shall be a separation of church and state" and end with the affirmation that "we are a religious people whose institutions presuppose a Supreme Being."[20] At that time, Catholics and Jews were still somewhat marginal members of American society. Blacks were thoroughly subordinated. Popular culture faithfully represented the white Anglo-Saxon Protestant ethos. And most important, a traditional morality was dominant and effective. A male-governed family structure that largely excluded women from the world of commercial work; norms of personal conduct that emphasized self-reliance and self-restraint; respect for economic and political authority; unquestioning patriotism based on the conviction of unsullied American rectitude; pervasive expressions of religious faith – these were the main strands of that traditional morality.

Today, this cultural consensus is gone, replaced by pitched battles on numerous fronts. Although many forces contributed to the breakdown of consensus, the critical event was, I believe, the civil rights movement.

This movement had two important elements that are germane to our inquiry. First, it represented a clear collision between the juridical–liberal principles of our polity and the concrete practices of our society. Black leaders presented themselves not as revolutionaries but as conservatives, calling on white America to recall and revitalize its founding principles. These principles proved to be highly potent, stunning observers who believed in strict limits to the capacity of law to effect social transformation.

But the civil rights movement was more than an appeal to the moral equality of human beings and the political equality of citizens. It was also an effort to legitimize social difference. Black Americans, after all, had a distinctive group identity, forged in the crucible of slavery and discrimination. This identity was in no way incompatible with American principles. But it was very far from the dominant white culture. Black Americans argued that they could not rightly be asked to surrender their distinctiveness as the price of full admission into U.S. society. What makes Americans a nation, they argued, was voluntary adherence to shared political and moral principles, not forced assimilation to the mores of any social group. This argument, too, carried the day, and many long-suppressed elements of the black experience began to enter the mainstream of American culture.

The civil rights movement was pivotal, I suggest, not just because it so altered the condition of black Americans, but also because it became an inspirational metaphor for other aggrieved groups. In ensuing years, the subordination of women to men, of youth to age, of heterodox sexuality to traditional families, of nonbelief to religion – all these hierarchies and more were challenged in the name of freedom, equality, and the recognition of legitimate differences.

The assault on traditional morality was driven, as well, by two other forces.

It is a commonplace to stress the individualism of American culture. But, as Robert Bellah and his coauthors have reminded us, from the outset there has been a tension between Benjamin Franklin's "utilitarian" individualism (a lineal descendent of Lockean morality) and the "expressive" individualism of Emerson and Whitman. Each places the individual at the center of the moral universe. But while utilitarian individualism teaches that personal goals can be achieved in society only through adherence to moral and prudential maxims of self-restraint, expressive individualism argues that the fullness of existence craved by each person stands in opposition to the constraints of morality and society.[21] During the 1960s, this ancestral tension within the individualist tradition resurfaced in the form of generational warfare. Unlimited self-expression was held to be not only good in itself but fully compatible with – indeed, mandated by – the classic liberal distinction between the public and private spheres.

The assault on traditional morality was also spurred on by the Supreme Court. Key decisions on school prayer, pornography, criminal justice, and abortion sharpened the line between public and private, widened individual freedom, and emphasized the requirement of state neutrality in areas previously seen as the legitimate arena for collective moral judgment.

In short, during the past generation, the long-standing balance between juridical liberal principles and a complex of traditional moral beliefs, many of which were reinforced by religion, was disrupted, with juridical liberalism in the ascendancy and tradition in retreat. In key respects, these developments were long overdue. Many "traditional" practices, chief among them racial and gender discrimination, violated liberal principles and required vigorous public repudiation. But the relentless extension of the revolt against tradition increasingly relied on the far more controversial premise that traditionalism *as a whole* was opposed to the actualization of liberal principles.

Not surprisingly, these developments were received differently in diverse sectors of society. Among groups constrained or aggrieved by traditional practices, the rise of the secular, putatively neutral state was interpreted as the civil rights movement writ large – that is, as the long-overdue decision to live up to our founding principles. Among the partisans of what I am calling the tradition, the response was quite different. From their standpoint, the new assertion of strict state neutrality on matters of morals and religion was anything but neutral. Indeed, the defenders of the tradition saw it as an assault on the very foundations of public order.

It was not long before this conflict began to dominate American party politics. By the early 1980s, religious fundamentalists and other partisans of traditional morality were among the most politically active groups in the country. And during 1984, a debate erupted between the two candidates for the presidency about the proper role of religion in our society. At a prayer breakfast the morning after the Republican convention, Ronald Reagan defended a constitutional amendment favoring school prayer and denounced its opponents as intolerant of religion. In a series of statements, he went on to charge that the Democratic party had come to support an extreme doctrine of separation of church and state antithetical to both America's history and its principles; as he put it, "freedom *from* religion" rather than freedom *of* religion. This error was particularly grave, Reagan asserted, because America rests on a public morality of which religion is the indispensable foundation.

In response, Walter Mondale restated his understanding of church–state relations in a liberal polity:

> I believe in an America that honors what Thomas Jefferson first called the "wall of separation between church and state." That freedom has made our faith unadulterated and unintimidated. It has made Americans the most religious people on earth.
>
> I believe in an America where government is not permitted to dictate the religious life of our people; where religion is a private matter between individuals and God, between families and their churches and synagogues, with no room for politicians in between.
>
> To ask the state to enforce the religious life of our people is to betray a telling cynicism about the American people.
>
> Moreover, history teaches us that if that force is unleashed, it will corrupt our faith, divide our nation, and embitter our people.[22]

On the surface, this is a familiar argument. But note a complication. The doctrine of the wall between church and state is defended as essential not only to politics but also to religion. To intermingle them, at least in the manner proposed by the fundamentalists, would be both to endanger liberty and to corrupt piety.

This point has deep roots in our history. Thomas Jefferson viewed the wall of separation between church and state primarily as protection for individual intellectual and political freedom against clerical or sectarian oppression. But as Mark DeWolfe Howe has observed, the first American known to have used the wall of separation metaphor was not Thomas Jefferson but, rather, the seventeenth-century Baptist Roger Williams. Williams argued that the purity of the Christian faith had always depended on its removal from what he called "the wilderness of the world," and that any effort by Christian churches to dominate rather than abstain from politics would lead Christians into temptation, not deliver the world from evil.[23]

As late as 1965, this was the view of the best-known contemporary Baptist, Jerry Falwell. "Believing in the Bible as I
do," Falwell declared, "I would find it impossible to stop
preaching the pure saving Gospel of Jesus Christ, and begin
doing anything else – including fighting communism. . . .
Preachers are not called to be politicians but to be soul win-
ners."[24] As late as 1975, this was the view of most Americans
who regarded themselves as evangelical Christians. But by
1980, Falwell and his followers had reversed course and
plunged headlong into the world.

The impetus for this new activism was the clash between
juridical liberalism and the moral tradition – a clash that
thoughtful opponents of the traditionalists were compelled
to ponder. Here, for example, is what Walter Mondale said:

> Over the last generation, waves of change have swept our
> nation. No institution has been untouched. Religion, marriage,
> business, government, education – each has been questioned,
> and each has struggled toward new foundations and new
> rules.
>
> By and large, it has been healthy for us. . . . But change is
> not easy. Many Americans have been upset to see traditions
> questioned. They have watched durable values give way to
> emptiness. And too often they have seen that void filled reck-
> lessly or self-indulgently . . .
>
> From the turbulence and unease, a great yearning has been
> born in America in recent years. It is a quest for stable values.
> It is a search for deeper faith. And it deserves welcome and
> respect . . .
>
> But the yearning for traditional values is not a simple tide.
> It has undertows. And in the hands of those who would exploit
> it, this legitimate search for moral strength can become a force
> of social divisiveness and a threat to individual freedom.
>
> The truth is, the answer to a weaker family is not a stronger
> state. It is stronger values. The answer to lax morals is not
> legislated morals. It is deeper faith, greater discipline, and
> personal excellence.[25]

This argument rests on two key premises: First, the
changes that have swept through U.S. society in the past

generation are on balance not only consistent with but actually supportive of Americans' basic principles. Second, to the extent that these changes have a darker underside, the remedy lies not in state action but, rather, in individual moral responsibility.

One need not be a partisan of moral traditionalism – let alone religious fundamentalism – to wonder whether recent American social history is not more ambiguous than these premises would suggest. On the issue of whether the cultural revolution of the past generation has left the United States better or worse off, a case can be made for both sides. Although the civil rights movement is widely acknowledged to have righted ancient wrongs, epidemics of crime, drugs, and teenage pregnancy have exacted a fearful toll. And on the issue of whether the remedy for these ills appropriately lies in the private or the public sphere, traditionalists argue that because public action has contributed to the problem, countervailing public action must be part of the solution. If the state, hiding behind a veil of neutrality, has acted anything but neutrally in tearing down traditional barriers against immoral behavior, then calls for a public change of course are not on their face implausible.

V

To some extent, this disagreement revolves around differing interpretations of "neutrality." Juridical liberals typically argue as follows: Toward every action, the public authority can take one of three stances. It may command the performance of the action; it may prohibit the action; or it may promulgate neither commands nor prohibitions, in which case individuals may choose for themselves. In this last case, the state is said to be neutral, because it offers no authoritative judgment. Thus, the state commands jury duty, prohibits murder, and permits – but takes no stand on – abortion.

Traditionalists do not accept this stance as an adequate account of neutrality. To permit a certain class of actions, they argue, is to make the public judgment that those actions are not wrong. No one denies that the state should prohibit murder. To permit abortion is therefore to determine (at least implicitly) that abortion is not murder. But this is precisely the issue between proponents and opponents of abortion. Permitting abortion cannot be construed as neutrality, because it rests on a substantive moral judgment that is anything but neutral.

At this juncture in the argument, liberal theorists typically resort to history. The Lockean doctrine of toleration was an effort to reestablish the possibility of decent politics in the context of insoluble disagreements about fundamental religious questions. The contemporary doctrine of state neutrality, liberals argue, arises as a necessary generalization of religious toleration. In a complex, diverse modern society, agreement on a wide range of moral questions simply cannot be expected. When – as in the case of abortion – warring views cannot be reconciled, neither side can rightly use the coercive power of the state to enforce its views. The state is declaring neither that abortion is murder nor that it is not murder. Rather, the state is announcing that it is incompetent to make such a judgment. There is, liberal theorists insist, a vast difference between the proposition that "abortion is not murder" and the proposition that "we do not and cannot know whether or not abortion is murder." The latter proposition, an instance of what I earlier called epistemological neutrality, is all that permission really entails. Thus, liberals conclude, the traditionalists are wrong. In permitting abortion, the state is not denying traditionalist premises but only refusing to endorse them.

But traditionalists have some history of their own on which to fall back. From their perspective, abortion is like slavery – an issue that deeply divides the community, but about which one party to the dispute can be known to be right and the other wrong. The agnostic thesis underlying state neutrality is thus parallel to the position Stephen Douglas upheld in his famous debates with Abraham Lincoln – and just as mistaken. We cannot be indifferent to fundamental (and decidable) questions of right and wrong, and we violate no

274

one's rights by putting public authority in the service of what is right. Yes, doing this in circumstances of deep moral disagreement risks discord and even violence. But how many Americans believe that the Civil War was too high a price to pay for the abolition of slavery?[26]

We may translate this traditionalist critique into somewhat more theoretical language. Liberals, contend the traditionalists, are preoccupied with the *fact* of moral disagreement and give short shrift to the *content* of disagreement. This tendency flows from the liberal decision to give pride of place to two key goals: avoiding oppression and preserving civil tranquillity. Oppression is minimized when the state refrains, insofar as possible, from condemning or otherwise stigmatizing any individual's moral choices. Tranquillity is maximized when all parties within a society have fair (though not unlimited) scope to lead their lives as they see fit. This, say the traditionalists, is a public morality of sorts, but it is an inadequate morality. Tranquillity is an important good, but not the highest good. And it is not oppression when right conduct is commanded and wrongful acts are prohibited.

We can place this controversy within the matrix, earlier analyzed, of Locke's case for toleration. Traditionalists argue that the reach of *epistemological neutrality* is narrower than commonly supposed, because a range of controversial moral propositions can be rationally established. They deny the relevance of *conscience-based neutrality*, in part because many current controversies involve action, which is subject to coercion, rather than belief, which is not; in part because in matters of belief there is an alternative to the extremes of coercion and indifference: public education backed by the moral authority of political leaders. Traditionalists are at pains to deny the charges embedded in *character-based neutrality*. Their aim is to correct, not to dominate. Besides, how can they be guilty of lust for power when they only seek to defend themselves against the aggression of juridical liberals? *Rights-based neutrality*, they contend, goes too far when it debars the state from prohibiting conduct that can be known to be wrong. And *prudential neutrality* accords too high a value to public order and civil peace at the expense of the moral substance of society.

This analysis raises the question of whether the controversy between traditionalists and juridical liberals is a quarrel within liberalism, or rather between liberalism and an opposing understanding of politics. Is it possible to challenge the high priority of civil tranquillity and the strict limits to governmental power in moral issues without abandoning liberalism altogether?

These questions call our attention to a significant ambiguity in the contemporary traditionalist attack on juridical liberalism. One version of this critique maintains that in seeking to separate religion and religiously grounded values from the cognizance of the state, modern liberals are promoting a public life empty of moral meaning, a kind of collective nihilism that serves as the breeding ground for despotism. It follows that liberal democracy properly understood cannot do without religion.

The other version of the traditionalist critique is quite different. According to this argument, liberalism is not a moral vacuum but rests, rather, on a specific kind of public morality: secular humanism. The problem with this morality is that it deifies human subjectivity. It gives priority to untrammeled choice over normative constraints, and to rights over duties. And it gives rise to a society in which piety is on the defensive against a hostile public authority. Far from needing religion, this thesis concludes, liberalism is at war with religion. The contemporary cultural conflict reflects liberalism, not run amok, but rather making explicit what was from the start inherent in its principles. Liberalism can see no arguments against equal rights for homosexuals; a Scripture-based politics must view this possibility as an abomination. And compromise is impossible.

Some evidence can be adduced to support the latter version of the traditionalist critique. As was suggested earlier, the understanding of the state as restraining conflict rests on a substantive judgment about the worth of civil tranquillity relative to the worth of the positions of any of the contending parties. One may reach this conclusion by denying that moral and religious beliefs are matters of intersubjective knowledge as opposed to subjective conviction. Or one may reach it by arguing that the evils of coercion override the benefits of publicly promoting even rationally justified claims about virtue or the good life. But to give coercion pride of place as the *summum malum* is already to advance a nonvacuous thesis about the human good.

Some contemporary liberal theorists are aware of this. Judith Shklar, for example, argues that liberalism rests on a decision to regard cruelty as the "first vice," which must be avoided above all. But the prohibition against cruelty is not the same as full neutrality among competing doctrines and ways of life. Rather, it is itself a specific doctrine, and it creates a political order that tolerates actions and doctrines only to the extent that they do not undermine this highest value. Although it is certain that "as a matter of liberal policy we must learn to endure enormous differences in the relative importance that various individuals and groups attach to the vices," our forbearance is circumscribed by our prior decision to give a specific account of the vices pride of place.[27]

It is important to be clear about what this argument does and does not prove. I am not suggesting that the scope for diversity in liberal societies is no greater than in closed or theocratic communities. But I am suggesting (as I have before) that liberalism has a characteristic tendency, imparted to the members of liberal societies both directly (through systems of education and training) and indirectly (through the tacit norms conveyed by political and social practices). The moral commitments of liberalism influence – and in some cases circumscribe – the ability of individuals within a liberal society to engage fully in particular ways of life. If, to be wholly effective, a religious doctrine requires control over the totality of individual life, including the formative social and political environment, then the classic liberal demand that religion be practiced privately amounts to a substantive restriction on the free exercise of that religion. The manifold blessings of liberal social orders come with a price, and we should not be surprised when those who are asked to pay grow restive.[28]

This line of argument would appear to support the thesis that the relation between traditionalism and the liberal state is one of opposition rather than mutual support. But on the other side stands the evidence of much historical research. In addition to the arguments of Washington and Jefferson cited earlier, the studies of scholars such as Walter Berns, Michael Malbin, and Mark DeWolfe Howe strongly suggest that the contemporary interpretation of the First Amendment is at variance with the manner in which the founders understood it. As Howe put it:

> The American ideal of absolute equality between all religious opinions and sects indicated the government's official sympathy for the total religious undertaking. The neutrality . . . was not the neutrality of indifference but the neutrality that condemns favoritism among friends. . . . There is not, so far as I am aware, any indication that when the concept of neutrality in matters of religion first appeared in American decisions the judges conceived of the concept as one requiring an equality between religious and antireligious interests.[29]

The thesis that religion and the liberal political order can be mutually supportive is bolstered by contemporary sociological evidence as well. A recent follow-up to the classic *Middletown* study of the 1920s indicates that the people of Muncie, Indiana, are dramatically more religious than they were sixty years ago – and dramatically more tolerant: "We cannot turn up a group whose religious chauvinism comes anywhere near the level that was normal in 1924. . . . In a liberal perspective, these findings are almost too good to be true."[30] Today, as when Tocqueville wrote, the level of religious commitment among Americans is demonstrably higher than is the case for all other Western countries.[31] It is difficult to believe that this fact is unrelated to the extraordinary stability of republican values and institutions in the United States.

These conflicting theses – that traditionalism and liberalism are opposed, and that they are mutually supportive – can be reconciled. My suggestion is that there is a substantial area of overlap between these two forces, as well as significant areas of conflict. In some measure, religion and liberal politics need each other. Religion can undergird key liberal values and practices; liberal politics can protect – and substantially accommodate – the free exercise of religion. But this relationship of mutual support dissolves if the respective proponents lose touch with what unites them. Pushed to the limit, the juridical principles and practices of a liberal society tend inevitably to corrode moralities that rest either on traditional forms of social organization or on the stern requirements of revealed religion. Pushed to the limit, tradition and religion can end by denying the diversity – and the freedoms – at the heart of liberal society.

So, for example, the fundamentalist effort to reconstitute the moral foundations of our institutions goes astray. As Harvey Mansfield, Jr., has written:

> The Moral Majority . . . is concerned above all with the souls of Americans, but it has difficulty in finding a universal definition of the healthy individual suitable for a free, secular society. . . . The Moral Majority seems to want to abolish the distinction between state and society.[32]

It is hard to be reassured by the call for a "Christian Commonwealth," by the claim that "God does not hear the prayers of a Jew," or by the definition of an anti-Semite as "someone who hates Jews more than he ought to" – all statements made in the 1980s by leading fundamentalist ministers. But equally, liberal theorists (and activists) who deny the very existence of legitimate public involvement in matters such as family stability, moral education, and religion are unwittingly undermining the values and institutions they seek to support.

VI

The foregoing analysis, if correct, suggests two great tasks for contemporary liberals. On the level of political practice, ways must be found to deescalate the conflict between traditionalism and juridical liberalism. On the level of political theory, an authentically liberal account of goods and virtues must be articulated and linked, to the extent possible, with the traditionalist understanding.

In Part III, I sketched such an account. I want now to suggest how it connects with traditionalism. To do so, let me distinguish two forms of traditionalism. The first, which I will call *intrinsic*, is crystallized in sentiments of the form "X is unnatural, disgusting, ungodly (or whatever)" and moves directly to the proposition that anything judged innately unacceptable by such standards may be legally prohibited. The second form of traditionalism, which I call *functional*, rests its case on asserted links between certain moral principles and public virtues or institutions needed for the successful functioning of a liberal community. So, for example, an intrinsic traditionalist might deplore divorce as a violation of divine law, whereas a functional traditionalist might object to it on the grounds (for which considerable empirical evidence can be adduced) that children in divorced families tend to suffer kinds of economic and psychological damage that reduce their capacity to become independent and contributing members of the community.

Let me now apply this distinction to the question at hand. Liberalism is, and must remain, wary of intrinsic traditionalism. It must seek to minimize, if it cannot wholly eliminate, the role of personal moral sentiment in coercive public policy. In this respect, anyway, the objections H. L. A. Hart and Ronald Dworkin raised against Lord Devlin must be accorded great weight.[33] It is on this basis that many elements of historic American moral/religious traditionalism – in particular, hierarchies of race, gender, and ethnicity – have properly been rejected, as unacceptable bases for public policies.

But these considerations do not warrant the much broader

conclusion, embraced by so many contemporary liberals, that traditionalism as such is suspect. In the first place, even intrinsic traditionalism may have an important role within liberal societies. Recall that the premise "B has a right to do X" does not warrant the conclusion "It would be right for B to do X." Between rights and rightness lies a vast terrain where moral argumentation and (in some cases) forms of public persuasion have a legitimate role. Recall also that there may well be public policy disputes in which deep feeling forms an ineliminable component of argumentation on all sides. In such cases it would be self-defeating (indeed, impossible) to rule the public sphere altogether off-limits to such considerations.[34]

Finally (and most critically for present purposes), the liberal case against intrinsic traditionalism leaves the claims of functional traditionalism untouched. If a plausible (not necessarily conclusive) link can be forged between some aspect of traditional morality (e.g., the intact two-parent family) and some feature of liberal public purposes, institutions, or conduct, then a rational basis exists for liberal public policy that endorses and helps sustain that aspect of the tradition. In the zeal of the past generation to expand individual choice and affirm autonomy, liberals have largely overlooked the possible existence of reasonable public arguments for traditionalism. In current circumstances, it is time to reconsider the adequacy of individualistic voluntarism as the guide to liberal public policy and jurisprudence.

VII

So much for the theoretical deescalation of the clash between juridical liberalism and traditionalism. The domain of constitutional adjudication affords an important angle of view into the practical challenge. A recent Supreme Court case exemplifies the clash between juridicalism and traditionalism while suggesting strategies for ameliorating this conflict.

The case I wish to discuss – *Wallace* v. *Jaffree*[35] – deals with the vexed issue of school prayer. The specific facts of the case are not germane to our inquiry. Nor is the holding, which turned on obscure points of legislative history. The importance of this case, rather, lies in the middle way it suggests between administered vocal school prayer, on the one hand, and the total expulsion of religious expression from public schools, on the other.

Although traditionalists would like to return to the status quo ante of the 1950s, it is clear that formal, prescribed school prayer cannot pass constitutional muster, for the simple reason that it is impossible to construct an official prayer that is truly impartial among religious faiths. The First Amendment arguably does not require state neutrality between religion and irreligion. But it surely forbids sectarian favoritism. In the contemporary circumstances of deep religious pluralism, this prohibition rules out any and all publicly administered prayers.

The First Amendment need not, however, rule out a state-sponsored moment of silence in the public schools – a practice now permitted or required by the laws of twenty-five states. Concurring in *Wallace* v. *Jaffree*, Justice O'Connor argues the case for a moment of silence in persuasive terms:

> A state sponsored moment of silence in public schools is different from state sponsored vocal prayer or Bible reading. First, a moment of silence is not inherently religious. Silence, unlike prayer or Bible reading, need not be associated with a religious exercise. Second, a pupil who participates in a moment of silence need not compromise his or her beliefs. During a moment of silence, a student who objects to prayer is left to his or her own thoughts, and is not compelled to listen to the prayers or thoughts of others. For these simple reasons, a moment of silence statute does not stand or fall under the Establishment Clause.

From many different points of view, a moment of silence should be regarded as a principled resolution of a bitter controversy. It does not favor any sect or doctrine – the "narrow" requirement of the First Amendment as interpreted by scholars such as Howe, Berns, and Malbin. It does not even favor religion over irreligion – the "broad" requirement of the First Amendment as interpreted by the Court in such cases as *Everson* v. *Board* and *Abington* v. *Schempp*. And it has the inestimable practical advantage of driving a wedge between legitimate parental concerns, on the one hand, and theocratic ambitions or antireligious ire on the other.[36]

I turn now from constitutional adjudication to public policy – specifically, family policy.

On January 21, 1990, the *Washington Post* published the results of its nationwide inquiry into the public mood. The title: "Introspective Electorate Views Future Darkly." The thesis: The public believes America is in decline for many reasons, chief among them "moral decay." The public's prime explanation for moral decay: "the breakdown of the family."

These worries are hardly the product of an overheated popular imagination. In 1989, more than one-quarter of all infants were born out of wedlock. For black infants, that figure exceeded 60 percent.[37]

The phenomenon of children born out of wedlock has been extensively chronicled by the media and intensively studied by academics. But the number of single-parent children produced by divorce and separation has been rising far more rapidly.[38] From 1940 to 1960, the annual U.S. divorce rate was essentially stable. From 1960 to 1985, by contrast, it skyrocketed 250 percent.[39] In 1960, the United States had 35 divorced persons per 1,000 married persons. By 1985, that figure has nearly quadrupled, to 130.[40] So when we talk about the "breakdown of the family" and its consequences for children, family break*up* is even more significant than is the failure of families to form in the first place.[41]

We have known for some time about the economic consequences of family breakdown. As David Ellwood observes, "The vast majority of children who are raised entirely in a two-parent home will never be poor during childhood. By contrast, the vast majority of children who spend time in a single-parent home will experience poverty."[42] In 1984, the rate of poverty before government transfer payments in single-parent families was about 50 percent, whereas the comparable figure for two-parent families was 15 percent.

A closer look at the statistics only intensifies the difference. Some 80 percent of children growing up in two-parent families experienced no poverty whatever during the first ten years of their lives, whereas only 27 percent of the children in single-parent households were so fortunate. Only 2 percent of children in two-parent families experienced persistent poverty (7 years or more), whereas a full 22 percent of children in single-parent households literally grew up poor.[43] It is no exaggeration to say that the best antipoverty program for children is a stable intact family.

If the economic effects of family breakdown are clear, the psychological effects are just now coming into focus. Karl Zinsmeister summarizes an emerging consensus:

> There is a mountain of evidence showing that when families disintegrate, children often end up with intellectual, physical, and emotional scars that last for life. . . . We talk about the drug crisis, the education crisis, and the problems of teen pregnancy and juvenile crime. But all these ills trace back predominantly to one source: broken families.[44]

From the standpoint of the economic well-being and sound psychological development, the evidence indicates that the intact two-parent family is generally preferable to the available alternatives. It follows that a prime purpose of sound family policy is to strengthen such families by promoting their formation, assisting their efforts to cope with contemporary economic and social stress, and retarding their breakdown whenever possible. This is of course not the only purpose: Family policy must also seek to ameliorate the consequences of family breakdown for children while recognizing that some negative effects cannot be undone.

Of course, a general preference for the intact two-parent family does not mean that this is the best option in every case. That proposition would be absurd. Nor does it mean that all single-parent families are somehow "dysfunctional."

That proposition would be not only false but also insulting to the millions of single parents who are struggling successfully against the odds to provide good homes for their children. The point is only that at the level of society-wide phenomena, significant differences do emerge, differences that can and should shape the conduct of social policy.

Nor, finally, should the endorsement of the two-parent family be mistaken for nostalgia for the single-breadwinner "traditional" family of the 1950s. Setting aside all other variables, it cannot be doubted that much of the surge of women into the work force since the 1960s has come in reaction to economic stress. As inflation-adjusted hourly wages have fallen in response to international competition and stagnant productivity, only increased female labor-force participation has enabled families to maintain their purchasing power. For better or worse, the new reality for most American families is that two earners are now needed to maintain even a modestly middle-class way of life. The point of a policy that takes its bearings from the two-parent family is not to turn the clock back, but rather to help such families stay together and deal more effectively with contemporary economic and social challenges.

My focus is on what must be a key objective of our society: raising children who are prepared – intellectually, physically, morally, and emotionally – to take their place as law-abiding and independent members of their community, able to sustain themselves and their families and to fulfill their duties as citizens. Available evidence supports the conclusion that on balance, the intact two-parent family is best suited to this task. We must thus resist the easy relativism of the proposition that different family structures represent nothing more than "alternative life-styles" – a belief that impeded the Carter administration's efforts to develop a coherent family policy and that continues to cloud debate even today.[45]

We must also reject the thesis that questions of family structure are purely private matters not appropriate for public discussion and response. After all, the consequences of family failure affect society at large. We all pay for systems of welfare, criminal justice, and incarceration as well as for physical and mental disability; we are all made poorer by the inability or unwillingness of young adults to become contributing members of society; we all suffer if our society is unsafe and divided. There is a fundamental distinction between social institutions and practices that affect only the parties consenting to them and those that affect everyone. Whenever institutions and practices have such pervasive consequences, society has the right to scrutinize them and, where possible, to reshape them in light of its collective goals.

This suggests that there is a deep difference between families with children and those without them. Families without children may well approximate arrangements that touch the vital interests of their immediate members only, and principles of individual freedom and choice may be most appropriate. By contrast, families with children are engaged in activities with vast social consequences. Moral categories such as duty, continuing responsibility, and basic interests come into play in addition to, and as restraints on, voluntaristic individualism. Society is justified, then, in treating these two types of families quite differently in the structure of law and policy.

One prime candidate for this strategy of differentiation is the law of divorce. To begin with, because of the shattering effects of divorce on children, it would be reasonable to introduce "braking" mechanisms that require parents contemplating divorce to pause for reflection. There is transatlantic precedent for such procedures. A report from Britain's Law Commission has recommended that such couples "notify the courts of their intention, then spend at least nine months resolving crucial details of the divorce. Their first obligation would be to decide the future of their children before settling questions of property and maintenance. Only then could couples return to court for a divorce." As a recent account notes, "By encouraging parents to look at the consequences of a family breakup rather than at the alleged cause or excuse for it, the commission hopes couples will improve their prospects of saving the marriage."[46]

Of course, such a pause for reflection does not always – perhaps not even usually – succeed in warding off divorce. It is then necessary to turn to phase two: the reform of procedures affecting the economics of divorce for families with children. As Mary Ann Glendon, a leading American student of the law of divorce, has observed, "When almost three-fifths of all divorces in the United States involve couples with minor children, it is astonishing that our spousal support law and marital property law treat that situation as an exception to the general rule." She goes on to recommend a set of guidelines for divorces with children:

> A "children first" principle should govern all such divorces.
> . . . [T]he judge's main task would be to piece together, from property and income and in-kind personal care, the best possible package to meet the needs of the children and their physical custodian. Until the welfare of the children had been adequately secured in this way, there would be no question or debate about "marital property." All property, no matter when or how acquired, would be subject to the duty to provide for the children.[47]

This argument illustrates the key distinction between intrinsic and functional traditionalism discussed earlier. The intrinsic traditionalist might object to all divorce as (say) a violation of divine or natural law and would seek to restrict it to the narrowest possible grounds, or perhaps even prohibit it altogether. For the functional traditionalist, by contrast, the central issue is the relationship between family structure and the requirements of liberal politics. To the extent that children from broken families are less able to become independent and contributing members of the liberal economy, society, and polity, divorce becomes a public issue and the implementation of a more restrictive legal regime becomes a serious possibility.

The case I want to make may be summarized in three propositions. First, functional traditionalism represents a perspective and mode of argument consistent with, and supportive of, liberal politics. Second, in many important policy areas significant evidence exists to bolster a functional tra- ditionalist argument. And finally, functional traditionalism represents the basis on which the cultural cleavages of the past generation may best be ameliorated. For it is through this perspective that common ground may be found between partisans of voluntaristic individualism and proponents of social duty, between those who applaud and those who de- plore the social changes of the past generation, between those who oppose and those who demand state action on moral questions.

Of course, no perspective can possibly eliminate deep con- flict. Liberalism rightly understood will continue to antago- nize both extreme voluntarists and intransigent moralists. But it will also create the largest possible space for public discussion among men and women of good will, and for the noncoercive resolution of inevitable differences. We cannot hope to go farther than this in practice, and if we go farther in theory, it is only because our abstractions have lost touch with the concrete phenomena of social difference.

VIII

Some years ago, James Q. Wilson traced the evolution of American scholarship from the morally neutral economic analysis characteristic of the mid-1960s to a renewed focus on individual character. In the long run, he argued, "the public interest depends on private virtue."[48]

Addressing himself to this issue, Wilson invoked the au- thority of Aristotle – a suggestive move indeed. Among Ar- istotle's core virtues are moderation and justice – a familiar fact that suggests a hypothesis about the contemporary moral controversy between juridical liberals and traditionalist conservatives.

Traditionalists charge liberals with ignoring or undermin- ing self-discipline and self-restraint in such matters as sex- uality, the work ethic, and respect for law. Liberals charge traditionalists with ignoring or undermining the demands of fairness, particularly with regard to the least fortunate members of society.

Each side, I believe, has grasped a portion of the truth. Conjoined, their insights point toward a more fully adequate public morality for a modern liberal republic.

Moral virtue is more than individual self-restraint. It is also the display of due concern for the legitimate claims of others. Conversely, moral virtue is more than a system of rational demands we make on one another. It requires, as well, taking responsibility for oneself and cultivating one's humanity while tempering one's passions and desires. To put this point another way, what Wilson calls "private virtue" properly governs both individual conduct *and* the social context within which that conduct occurs. Sound moral analysis takes into account the myriad ways in which social context, beginning with family and neighborhood, encourages or discourages the formation of good character.

But contextual understanding cannot properly absolve individuals of ultimate responsibility for their own conduct. The necessary presumption of human freedom must not be replaced with the debasing psychology of victimization. To slight either side of this moral equation is to engage in a form of ideological special pleading that precludes sound social policy. To strike a principled balance between them is to begin the task of reconstituting public morality in a liberal polity.

Chapter 13

Partisanship and inclusion

Throughout this book, I have sought to argue against neutralist accounts of liberalism and to replace them with an
account focused on liberal goods and virtues and on the
means whereby they may be attained (or engendered). A
leitmotif of my critique has been what I see as a subtle irony:
Neutralist liberalism, whose guiding intention is the widest
possible inclusiveness for differing ways of life subject only
to the requirements of social justice, turns out to be far more
partisan and exclusionary than its proponents are readily
willing to admit. The substantive liberalism I advocate, by
contrast, is actually less biased against many ways of life
than is the thesis I reject. In this respect, among others, it is
more political than is the self-styled "political liberalism."

In this concluding chapter, I focus on the complex interplay
of partisanship and inclusion. Section I explores the extent
to which liberal principles of public justice can and do shape
the content of private lives and associations. Section II discusses ways of minimizing moral coercion in liberal polities.
Section III indicates how the characteristic outcomes produced by liberal principles and institutions can be deployed
to develop a normatively substantive and empirically realistic
defense of liberal politics.

I

As we saw in Chapter 5, political liberals such as John Rawls
and Charles Larmore acknowledge that liberal regimes do

not (and cannot) satisfy the requirements of "neutrality of outcome," for two reasons: Some ways of life are flatly ruled out as impermissible, and other (permissible) ways of life tend to lose out. Moreover, the defenders of political liberalism acknowledge that the losers are not selected randomly but, rather, form a pattern. As Larmore puts it, "Ways of life that depend upon close and exclusive bonds of language and culture . . . may lose, within a liberal society also tolerating quite different and more open ways of life, some of the authority and cohesion that they would have if they formed complete societies unto themselves."[1] As Rawls says, "We must accept the facts of common-sense political sociology."[2]

I want to focus on a key dispute as to the consequences of liberal principles for individual lives and associations within liberal polities. One approach, stressed by Rawls and by Larmore, is that the constraints of social unity have only modest effects. We can divide ourselves without excessive difficulty between our responsibilities as citizens and our desires as seekers after love, money, truth, salvation, or whatever. To be sure, the core political principles are "overriding" in the sense that private actions and associations must give way in cases of direct conflict with public norms. But this does not mean that these norms are "pervasive"; that is, the substance of private life need not be comprehensively reconstructed in light of liberal public principles. For example, although liberal democracy requires toleration and equal respect, the U.S. Catholic Church may conduct its internal affairs on the basis of quite different considerations. If we can bring ourselves to discard the "cult of wholeness" – the dogmatic belief that society must mirror or "express" the reigning structure of the polity – we shall be able to see how liberal politics is compatible with – leaves essentially unaffected – the widest possible range of private lives.[3]

The other approach, developed in a book by Stephen Macedo, is to argue that liberal principles of social unity have effects "all the way down," on intermediate associations and individuals within liberal societies. In Larmore's terms, political principles cannot be overriding without becoming pervasive. Aristotle was right: Core political principles shape the character of every aspect of the community. Like every other form of political community, liberalism is a regime. Wholeness – the inner unity of state and society, public and private – is not a cult, but rather a fact.[4]

To sharpen the debate, let me try to enumerate the ways in which liberal public principles may be thought to affect groups and individuals. (In many respects, this list simply brings together considerations scattered through Macedo's book.)

1. In practice, it is no easy matter to flesh out the theoretical distinctions between public and private, political and nonpolitical. Rather than drawing a sharp line, these distinctions demarcate an endlessly contested battle zone. An example of this is the tendency to employ constitutional law to extend the sway of liberal public values throughout the society. Racial discrimination is banned not only in voting but also in housing and employment; gender discrimination is prohibited in "private" clubs; due process rights are extended to welfare recipients and high school students. We can, of course, argue about the appropriateness of any or all of these measures. The fact remains that in many cases a link may plausibly be adduced between "private" behavior and "public" opportunity.

2. Beyond the formal, legal, willed extension of public values lies their informal gravitational influence on individuals and institutions. Witness an extraordinary meeting held in the Vatican between U.S. Catholic bishops and representatives of the Pope: The Roman prelates inveighed against what they saw as the laxity of the American Church. American bishops responded with a fascinating disquisition in which they pointed out, inter alia, that liberal political culture encourages rational criticism of all forms of authority, a tendency the American Church is not free to disregard. The notion of unquestioned authority that seems unimpeachable to a Polish Pope is almost unintelligible to U.S. Catholics, and the American Church has been significantly reconstructed in response to the influence of liberal public culture.

Another example is the core liberal notions of free choice and contractual relations, which have permeated the previously sacramental understanding of marriage and the family. The notion of an irreversible, constitutive commitment has been undermined by notions of liberation and autonomy: "Till death do us part" has been replaced by "till distaste drive us apart." It is possible to resist, of course, in the same way that exceptionally strong swimmers can overcome swift currents. My point is only that there are powerful if informal liberal currents against which resistance is at best difficult.

3. As previously discussed, liberalism is not equally hospitable to all ways of life or to all subcommunities. Ways of life that require self-restraint, hierarchy, or cultural integrity are likely to find themselves on the defensive, threatened with the loss of both cohesion and authority.

4. What I have called the primacy of the political – the fact that Rawlsian principles of social unity trace the limits of diversity and trump individual and group claims to the contrary – has an important effect on the content of practices within liberal societies. For example, polygamy was an integral part of Mormonism, contained in the direct revelation to the founders of the Church. Under pressure from the Supreme Court (and federal law enforcement authorities, backed by the military), the Mormons eventually abandoned the practice. (Resistance by Mormon fundamentalists continues to this day, however.)

Liberal social unity thus recapitulates the structure of Locke's toleration doctrine. At a critical point in the argument, Locke subordinates permissible religious practices to the requirements of civil peace and order. As Macedo correctly observes, the faithful may well resist this subordination – particularly those who take "I come bringing not peace, but the sword" quite literally.

In this regard, anyway, it is a mistake to believe that liberalism takes religion, or anything else, off the public agenda. To be sure, a zone of private conscience is established. But as soon as beliefs are translated into individual or group practices, public scrutiny is possible and legitimate. Indeed, twentieth-century First Amendment litigation is a testimony to the multifaceted tension between particular religions and the common polity. Not long ago, there was renewed controversy over legal restraints on the sacramental use of peyote in certain religious communities, a dispute in which the Oregon supreme court endorsed the free exercise claims of native Americans and the U.S. Supreme Court endorsed as legitimate the public purposes animating the restrictive law adopted by the Oregon legislature.

5. Finally, there is the question of the impact of the critical reflection needed to understand, to accept, and to apply liberal principles of social justice on other commitments we may have. Even if the original position is only a "device of representation," it represents a moral point of view into which we as individuals must be able to enter in order to determine our rights and duties as citizens of the liberal polity. The ability to separate ourselves reflectively from our other commitments is bound to have an effect on our ability to maintain those commitments, especially the ones resting on tradition, unquestioned authority, and faith. (This will be so, I believe, even if, as Larmore suggests, necessary critical reflection involves only possible conflicts between personal commitments and overarching liberal principles, that is, even if it does not require reflection on the worth of those commitments considered in themselves.) The extent of that effect is an empirical question. But I believe that the Burkean sociological tradition has a point: Any liberal commitment to key elements of both Socratic and Enlightenment rationalism has important corrosive effects on a wide range of psychological and social structures.

Taken together, these observations make a strong case against any sharp distinction between "overriding" and "pervasive" principles of the public order. This does not mean, however, that the regime character of liberalism is just the same as that of other polities.

First, liberal public principles permit, and make possible, a range of individual and associational activities that must be regarded as wide when compared to the major alternatives revealed by historical inquiry and contemporary transnational studies. Liberal public principles are not neutral, but they are pluralistic, hence consistent with a very considerable measure of social diversity.

Second, at least some highly "traditional" ways of life can survive, even thrive, within liberal polities. (Consider, for example, the lush profusion of Orthodox and Hasidic Jewish groups now flourishing in Brooklyn.) One might even see such groups as the beneficiaries of a sociological backlash, which Erich Fromm once ominously characterized as the "escape from freedom." For some individuals, the relative openness of liberal society engenders a sense of confusion and fear rather than exhilaration, and a corresponding desire to flee from the burdens of self-determination to the comforts of submission to authority.

Third, key features of liberal societies make possible a substantial measure of withdrawal and insulation for dissenting groups. In the United States, anyway, formal political participation is optional; equality of opportunity means, among other things, that individuals may choose whether to work at all (there is no legally defined crime of "parasitism" in liberal societies); the alternative of private academies makes it possible to nullify what some see as the secular humanism of the public schools; freedom of movement permits physical withdrawal, even isolation; and so forth.

Finally, it seems possible for liberal societies to manage the inevitable conflict with marginal groups in a spirit of maximum feasible accommodation. In the famous *Yoder* case, for example, the Supreme Court exempted Amish children from certain educational requirements, with the explicit aim of minimizing the erosion of the Amish community. This decision has been widely, and in some respects persuasively, criticized as resting on a selective endorsement of the Amish way of life – that is, on nonneutral principles.[5] But it is also possible to interpret *Yoder* as the particularized, but neither uncharacteristic nor unprincipled, practice of liberal generosity.

In short, liberal public principles should be seen as more

than simply overriding but less than fully pervasive. Perhaps a metaphor will clarify this hard-to-describe "inbetweenness." Think of a society based on liberal public principles as a rapidly flowing river. A few vessels may be strong enough to head upstream. Most, however, will be carried along by the current. But they can still choose where in the river to sail, and where along the shore to moor. The mistake is to think of the liberal polity either as a placid lake or as an irresistible undertow.

One final point: The existence of the liberal "current," the necessity it imposes on some groups to buck it, means that the life of those groups is in a sense pervasively altered. An activity carried out in the spirit of vigilant resistance is not exactly the same as the formally similar activity conducted in neutral or supportive circumstances. (A homely microexample: Conducting a family dinner before the invention of television is not the same as conducting that dinner with the strenuously resisted possibility of turning on the television.) So liberal public principles are pervasive in the sense that they structure a set of influential tendencies in reference to which all activities and choices are compelled to be defined.

II

Contemporary liberal theory is preoccupied with the threat of moral coercion – the use of public authority to compel individuals to speak, or act, against their deepest convictions. The variegated quest for "neutrality" is basically the endeavor to define a form of social life free of moral coercion, so understood, in circumstances of deep moral disagreement. But the neutral society is intended to be founded on more than a peace treaty among forces too weak to overawe one another. It is constituted, rather, by a substantive, if parsimonious, moral framework to which all (morally serious) individuals can conscientiously assent and faithfully adhere. Neutralist liberalism, in Larmore's phrase, is not just another "controversial and partisan vision of the good life," not just another contender for dominance in the ongoing process of moral conflict. It is, rather, a "plausible solution" of the dangerous, even deadly, problems engendered by the simple fact of that conflict.[6]

The difficulty is this. The more seriously one takes liberalism as a core moral commitment, the less likely it is that one's other personal moral commitments will emerge unscathed. As we have seen, the more one examines putatively neutral liberal principles and public discourse, the more impressed one is likely to become by their decidedly nonneutral impact on different parts of diverse societies. Liberalism is not and cannot be the universal response, equally acceptable to all, to the challenge of social diversity. It is ultimately a partisan stance. As Jeremy Waldron puts it, the liberal must concede that

> his conception of political judgement will be appealing only to those who hold their commitments in a certain 'liberal' spirit. ... But if this line is taken, we must abandon any claim about the 'neutrality' of liberal politics. The liberal will have to concede that he has a great many more enemies (real enemies – people who will suffer under a liberal dispensation) than he has usually pretended to have.[7]

Let me put this in Rawls's terms. In choosing principles for the basic structure behind a veil of ignorance, each individual will be aware of the bias of liberalism, that is, will know that there is a chance that his or her conception of the good will turn out to be systematically disfavored. Given this, I suggest, each person will subscribe to the basic structure only with the proviso that it permit that individual to lead his or her life without massive moral compromise. For if not, what Rawls calls the "strains of commitment" would be too great.

In circumstances of deep moral division, the ultimate liberal hope – unanimous, conscientious, and stable endorsement of core political principles – cannot be realized. But the defeat of this hope is far from fatal for the liberal enterprise. Here are three reasons why.

First, even if liberal orders do not and cannot *eliminate* moral coercion, they may still be defended as the form of political authority that *minimizes* such coercion. The scope of acceptable diversity in liberal societies may be wider than in any of the feasible alternatives.

Second, liberalism may be defended as legitimate even though not every member of the community is morally obligated to it. As both Kent Greenawalt and Jeremy Waldron have argued, it is a mistake to interdefine legitimacy and obligation: Legitimate authority does not entail an obligation to obey on the part of all individuals, and the absence of the obligation to obey on the part of some does not entail the illegitimacy of authority.[8]

More precisely, the case is this: A society can be legitimate if the preponderance of its members conscientiously subscribe to it while the rest stand in what Rawls would call a modus vivendi relationship to it. Those in the latter category will seek in the long run to alter the basic structure of society as their relative bargaining position improves, and in the short run they may feel compelled to engage in selective nonobedience. These sorts of reservations are tolerable (within limits); in any event, they are inevitable.

Finally, there are strategies a liberal society can adopt to mute the coercive consequences of its own unavoidable biases. For example, as I argued in Chapter 11, public education in the liberal state should focus on the core requirements of competent economic, social, and political performance expected of all citizens. When public education expands this focus – for example, by trying to infuse all students with a Socratic-critical attitude toward different ways of life (including their own) – it generates unnecessary and damaging conflict with many ways of life that would otherwise be tolerably comfortable.

A high task of liberal statesmanship is to attend to inevitable moral conflict, not by pretending that the liberal state is neutral but, rather, by working toward the greatest possible accommodation with dissenters that is consistent with liberalism's core commitments. Properly practiced, I believe, liberal statesmanship can create a "social space" far more extensive than that afforded by any other form of social organization. What it cannot do is abolish partiality and moral coercion altogether.

The real question, then, concerns the content of the substantive agreement that liberal society requires. I think that political liberalism is on the right track in insisting that this agreement must be relatively parsimonious. But political liberalism is, I believe, mistaken in its belief that notions such as neutral rational dialogue and equal respect will suffice. Not only does the defense of these notions bring other morally relevant considerations into play; so, too, does the movement from abstract concepts to more concrete conceptions – as I have tried to show in the case of equal respect. As I argued negatively in Chapter 4 and affirmatively in Chapter 8, liberal social philosophy cannot get along without a conception of the good – if you will, a kind of minimal perfectionism.

Now it may be that, ultimately, political liberals will not want to dissent from this proposition. Stephen Holmes, for example, acknowledges that fully general, abstract neutrality makes no sense, but he insists that neutrality was never intended to meet this criterion. Rather, neutrality is contextual: It can be established only *"relative* to specific factions or individuals. . . . Formal rules tolerate certain content and prohibit other content. . . . [n]o instrument can be pliantly adapted to every conceivable function."[9]

This thesis has the ring of truth, historically as well as philosophically. But it then raises the question, Relative to *what* should the polity strive to maintain a neutral stance? Larmore, for example, sees political liberalism as a way of detaching liberalism from the values of autonomy and individuality – that is, of achieving public neutrality between the heirs of Kant and Mill, on the one hand, and the neoromantic critics of "individualism," on the other.[10] I do not wish to dwell here on the irony of attempting to resolve this dispute on the basis of an avowedly Kantian conception of equal respect. The point, rather, is that this conception of

the contemporary forces standing in greatest need of neu-
tralization or accommodation is hardly uncontroversial. Contemporary neoromanticism – the appeal to the values of
tradition and belonging – has little support (at least in America; Europe may be a different story) outside the academy
and among a narrow stratum of baby-boomers nostalgic for
the dreams of the 1960s. By contrast, many present-day religious believers in America have found themselves increasingly driven into opposition to liberalism, and their revolt
has created one of the great political cleavages of our time.
If our goals include the widest possible accommodation, this
(or some other politically significant division) is surely a more
plausible point of departure than a debate that, at least in
the United States, is almost exclusively academic.

Judged by this standard, political liberalism is not an obviously promising point of departure. Stuart Hampshire puts
this well:

> Political liberalism includes a definite, although incomplete,
> conception of the good which prevails principally among free-
> thinking liberals in politically sophisticated societies. For such
> persons the liberty of the individual is the first essential ele-
> ment in the good. So-called procedural justice, as Rawls spec-
> ifies its content, is not acceptable as justice in the judgment of
> those, for instance, who accept all the traditional authority of
> the Catholic Church in moral matters; Rawls's just institutions
> will permit freedom of choice in areas where the devout believe
> such freedom ought not to be allowed.[11]

The question of what should be politically accommodated
or neutralized, and how, cannot be resolved on the basis of
concepts such as neutrality, dialogue, and equal respect. It
calls upon us to consider the relative impact of public involvement in, or withdrawal from, a specific set of controverted issues, and to conduct that assessment in light of
interests (peace, security, freedom from pain and humiliation, or whatever) that human beings and citizens take to be
fundamental. The liberal theory of the human good, or well-
being, developed in Chapter 8, seeks to provide a widely

acceptable basis for such an assessment. But it will not, and cannot, satisfy everyone.

III

The strategy for justifying the liberal state that seeks to dispense with all specific conceptions of the good cannot succeed. Defenders of the liberal state must either accept the burden of inquiry into the human good or abandon their enterprise altogether.

This does not mean that the minimal theory of the good identified in Chapter 4 – life, purposiveness, rationality – on which contemporary liberal theorists tacitly rely would suffice, if only it were explicitly recognized and defended. Nor, on the other hand, need it be discarded altogether. Rather, as I argued in Chapter 8, this minimal theory must be expanded to encompass the full theory of the good latent in liberal practice. For example, liberal societies rest, as well, on the belief that the development of individual capacities is an important element of the good and that liberal societies are, on balance, the most conducive to individual development. Liberal societies believe that individuals are, at least in part, responsible for the use they make of opportunities for development and are entitled to make claims on resources on the basis of what they have achieved. Liberal societies claim to be more just than those societies that deny the moral force of claims based on achievement, as well as those societies that ignore claims based on need. And finally, liberal societies contend that their organization reflects, as none other can, two fundamental truths of the human condition: the diversity of human types and the inherent incapacity of the public sphere to encompass more than a portion of human activity or to fulfill more than a part of human aspiration.

A justification of the liberal order, constructed on this foundation, would contain, at a minimum, the following elements.

1. *Social peace:* Through social arrangements and political mechanisms directed toward the compromise of difference

and the amelioration of conflict, liberal societies reduce the probability that disagreements among their members will degenerate into armed strife that endangers human life.

2. *Rule of law:* Through comprehensive, effective, and relatively autonomous systems of law, liberal societies minimize arbitrariness and create a framework of reasonably stable expectations conducive to the planned pursuit of individual purposes.

3. *Recognition of diversity:* Although, as we have seen, liberal societies are not equally hospitable to every way of life, they are unusually sensitive to the diversity of individual tastes, talents, and life plans. Relatively few members of liberal societies lack significant opportunities to pursue their individual purposes.

4. *Tendency toward inclusiveness:* The liberal devotion to rationality tends to erode arbitrary distinctions among human beings. Liberal societies tend, therefore, to treat steadily increasing percentages of their members as full and equal citizens rather than as political subjects or social subordinates.

5. *Minimum decency:* Liberal societies tend to reduce the incidence of the two greatest affronts to basic decency in human relations: wanton brutality as an instrument of governance or social control, and the desperate poverty that constricts all hopes and obstructs the pursuit of all purposes.

6. *Affluence:* Liberal societies are at least compatible with economies that generate high levels of discretionary resources, the sine qua non for the pursuit of all purposes, collective as well as individual. Judged from a historical or comparative perspective, limited periods of reduced growth rates as in the 1980s do not significantly affect this generalization.

7. *Scope for development:* Liberal societies offer a wide range of opportunities for the development of individual talent and excellence, by providing individuals with a multiplicity of institutions devoted to education and training on many different levels of rigor and complexity and by devoting significant social resources to developmental opportunities. The classic liberal doctrine of equality of opportunity combines

this positive valuation of individual development with the proposition that only individual talents and capacities – not differences of birth, wealth, or background – are relevant bases for allocating developmental opportunities.

8. *Approximate justice:* No one would wish to argue that liberal societies comply with strict standards of distributive justice; but overall, liberal societies have displayed a tendency toward justice. Their characteristic allocation of resources is the product of the three principles that form the basis of distributive justice: need-based claims stemming from the simple fact of individual existence, desert-based claims arising from differences of individual endeavor and contribution, and choice-based claims arising from the individual disposition of assets legitimately held. That these components of social justice are institutionalized in the liberal polity is, of course, not sufficient to guarantee just outcomes, which depend on the unending quest for an appropriate balance between the equality of human needs and the inequality of human capacities.

9. *Openness to truth:* No polity is completely comfortable with the unfettered pursuit and promulgation of truth. But liberal societies are to an unusual degree open to truth. This fact is reflected in the diversity of their universities and research institutes, public and private, and in the freedom of scholars to investigate what they please and to communicate with their peers and with the public. It is reflected, as well, in their political institutions: in the freedom and diversity of the press; in the volume of officially generated information and argument in the public domain; and in a decision-making process dominated by norms of publicity, access, and discussion as opposed to concealment or coercion. Of course, the value of truth has been repeatedly denied and the norm of truth repeatedly violated in liberal societies. On the other hand, both public beliefs and public institutions in liberal societies have tended to oppose, and when possible to countermand, these betrayals.

10. *Respect for privacy:* Liberal polities recognize that not everything of importance to human beings occurs in the pub-

lic sphere or can be regulated by public decisions. Alongside the public domain lies a sphere of private sentiments and affections. Moreover, there is, as Hegel suggested, a realm of "absolute spirit" – art, religion, and philosophy. Each of these, although it affects and draws sustenance from the political sphere, in part escapes and transcends it. A sign of their inherent transcendence is the perversions that result when the political order attempts to extend total control over them: bombastic poetry, sculpture, and architecture; lifeless ceremony and false piety; Lysenkoist biology and Aryan physics; servile ideology cloaked in the proud robe of autonomous reason. The public and private domains are linked in a complex web of reciprocal impact and dependence. Accordingly, the achievement of appropriate relations between them is an endless task of imperfect adjustment. But at least liberal societies, unlike most others, are conscious of the necessity of this task and build this consciousness into their guiding principles and basic institutions.[12]

In the past generation, thinkers along the political spectrum from Irving Kristol to Jurgen Habermas have contended that liberalism is dependent on – and has depleted – the accumulated moral capital of revealed religion and premodern moral philosophy. If the argument of this book is correct, they are mistaken. Liberalism contains *within itself* the resources it needs to declare and to defend a conception of the good and virtuous life that is in no way truncated or contemptible. This is not to deny that religion and classical philosophy can support a liberal polity in important ways. Indeed, as I suggested in Chapter 12, many of America's founders embraced just such an understanding of the tradition they had inherited. But it is to deny that liberalism draws essential content and depth from these sources.

Notes

1. INTRODUCTION

1 Michael Oakeshott, *On Human Conduct* (Oxford: Clarendon Press, 1975). For a subtle discussion that reaches a more favorable conclusion, see David R. Mapel, "Civil Association and the Idea of Contingency," *Political Theory* 18, 3 (August 1990): 392–410. See also Richard Flathman, *The Practice of Political Authority* (Chicago: University of Chicago Press, 1980), pp. 51–71; and Flathman, *Toward a Liberalism* (Ithaca: Cornell University Press), chs. 1–3.

2 See, from very different standpoints, the responses to Francis Fukuyama's now-famous "end-of-history" thesis in *The National Interest* 16 (Summer 1989): 19–35; and Stephen Holmes, "The Permanent Structure of Antiliberal Thought," in Nancy Rosenblum, ed., *Liberalism and the Moral Life* (Cambridge, Mass.: Harvard University Press, 1989), pp. 227–53. Rosenblum's introduction to that volume provides a useful overview.

3 Richard Flathman, *Toward a Liberalism*, pp. 217–18.

4 Flathman, *Toward a Liberalism*, p. 219.

5 Judith Shklar, "The Liberalism of Fear," in Rosenblum, *Liberalism and the Moral Life*, pp. 21–38.

6 This is the basis on which I would build my reply to the kinds of concerns Judith Shklar expresses in "Injustice, Injury, and Inequality: An Introduction," in Frank Lucash, ed., *Justice and Equality: Here and Now* (Ithaca: Cornell University Press, 1986). See especially her discussion of equality of opportunity, pp. 20–23.

7 On the political consequences of cultural divisions, see Michael Barone, *Our Country* (New York: Free Press, 1990); Thomas Byrne Edsall, "The Hidden Role of Race," *The New Republic*,

July 30 – August 6, 1990, pp. 35–40; William A. Galston and Elain C. Kamarck, *The Politics of Evasion* (Washington, D.C.: Progressive Policy Institute, 1989).

8 Louis Hartz, *The Liberal Tradition in America* (New York: Harcourt, Brace, and World, 1955); Robert E. Lane, *Political Ideology* (New York: Free Press, 1962); Jennifer Hochschild, *What's Fair?: American Beliefs About Distributive Justice* (Cambridge, Mass.: Harvard University Press, 1981).

9 I began thinking and writing about this question a decade ago in my "Defending Liberalism," *American Political Science Review* 76 (1982): 621–29. Since then a substantial literature has developed. A significant addition to the literature is Robert Goodin and Andrew Reeve, *Liberal Neutrality* (London: Routledge, 1989). Other important contributions include Larry Alexander and Maimon Schwarzschild, "Liberalism, Neutrality, and Equality of Welfare vs. Equality of Resources," *Philosophy and Public Affairs* 16, 1 (Winter 1987): 85–110; Richard Arneson, "Neutrality and Utility," *Canadian Journal of Philosophy* 20, 2 (June 1990): 215–40; Bruce Douglass, Gerald Mara, and Henry Richardson, eds., *Liberalism and the Good* (New York: Routledge, 1990); Richard Flathman, "Egalitarian Blood and Skeptical Turnips," in Flathman, *Toward a Liberalism* (Ithaca: Cornell University Press, 1989), ch. 7; Patrick Neal, "Liberalism and Neutrality," *Polity* 17, 4 (Summer 1985): 664–84, "A Liberal Theory of the Good?" *Canadian Journal of Philosophy* 17,3 (September 1987): 567–82, and "Justice as Fairness: Political or Metaphysical?" *Political Theory* 18, 1 (February 1990): 24–50; Peter de Marneffe, "Liberalism, Liberty, and Neutrality," *Philosophy and Public Affairs* 19, 3 (Summer 1990): 253–74; David Paris, "The Theoretical Mystique: Neutrality, Plurality and the Defense of Liberalism," *American Journal of Political Science* 31, 4 (November 1987): 909–39; Michael J. Perry, "Neutral Politics?" *Review of Politics* 51, 4 (1989): 479–509. Joseph Raz, *The Morality of Freedom* (Oxford: Clarendon Press, 1986), chs. 5 and 6, and "Facing Diversity: The Case of Epistemic Abstinence," *Philosophy and Public Affairs* 19, 1 (Winter 1990): 3–46; Richard Rodewald, "Does Liberalism Rest on a Mistake?" *Canadian Journal of Philosophy* 15, 2 (June 1985): 231–51; Thomas A. Spragens, Jr., "Reconstructing Liberal Theory: Reason and Liberal Culture," in Alfonso J. Damico, ed., *Liberals on Liberalism* (Totowa, N.J.: Rowman and Littlefield, 1986), pp. 34–53; Robert

Thigpen and Lyle Downing, "Liberalism and the Neutrality Principle," *Political Theory* 11, 4 (November 1983): 585–600; Jeremy Waldron, "Theoretical Foundations of Liberalism," *The Philosophical Quarterly* 37, 147 (April 1987): 127–50.

Two theorists who broached the neutrality issue in the 1970s are Brian Barry, *The Liberal Theory of Justice* (Oxford: Clarendon Press, 1973); and Vinit Haksar, *Equality, Liberty, and Perfectionism* (Oxford: Oxford University Press, 1979).

10 On the current British situation, see Alan Ryan, "From 1688 to 1791 by Way of 1990," in Michael Lacey and Knud Haakonssen, eds., *A Culture of Rights: The Bill of Rights in Philosophy, Politics, and Law – 1791 and 1991* (Cambridge: Cambridge University Press, in press).

2. PEIRCE'S CABLE AND PLATO'S CAVE

1 Richard Bernstein, *Beyond Objectivism and Relativism: Science, Hermeneutics, and Praxis* (Philadelphia: University of Pennsylvania Press, 1985).

2 Richard Rorty, *Contingency, Irony, and Solidarity* (Cambridge: Cambridge University Press, 1989), p. 50.

3 Rorty, *Contingency, Irony, and Solidarity*, p. 48.

4 Charles Larmore, review of Alasdair MacIntyre's *Whose Justice? Which Rationality?*, in *Journal of Philosophy* 86, 8 (August 1989): 437–38.

5 Rorty, *Contingency, Irony, and Solidarity*, p. 50.

6 Larmore, review of MacIntyre, p. 438.

7 John Rawls, "Political Constructivism and Public Justification," unpublished.

8 For a fuller discussion of MacIntyre, and also Walzer, see Chapter 3.

9 Thomas Nagel, *The View from Nowhere* (Oxford: Oxford University Press, 1986), p. 10.

10 Michael Walzer, *Interpretation and Social Criticism* (Cambridge, Mass.: Harvard University Press, 1987). For further discussion see Chapter 3, Section I.

11 James Fishkin, *Justice, Equal Opportunity, and the Family* (New Haven: Yale University Press, 1983).

12 John Rawls, "The Domain of the Political and Overlapping Consensus," unpublished.

13 Quoted in Bernstein, *Beyond Objectivism and Relativism*, p. 224.

14 John Rawls, "The Independence of Moral Theory," *Proceedings and Addresses of the American Philosophical Association* 48 (1974–75): 6.

15 Walzer, *Interpretation and Social Criticism*, pp. 23–25. For Walzer's most direct affirmation of (minimalist) universalism, see his review of Stuart Hampshire's *Innocence and Experience* in *The New Republic* (January 22, 1990): 39–41.

16 H. L. A. Hart, *The Concept of Law* (Oxford: Clarendon, 1961), p. 188.

17 Judith Shklar, *Ordinary Vices* (Cambridge, Mass.: Harvard University Press, 1984); Shklar, "Giving Injustice Its Due," *The Yale Law Journal*, 98 (1989): 1135–51; and Shklar, "Injustice, Injury, and Inequality," in Frank Lucash, ed., *Justice and Equality: Here and Now* (Ithaca: Cornell University Press, 1986).

18 Stuart Hampshire, *Morality and Conflict* (Cambridge, Mass.: Harvard University Press, 1983), pp. 142–43.

19 On some plausible interpretations this is true of even the most ardent contemporary localists. For example, Larmore insists that "MacIntyre is not making the self-defeating claim that there is no idea of rationality shared by all traditions. The norm of avoiding logical inconsistency belongs to neutral ground, as does presumably the norm of progressiveness" (Larmore, review of MacIntyre, p. 439). And Rorty's notion of human solidarity, which rests on the alleged distinction between "questions about pain" and "questions about the point of human life," looks suspiciously like a universalism that dares not speak its name (Rorty, *Contingency, Irony, and Solidarity*, p. 198). On this point, see Richard Flathman, review of *Contingency, Irony, and Solidarity*, *Political Theory* 18, 2 (May 1990): 308–12.

20 Bernard Williams, *Moral Luck* (Cambridge: Cambridge University Press, 1981); Martha Nussbaum, *The Fragility of Goodness* (Cambridge: Cambridge University Press, 1986); Charles Larmore, *Patterns of Moral Complexity* (Cambridge: Cambridge University Press, 1987).

21 David Mapel, *Social Justice Reconsidered: The Problem of Appropriate Precision in a Theory of Justice* (Urbana: University of Illinois Press, 1989).

22 Fishkin, *Justice, Equal Opportunity, and the Family*, p. 193.

23 Brian Barry, *Political Argument* (London: Routledge and Kegan Paul, 1965), pp. 3–8.

3. CONTEMPORARY CRITICS OF LIBERALISM

1 One vigorous effort to do this is Stephen Holmes, "The Permanent Structure of Antiliberal Thought," in Nancy L. Rosenblum, ed., *Liberalism and the Moral Life* (Cambridge, Mass.: Harvard University Press, 1989), pp. 227–53. Jeremy Waldron surveys criticisms of liberal-rights theory in Waldron, ed., *Nonsense upon Stilts* (London: Methuen, 1987), ch. 6. Will Kymlicka takes on two leading "communitarians" (Charles Taylor and Michael Sandel) in his *Liberalism, Community, and Culture* (Oxford: Clarendon Press, 1989), chs. 4 and 5.

2 In singling out Walzer, Unger, and MacIntyre for discussion in this chapter, I do not mean to suggest that they represent anything like a unified antiliberal position, let alone a single affirmative program. Indeed, one is likely to come away with a livelier sense of their differences than of their agreements. Of the three, Walzer is the most sympathetic to liberalism; his strategy is to argue that a consistent and realistic liberalism rests on shared social understandings and overlaps democratic socialism. Unger appropriates the liberal discourse of rights for his own democratic/redistributive/expressive purposes and even ventures to characterize his position as "superliberalism." Of the three, MacIntyre is probably the most systematically hostile to the vocabulary, theory, and practice of liberalism. Indeed, antiliberalism is one of the few consistent elements of a philosophical quest that has led him from Trotsky to Aristotle to (most recently) Thomas Aquinas.

3 Jeremy Waldron, *Nonsense upon Stilts*, p. 229; Nancy Rosenblum, *Another Liberalism* (Cambridge, Mass.: Harvard University Press, 1987), pp. 165–66.

4 Kymlicka, *Liberalism, Community, and Culture*, p. 72, n. 6.

5 Nancy Rosenblum, "Moral Membership in a Postliberal State," *World Politics* 36, 4 (July 1984): 586.

6 Michael Walzer, *Spheres of Justice* (New York: Basic Books, 1983), p. 29.

7 Walzer, *Spheres of Justice*, p. 9n.

8 Walzer, *Spheres of Justice*, p. 250n.

9 Michael Walzer, *Interpretation and Social Criticism* (Cambridge, Mass.: Harvard University Press, 1987), pp. 41–43.

10 Walzer, *Interpretation and Social Criticism*, pp. 9–11; Walzer, *Spheres of Justice*, p. xiv.

11 Walzer, *Spheres of Justice*, p. 314.
12 See Richard Rorty, "Solidarity or Objectivity?" in John Rajchman and Cornel West, eds., *Post-analytic Philosophy* (New York: Columbia University Press, 1985), pp. 3–19.
13 Walzer, *Spheres of Justice*, p. 314.
14 Michael Walzer, *Just and Unjust Wars* (New York: Basic Books, 1977), p. 54.
15 See Walzer, *Spheres of Justice*, p. xv.
16 Walzer, *Interpretation and Social Criticism*, pp. 24–25. In a recent review of Stuart Hampshire's *Innocence and Experience*, Walzer has further clarified his position. He now contends that the alleged battle between moral universalists and moral relativists is "mock-epic" because both positions are "caricatures." The real argument, he insists, is between "moral minimalists and moral maximalists, the first group seeking to limit the impact of universal principles (which they acknowledge), the second seeking to extend their reach (but not everywhere)." Moral minimalism seeks to throw up barriers "against evils about which there could be no disagreement" while opening up space for the rich and diverse "furnishing of the cultural imagination" ("The Minimalist," *The New Republic*, [January 22, 1990]: 39–41). I agree completely with this sensible formulation, which invites the classic liberal inquiry into the principles and institutions most conducive to warding off these evils. I would observe only that the minimalist/maximalist thesis necessitates some qualification of propositions that Walzer previously seemed to advance as general and unqualified.
17 Walzer, *Interpretation and Social Criticism*, p. 45.
18 Walzer, *Spheres of Justice*, p. 314.
19 Walzer, *Interpretation and Social Criticism*, pp. 46–48.
20 Walzer, *Interpretation and Social Criticism*, pp. 62–64.
21 See Michael Walzer, "Philosophy and Democracy," *Political Theory* 9, 3 (August 1981): 393.
22 Walzer, *Interpretation and Social Criticism*, p. 24.
23 Michael Walzer, *Radical Principles* (New York: Basic Books, 1980), p. 13.
24 Walzer, "Philosophy and Democracy," p. 383.
25 Walzer, *Spheres of Justice*, pp. 303–4.
26 Walzer, *Spheres of Justice*, p. 285.
27 Walzer, *Interpretation and Social Criticism*, pp. 20–21.
28 Walzer, *Spheres of Justice*, pp. 286–87.

29 Walzer, *Spheres of Justice*, p. 99.

30 Walzer, "Philosophy and Democracy," pp. 389–93.

31 For the argument of this paragraph, see Walzer, "Philosophy and Democracy," passim.

32 Michael Walzer, "Liberalism and the Art of Separation," *Political Theory* 12, 3 (August 1984): 326.

33 Walzer, "Philosophy and Democracy," p. 384; Walzer, *Spheres of Justice*, pp. 282–4.

34 Walzer, *Spheres of Justice*, p. 15n.

35 Walzer, "Liberalism and the Art of Separation," p. 328.

36 Daniel Bell, *The Cultural Contradictions of Capitalism* (New York: Basic Books, 1976), p. 14.

37 Robert Unger, *Politics*, in three volumes: vol. 1: *Social Theory: Its Situation and Its Task*; Vol. 2: *False Necessity: Anti-necessitarian Social Theory in the Service of Radical Democracy*; and Vol. 3: *Plasticity into Power: Comparative-Historical Studies on the Historical Conditions of Economic and Military Success* (all three, Cambridge: Cambridge University Press, 1987).

38 Unger, *Passion: An Essay on Personality* (New York: Free Press, 1984), p. 297.

39 Unger, *Passion*, p. 296.

40 Unger, *Passion*, pp. 109, 111, 114.

41 Unger, *False Necessity*, p. 579.

42 Unger, *Passion*, p. 165.

43 Unger, *Social Theory*, p. 65.

44 Unger, *Passion*, p. 73.

45 Unger, *False Necessity*, p. 524.

46 Unger, *False Necessity*, pp. 514–15.

47 Unger, *False Necessity*, p. 558.

48 Unger, *False Necessity*, pp. 572–73.

49 Unger, *Social Theory*, pp. 10, 145–46.

50 Unger, *False Necessity*, pp. 8–9.

51 Robert Unger, *The Critical Legal Studies Movement* (Cambridge, Mass.: Harvard University Press, 1986), p. 94.

52 Unger, *Passion*, p. 267.

53 Unger, *Social Theory*, p. 46.

54 Alasdair MacIntyre, *After Virtue* (Notre Dame: University of Notre Dame Press, 1981), p. 22. In this critique of MacIntyre I shall focus on *After Virtue*, where his critique of liberalism is most fully developed, rather than his more recent *Whose Justice? Which Rationality?* (Notre Dame: University of Notre Dame

Press, 1988). Although, as Charles Larmore has pointed out, there are some significant shifts between the two books, none affect the issues discussed here. As MacIntyre himself declares, the changes of mind since *After Virtue* do not affect "any of its main contentions" (*Whose Justice? Which Rationality?* p. x). My procedure simply takes him at his word.

55 MacIntyre, *After Virtue*, pp. 244–45.
56 MacIntyre, *After Virtue*, p. 33.
57 MacIntyre, *After Virtue*, p. 50.
58 MacIntyre, *After Virtue*, p. 56.
59 MacIntyre, *After Virtue*, p. 241.
60 MacIntyre, *After Virtue*, pp. vii–viii, 103, 242–44.
61 MacIntyre, *After Virtue*, p. 241.
62 MacIntyre, *After Virtue*, p. 34.
63 MacIntyre, *After Virtue*, pp. 22–23.
64 MacIntyre, *After Virtue*, p. 103.
65 MacIntyre, *After Virtue*, p. 236.
66 Although explicit concern for the virtues is not as absent as many analysts suppose. See Chapter 10. And for a reading of the Declaration of Independence that restores its reliance on virtue and duty without embracing Garry Wills's affective communitarian interpretation, see my "Practical Philosophy and the Bill of Rights: Perspectives on Some Contemporary Issues," in Michael Lacey and Knud Haakonssen, eds., *A Culture of Rights: The Bill of Rights in Philosophy, Politics, and Law – 1791 and 1991* (Cambridge: Cambridge University Press, in press).
67 MacIntyre, *After Virtue*, p. 183.
68 MacIntyre, *After Virtue*, p. 21.
69 For an elaboration, see Chapter 12.
70 MacIntyre, *After Virtue*, p. 134.
71 Isaiah Berlin, *Four Essays on Liberty* (London: Oxford University Press, 1969), p. 169.
72 MacIntyre, *After Virtue*, pp. 6–7.
73 MacIntyre, *After Virtue*, p. 208.
74 To be sure, rights may be understood as reflecting a privileged status for certain human goods or interests that are taken to be fundamental. But notoriously, rights themselves come into conflict with one another. What then?
75 MacIntyre, *After Virtue*, p. 208.
76 MacIntyre, *After Virtue*, p. 119; emphasis added.
77 Berlin, *Four Essays on Liberty*, p. 172.

78 For stimulating examinations of Walzer, see Nancy Rosenblum, *Another Liberalism*, pp. 165–74; and Ian Shapiro, *Political Criticism* (Berkeley: University of California Press, 1990), ch. 3. For Unger, see Robin W. Lovin and Michael J. Perry, eds., *Critique and Construction: A Symposium on Roberto Unger's Politics* (Cambridge: Cambridge University Press, 1990).

4. LIBERALISM AND THE NEUTRAL STATE

1 Brian Barry, *The Liberal Theory of Justice* (Oxford: Clarendon Press, 1973), p. 126.
2 John Rawls, *A Theory of Justice* (Cambridge, Mass.: Harvard University Press, 1971), p. 19.
3 Ronald Dworkin, "Liberalism," in Stuart Hampshire, ed., *Public and Private Morality* (Cambridge: Cambridge University Press, 1978), p. 127.
4 Bruce Ackerman, *Social Justice in the Liberal State* (New Haven: Yale University Press, 1980), p. 11.
5 In *A Theory of Justice*, Rawls's "primary goods" represented another example of neutral universal means. But as we shall see in Chapter 6, he has subsequently revised his account so as to link primary goods with a restricted set of important interests.
6 Immanuel Kant, "On the Common Saying, 'This May Be True in Theory, but It Does Not Apply in Practice,' " in Hans Reiss, ed., *Kant's Political Writings* (Cambridge: Cambridge University Press, 1970), p. 73. See also *The Metaphysical Elements of Justice*, trans. John Ladd (Indianapolis: Bobbs-Merrill, 1965), p. 35.
7 Kant, "On the Common Saying," p. 85; emphasis added.
8 Immanuel Kant, *The Metaphysical Principles of Virtue*, trans. James Ellington (Indianapolis: Bobbs-Merrill, 1964), p. 145.
9 Kant, *The Metaphysical Principles of Virtue*, p. 44.
10 George Kelly, *Idealism, Politics and History: Sources of Hegelian Thought* (Cambridge: Cambridge University Press, 1969), pp. 170–74.
11 Charles Taylor, "What's Wrong with Negative Liberty" in Alan Ryan, ed., *The Idea of Freedom: Essays in Honour of Isaiah Berlin* (Oxford: Oxford University Press, 1979), p. 183. See also Richard Flathman, *Toward a Liberalism* (Ithaca: Cornell University Press, 1989), ch. 4.

12 Gerald Dworkin, "Paternalism," in Richard Wasserstrom, ed., *Morality and the Law* (Belmont, Cal.: Wadsworth, 1971), pp. 107–26; Douglas Husak, "Paternalism and Autonomy," *Philosophy and Public Affairs* 10 (1981): 27–46. Even Joel Feinberg, whose stance is far more hostile to paternalism than that of Dworkin and Husak, is prepared to countenance what he terms "soft paternalism" in circumstances in which the action in question is substantially nonvoluntary. See Feinberg, *Harm to Self* (New York: Oxford University Press, 1986), pp. 12–16.

13 See William A. Galston, *Justice and the Human Good* (Chicago: University of Chicago Press, 1980), pp. 55–56, 279–80.

14 See especially Ackerman, *Social Justice in the Liberal State*, pp. 368–69.

15 See Geoffrey Harrison, "Relativism and Tolerance," in Peter Laslett and James Fishkin, eds., *Philosophy, Politics, and Society;* 5th series (New Haven: Yale University Press, 1979), pp. 273–90; and Richard Tuck, "Skepticism and Toleration in the Seventeenth Century," in Susan Mendus, ed., *Justifying Toleration* (Cambridge: Cambridge University Press, 1988), pp. 21–35. I am indebted to Alfonso Damico for these references and for instructive discussion.

16 Ronald Dworkin, *Taking Rights Seriously* (Cambridge, Mass.: Harvard University Press, 1978), p. 272.

17 Ackerman, *Social Justice in the Liberal State*, pp. 54, 57, 373–74.

18 Rawls, *A Theory of Justice*, sects. 15, 23, 86–7. For a parallel effort to examine the hidden presuppositions of Rawls's theory (and, more broadly, of neutralist liberalism), see Vinit Haksar, *Equality, Liberty, and Perfectionism* (Oxford: Oxford University Press, 1979). While I am broadly sympathetic with Haksar's strategy of argument, I disagree with many of his specific arguments. The details of this disagreement are not germane here.

19 John Rawls, "Kantian Constructivism in Moral Theory: *The Dewey Lectures 1980,*" *Journal of Philosophy* 77, 9 (September 1980): 525.

20 Thomas Hobbes, *Leviathan* (New York: Macmillan, 1962), pp. 123–24; emphasis added.

21 Rawls, *A Theory of Justice*, p. 515.

22 John Rawls, "Fairness to Goodness," *Philosophical Review* 84 (1975): 549.

5. LIBERALISM AND NEUTRAL PUBLIC DISCOURSE

I am deeply indebted to Richard Arneson, "Neutrality and Utility," *Canadian Journal of Philosophy* 20, 2 (June 1990): 215–40. While I do not agree with Arneson's defense of subjectivist utilitarianism, I can no longer tell where his critique of liberal neutrality leaves off and mine begins. I am also indebted to Charles Larmore for initially stimulating these reflections, and for a steady stream of helpful criticism.

1 Joseph Raz, *The Morality of Freedom* (Oxford: Clarendon 1986), p. 265.

2 John Rawls, "The Idea of an Overlapping Consensus," *Oxford Journal of Legal Studies* 7, 1 (1987): 1–25; David Gauthier, *Morals by Agreement* (Oxford: Oxford University Press, 1986).

3 Charles Larmore, "Comment on Stephen Macedo, 'The Politics of Justification' " (unpublished), p. 3.

4 Charles Larmore, "Political Liberalism," *Political Theory* 18, 3 (August 1990): 346.

5 John Rawls, "The Priority of Right and Ideas of the Good," *Philosophy and Public Affairs* 17, 4 (Fall 1988): 262.

6 Charles Larmore, *Patterns of Moral Complexity* (Cambridge: Cambridge University Press, 1987), p. 43.

7 Larmore, *Patterns of Moral Complexity*, p. 44.

8 Richard Arneson, "Neutrality and Utility," pp. 218–19.

9 See especially Thomas Nagel, "Moral Conflict and Political Legitimacy," *Philosophy and Public Affairs* 16, 3 (Summer 1987): 226–27, 236–37.

10 For an argument emphasizing sincerity of intention, see Robert Audi, "The Separation of Church and State and the Obligations of Citizenship," *Philosophy and Public Affairs* 18, 3 (Summer 1989): 259–96.

11 Ackerman, "Why Dialogue?" *Journal of Philosophy* 86, 1 (January 1989): 16.

12 Ackerman, "Why Dialogue?" pp. 16–17, 20.

13 Ackerman, "Why Dialogue?" p. 20.

14 Ackerman, "Why Dialogue?" p. 17.

15 Larmore, *Patterns of Moral Complexity*, p. 53.

16 Larmore, *Patterns of Moral Complexity*, p. 60.

17 Ackerman, "Why Dialogue?" p. 13.

18 Ackerman, "Why Dialogue?" p. 8.

19 Larmore, "Political Liberalism," pp. 348–49.
20 Larmore, "Political Liberalism," p. 349.
21 Larmore, *Patterns of Moral Complexity,* p. 68.
22 Nagel, "Moral Conflict and Political Legitimacy," p. 231.
23 Nagel, "Moral Conflict and Political Legitimacy," p. 232.
24 Nagel, "Moral Conflict and Political Legitimacy," p. 236.
25 John Rawls, "On the Idea of Free Public Reason" (unpublished), pp. 7, 12–13.
26 Nagel, "Moral Conflict and Political Legitimacy," pp. 234–35.
27 Kent Greenawalt, "Rescuing Liberal Democracy from Its Defenders" (unpublished), p. 10.
28 Amy Gutmann and Dennis Thompson, "Moral Conflict and Political Consensus," in R. Bruce Douglass et al., eds., *Liberalism and the Good* (New York: Routledge, 1990), pp. 125–34.
29 Gutmann and Thompson, "Moral Conflict and Political Consensus," p. 130.
30 Thomas Jefferson, quoted and discussed in Walter Berns, *The First Amendment and the Future of American Democracy* (Chicago: Gateway, 1985), p. 36.
31 Jon Gunneman, "A Theological Defense of the Brute: The Christian Stake in Liberalism" (unpublished), pp. 22–23.
32 Gunneman, "Theological Defense," p. 26.
33 It was only after this chapter had been drafted that two important treatments of neutral dialogue appeared in print: Michael J. Perry, "Neutral Politics?" *Review of Politics* 51, 4 (1989): 479–509, and Joseph Raz, "Facing Diversity: The Case of Epistemic Abstinence," *Philosophy and Public Affairs* 19, 1 (Winter 1990): 3–46. These articles should be consulted for arguments that in different ways parallel and complement the analysis offered in this chapter.

6. MORAL PERSONALITY AND LIBERAL THEORY

1 John Rawls, *A Theory of Justice* (Cambridge, Mass.: Harvard University Press, 1971).
2 John Rawls, "The Basic Liberties and Their Priority," in Sterling M. McMurrin, ed., *The Tanner Lectures on Human Values III (1982)* (Salt Lake City: University of Utah Press, 1982), p. 21n.
3 John Rawls, "Kantian Constructivism in Moral Theory: The

Dewey Lectures 1980," *Journal of Philosophy* 77, 9 (September 1980): 515–72.

4   Remarkably, this alteration in the *basis* of primary goods effects no changes whatever in the *enumeration* of these goods. Rawls simply sketches a brief explanation of why the interest in moral personality leads parties in the original position to pursue the primary goods set forth in *A Theory of Justice*. But the fit between the new basis of primary goods and their unchanged content seems less than perfect. For example, Rawls argues that basic liberties "allow for the development and exercise of the sense of ... justice" (DL, p. 526). This is in a way true. But one might rather argue that basic liberties allow for the development and expression of a *wide range* of moral positions and characteristics, many of which pull, directly or indirectly, against the sense of justice. Basic liberties enable those who doubt the rationality of justice, or scorn it altogether, to constitute a portion of the public culture that educates the young. In modern democracies anyway, basic liberties seem to promote license at least as much as self-restraint – hardly a promising backdrop for the inculcation of virtues, such as justice, that demand restraint. This problem is especially serious if, as Aristotle argued, an effective sense of justice cuts across the grain of human nature, at least for most people, and can be fostered only through a rigorously directive system of moral education, backed by the full power of political and social institutions. Thus, the question whether the sense of justice is more effectively promoted in an open society or in a suitably designed closed society cannot be regarded as settled.

5   John Rawls, "Fairness to Goodness," *Philosophical Review* 84 (October 1975): 537.

6   See Chapter 4.

7   For more than a decade, critics such as A. K. Sen have argued that Rawls's theory is in principle incapable of dealing with the problem of special needs. To the best of my knowledge, Rawls has never offered a full response. The Dewey Lectures simply rule the question out of court. Rawls stipulates that no party in the original position "suffers from unusual needs that are especially difficult to fulfill ... [T]he fundamental problem of social justice arises between those who are full and active ... participants in society" (DL, p. 546). He goes on to talk vaguely about extending the theory, so conceived, to hard

cases. But he never does so, and it is difficult to see how he could do so in a manner consistent with his basic approach. Unusual and costly needs present difficulties that simply cannot be addressed by an index of primary goods. For a discussion, see G. A. Cohen, "On the Currency of Egalitarian Justice," *Ethics* 99, 4 (July 1989): 906–44.

8 Bernard Williams, "Persons, Character and Morality," in Amelie Oksenberg Rorty, ed., *The Identities of Persons* (Berkeley: University of California Press, 1976), pp. 210, 215.

9 This is roughly the Platonic–Aristotelian view as I understand it. One can imagine a variant of the perfectionist interpretation that does give priority to justice, so defined.

10 In this respect, at least, Rawls is squarely in the Kantian tradition. Early on in the *Foundations of the Metaphysics of Morals*, ed. Robert Paul Wolff (Indianapolis: Bobbs-Merrill, 1969), Kant declares that nothing is good without qualification except a good will. He proceeds to examine the classical virtues – wisdom, courage, moderation – showing that each can be viewed as evil in certain circumstances. But he excludes justice from this critique, apparently because he cannot see how justice could ever be evil. Indeed, Kant comes very close to equating the good will with justice.

11 Robert Nozick, *Anarchy, State, and Utopia* (New York: Basic Books, 1974), pp. 224–27.

12 Michael Zuckert, "Justice Deserted: A Critique of Rawls' *A Theory of Justice*," *Polity* 13, 3: 477.

13 For related discussions, see George Sher, *Desert* (Princeton: Princeton University Press, 1987), chs. 2; and Vinit Haksar, *Equality, Liberty, and Perfectionism* (Oxford: Oxford University Press, 1979), chs. 2–4, 10.

14 For an exceptionally clear discussion, see James S. Fishkin, *Justice, Equal Opportunity, and the Family* (New Haven: Yale University Press, 1983).

15 Immanuel Kant, *The Doctrine of Virtue*, Mary J. Gregor, trans. (New York: Harper and Row, 1964), p. 111.

16 Patrick Riley, "Practical Reason and Respect for Persons in the Kantian Republic" (paper delivered at the 1981 Annual Meeting of the American Political Science Association).

17 This is the essence of my disagreement with Charles Larmore's defense of Rawls on this point. See Larmore, "Political Liberalism," *Political Theory* 18, 3 (August 1990): 354–57.

18 Obviously this parallel with Hegel cannot be extended very far. Hegel contended that to bring a community to full self-consciousness is to make manifest its latent contradictions. Rawls appears to believe that this very process is the vehicle for *eliminating* contradictions. Specifically, Rawls believes in the possibility of a recognizably liberal society (and theory) in which all significant internal tensions have been overcome.

19 For a fuller discussion of these points, see William A. Galston, *Justice and the Human Good* (Chicago: University of Chicago Press, 1980), pp. 13–16.

7. PLURALISM AND SOCIAL UNITY

1 To avoid misunderstanding, I stress here that in this chapter and throughout this book, I am using the term "pluralism" more or less as Rawls does – that is, as a synonym for diversity. It does not refer to the socioinstitutional pluralist theory debated in political science over the past generation. Nor does it refer to the moral theory of pluralism, which "asserts that there are many valid forms of human self-realization" (Charles Larmore, "Political Liberalism," *Political Theory* 18, 3 [August 1990]: 340). The thesis I set forth in Chapter 8 is in fact a species of moral pluralism, but that is not what is at issue in this chapter.

2 William A. Galston, "Defending Liberalism," *American Political Science Review* 76, 3 (September 1982): 625–26. A revised version of this article appears as Chapter 3 of this book.

3 John Rawls, "The Priority of Right and Ideas of the Good," *Philosophy and Public Affairs* 17, 4 (Fall 1988): 254.

4 John Rawls, "The Idea of an Overlapping Consensus," *Oxford Journal of Legal Studies* 7, 1 (1987): 4.

5 Rawls, "Overlapping Consensus," p. 5.

6 Rawls, "Overlapping Consensus," p. 13n.

7 Rawls, "Priority of Right," pp. 269–70.

8 Rawls, "Priority of Right," pp. 251–52.

9 John Rawls, "Dewey Lectures," p. 525. See note 3 to Chapter for full reference information.

10 Rawls, "Priority of Right," p. 251.

11 Rawls, "Priority of Right," p. 265.

12 Rawls, "Overlapping Consensus," pp. 9, 17, 21–2. See also

his "Priority of Right," pp. 252–53, 274–5, and also his "Dewey Lectures," pp. 552–53.

13 Bernard Williams, "Persons, Character and Morality," in Amelie Oksenberg Rorty, ed., *The Identities of Persons* (Berkeley: University of California Press, 1976), pp. 210, 215.

14 Rawls, "Priority of Right," p. 275.

15 Michael Sandel, "The Procedural Republic and the Unencumbered Self," *Political Theory* 12, 1 (February 1984): 90–91.

16 John Rawls, "Justice as Fairness: Political Not Metaphysical," *Philosophy and Public Affairs* 14, 3 (Summer 1985): 237–39; hereafter cited as "Political Not Metaphysical."

17 Amy Gutmann, "Communitarian Critics of Liberalism," *Philosophy and Public Affairs* 14, 3 (Summer 1985): 319. See also Rawls's own qualifications in "Political Not Metaphysical," p. 240n.

18 For a fuller discussion of the abortion controversy in the context of state neutrality, see Chapter 12.

19 Rawls, "Overlapping Consensus," p. 14.

20 Parallel arguments have been developed by Will Kymlicka in *Liberalism, Community, and Culture* (Oxford: Clarendon Press, 1989), pp. 55–56; and Robert Post, "Tradition, the Self, and Substantive Due Process: A Comment on Michael Sandel," *California Law Review* 77 (May 1989): 557–58. Post very pertinently refers to George Herbert Mead's distinction between the socially constituted "me-self" and the socially critical "I-self" as support for such a position.

21 John Rawls, *Theory of Justice* (Cambridge, Mass.: Harvard University Press, 1971), p. 587. In written communications and private conversations, Charles Larmore and Thomas Pogge suggested to me that there is no sharp break between the earlier and later Rawls and that this quotation is perfectly consistent with the conception of political philosophy Rawls now explicitly embraces. (See also Larmore, "Political Liberalism," p. 360, n. 29.) I confess that I am not convinced. But even if this exegetical point were granted, little of significance would change: My argument against Rawls's current conception would simply have to be read back into *Theory of Justice* as well.

22 Rawls, "Dewey Lectures," p. 518; Rawls, "Political Not Metaphysical," p. 225.

23 Rawls, "Political Not Metaphysical," p. 230.

24 Rawls, "Political Not Metaphysical," p. 229.

25 Rawls, "Dewey Lectures," pp. 524, 562.

26 I am indebted to Richard Arneson for this suggestion.

27 On this point, and to roughly the same effect, see also Jeremy
    Waldron, "Particular Values and Critical Morality," *California
    Law Review* 77, 3 (May 1989): 576; Kymlicka, *Liberalism, Com-
    munity, and Culture*, pp. 65–66; Ronald Dworkin, "What Justice
    Isn't," in his *A Matter of Principle* (Cambridge, Mass.: Harvard
    University Press, 1985), pp. 214–20.

28 Rawls, "The Dewey Lectures," p. 551.

8. LIBERAL GOODS

1 T. M. Scanlon, "Preference and Urgency," *Journal of Philosophy*
   72, 19 (November 6, 1975): 655–68.

2 Michael Ignatieff, *The Needs of Strangers* (New York: Viking
   Penguin, 1985), p. 136.

3 Amartya Sen, "Equality of What?" in Sterling McMurrin, ed.,
   The Tanner Lectures on Human Values (Salt Lake City: University
   of Utah Press, 1980), p. 213; "Well-being, Agency and Freedom: The Dewey Lectures 1984," *Journal of Philosophy* 82, 4
   (April 1985): 186.

4 Judith Shklar, *Ordinary Vices* (Cambridge, Mass.: Harvard University Press, 1984), pp. 8–9.

5 James Griffin, *Well-Being: Its Meaning, Measurement, and Moral
   Importance* (Oxford: Clarendon Press, 1986), pp. 58, 70.

6 Stuart Hampshire, *Innocence and Experience* (Cambridge, Mass.:
   Harvard University Press, 1989), pp. 28–29.

7 Hampshire, *Innocence and Experience*, pp. 137–42; Sen, "Equality of What?" p. 219; Martha C. Nussbaum, "Non-relative Virtues: An Aristotelian Approach," in Peter A. French, Theodore
   E. Uehling, Jr., and Howard K. Wettstein, eds., *Midwest Studies
   in Philosophy XII; Ethical Theory: Character and Virtue* (Notre
   Dame: University of Notre Dame Press, 1988), p. 38. See also
   Chapter 2.

8 Hampshire, *Innocence and Experience*, p. 33.

9 Immanuel Kant, *Foundations of the Metaphysics of Morals*, ed.
   Robert Paul Wolff (Indianapolis: Bobbs-Merrill, 1969), pp. 5–
   6.

10 Aristotle, *Nicomachean Ethics* 1178a: 8–21.

11 Nussbaum, "Non-relative Virtues," p. 42. For a converging

view from a very different point of departure, see Griffin, *Well-Being*, p. 70.

12 Nussbaum, "Non-relative Virtues," pp. 43–45.

13 Judith Shklar, "Giving Injustice Its Due," *Yale Law Journal* 98 (1989): 1135–51.

14 Hampshire, *Innocence and Experience*, pp. 90–91.

15 Aristotle, *Nicomachean Ethics* 1094b 13–28.

16 Richard E. Flathman, *Toward a Liberalism* (Ithaca: Cornell University Press, 1989), p. 116.

17 Scanlon, "Preference and Urgency," p. 655.

18 Sen, "Equality of What?" pp. 215–16. As the discussion in Chapter 6 suggests, the reformulated conception of primary goods offered in Rawls's Dewey Lectures and Tanner Lectures may evade this objection.

19 John Rawls, *A Theory of Justice* (Cambridge, Mass.: Harvard University Press, 1971), pp. 30–31; Rawls, "Social Unity and Primary Goods," in Amartya Sen and Bernard Williams, eds., *Utilitarianism and Beyond* (Cambridge: Cambridge University Press, 1982), pp. 168–69; G. A. Cohen, "On the Currency of Egalitarian Justice," *Ethics* 99, 4 (July 1989): 912–13.

20 Scanlon, "Preference and Urgency," p. 661.

21 Sen, "Well-being, Agency, and Freedom," pp. 195–200; Nussbaum, "Nature, Function, and Capability: Aristotle on Political Distribution," WIDER working paper (Helsinki), pp. 7–14.

22 Cohen, "On the Currency of Egalitarian Justice," p. 935.

23 Griffin, *Well-Being*, p. 47.

24 Richard J. Arneson, "Equality and Equal Opportunity for Welfare," *Philosophical Studies* 56, 1 (May 1989): 92–93.

25 Sen, "Equality of What?" p. 216.

26 Hampshire, *Innocence and Experience*, p. 87.

27 Nussbaum, "Nature, Function, and Capability," p. 38; Martha C. Nussbaum, *The Fragility of Goodness: Luck and Ethics in Greek Tragedy and Philosophy* (Cambridge: Cambridge University Press, 1986), ch. 8; William A. Galston, *Justice and the Human Good* (Chicago: University of Chicago Press, 1980), p. 59.

28 Griffin, *Well-Being*, ch. 5; Scanlon, "Preference and Urgency," pp. 662–63; Flathman, *Toward a Liberalism*, pp. 136–39; Sen, "Equality of What?" p. 208; Thomas Nagel, "Equality," in his *Mortal Questions* (Cambridge: Cambridge University Press, 1979), p. 125.

29 Griffin, *Well-Being*, pp. 81, 83–84, 91.

30 See, for example, John Finnis, *Natural Law and Natural Rights* (Oxford: Clarendon Press, 1980), chs. 3–4.
31 Flathman, *Toward a Liberalism*, pp. 114–16.
32 David Mapel, *Social Justice Reconsidered: The Problem of Appropriate Precision in a Theory of Justice* (Urbana: University of Illinois Press, 1989), pp. 84–93. Mapel goes on to argue that similar problems afflict Rawls's effort to construct a unitary index from the heterogeneous elements that comprise his primary goods. See also Arneson, "Equality and Equal Opportunity for Welfare," p. 91.
33 Sen, "Well-Being, Agency and Freedom," p. 198.
34 Douglas Besharov, "Crack Babies: The Worst Threat Is Mom Herself," *Washington Post*, August 6, 1989, B1.
35 For Michael Walzer's discussion, see his *Spheres of Justice* (New York: Basic Books, 1983), ch. 3.
36 For useful full-length treatments of need, see Garrett Thomson, *Needs* (London: Routledge and Kegan Paul, 1988); David Braybrooke, *Meeting Needs* (Princeton: Princeton University Press, 1987).
37 For the most detailed recent discussion, see George Sher, *Desert* (Princeton: Princeton University Press, 1987).
38 For an extended theoretical discussion of these points, see my *Justice and the Human Good*, ch. 6. For an empirical examination of the considerations bearing on the determination of "importance" within our society, see Karol Soltan, *The Causal Theory of Justice* (Berkeley: University of California Press, 1987).
39 John Rawls, "The Basic Structure as Subject," *American Philosophical Quarterly* 14, 2 (April 1977): 162, 163.
40 Mapel, *Social Justice Reconsidered*, p. 27.
41 Soltan, *The Causal Theory of Justice*, pt. II.

9. LIBERAL JUSTICE

1 See Chapters 6 and 7.
2 Ronald Dworkin, *Taking Rights Seriously* (Cambridge, Mass.: Harvard University Press, 1978), pp. 272–3.
3 For another treatment of this topic, with which I am in general agreement, see S. J. D. Green, "Competitive Equality of Opportunity: A Defense," *Ethics* 100 (October 1989): 5–32. See also James S. Fishkin, *Justice, Equal Opportunity and the Family* (New Haven: Yale University Press, 1983); and Ellen Frankel

Paul, Fred D. Miller, Jeffrey Paul, and John Ahrens, eds., *Equal Opportunity* (Oxford: Basil Blackwell, 1987).

4 William A. Galston, *Justice and the Human Good* (Chicago: University of Chicago Press, 1980), pp. 159–62.

5 Bernard Williams, "The Idea of Equality," in Peter Laslett and W. G. Runciman, eds., *Philosophy, Politics, and Society*, 2nd series (Oxford: Basil Blackwell, 1962), pp. 110–31.

6 Fishkin, *Justice, Equal Opportunity, and the Family*, chs. 1–3. Green's focus on equalization of educational opportunity, though sound, leaves Fishkin's central point intact; see Green, "Competitive Equality of Opportunity," pp. 30–32. For a skeptical view of equal educational opportunity, and by extension equal opportunity as such, see Christopher Jencks, "Whom Must We Treat Equally for Educational Opportunities to Be Equal?" *Ethics* 98, 3 (April 1988): 518–33.

7 Michael Zuckert, "Justice Deserted: A Critique of Rawls' *A Theory of Justice*," *Polity* 13 (1981): 477; Nozick, *Anarchy, State, and Utopia*, pp. 224–27; George Sher, *Desert* (Princeton: Princeton University Press, 1987), ch. 2.

8 Brian Barry extends this point pungently. In Rawls's hyperexpansive sense of moral arbitrariness, it must also be considered "radically contingent that the universe exists at all, that there is a planet capable of sustaining life, that human beings evolved on it, and so on. It seems to me that nothing of moral significance follows from this sort of radical contingency of everything. The only possible reply, when the issue is pitched at that level, is that things might have been different but they were not." Barry, "Equal Opportunity and Moral Arbitrariness," in Norman Bowie, ed., *Equal Opportunity* (Boulder, Colo.: Westview, 1988), p. 41.

9 On this point, see also Anthony T. Kronman, "Talent Pooling," in J. Roland Pennock and John Chapman, eds., *Human Rights: NOMOS XXIII* (New York: New York University Press, 1981), pp. 71–77.

10 G. A. Cohen, "Self-Ownership, World-Ownership, and Equality," in Frank S. Lucash, ed., *Justice and Equality: Here and Now* (Ithaca: Cornell University Press, 1986), pp. 110–12. For a broader discussion, see also G. A. Cohen, "On the Currency of Egalitarian Justice," *Ethics* 99, 4 (July 1989): 906–44.

11 Kronman, "Talent Pooling," pp. 76–77.

12 The same conclusion was reached by Green via a different

route (see "Competitive Equality of Opportunity," p. 16); by Alexander Rosenberg, "The Political Philosophy of Biological Endowments: Some Considerations," in Ellen Frankel Paul et al., eds., *Equal Opportunity*, pp. 1–31; and by Brian Barry, "Equal Opportunity and Moral Arbitrariness," in Bowie, ed., *Equal Opportunity*, pp. 33–43. For a warning against carrying the acceptance of social facts such as cultural differences or group attitudes too far, see James S. Fishkin, "Do We Need a Systematic Theory of Equal Opportunity?" in Bowie, ed., *Equal Opportunity*, pp. 18–20.

13 Norman Daniels ably discusses the issues just raised in his "Meritocracy," in John Arthur and William H. Shaw, eds., *Justice and Economic Distribution* (Englewood Cliffs, N.J.: Prentice-Hall, 1978), pp. 164–78. I am less sure than I once was, and than Daniels still is, that productivity represents the single best basis for understanding and justifying merit-based equality of opportunity. See the rest of Section III.

14 For a discussion, see George Sher, "Predicting Performance," in Ellen Frankel Paul et al., *Equal Opportunity*, pp. 188–203.

15 Galston, *Justice and the Human Good*, pp. 261–62.

16 Nozick, *Anarchy, State, and Utopia*, pp. 235–38.

17 John Schaar, "Equality of Opportunity, and Beyond," in J. Roland Pennock and John W. Chapman, eds., *Nomos 9: Equality* (New York: Atherton, 1967).

18 Michael Walzer, *Spheres of Justice: A Defense of Pluralism and Equality* (New York: Basic Books, 1983), p. 287.

19 For a more extended discussion of Walzer's views, see Chapter 3. For a more extended discussion of Jefferson in the context of liberal-democratic political excellence, see Chapter 10.

20 Judith Shklar, "Injustice, Injury, and Inequality: An Introduction," in Frank S. Lucash, ed., *Justice and Equality: Here and Now* (Ithaca: Cornell University Press, 1986), pp. 22–23. I do *not* mean to suggest that her stance toward equality of opportunity is wholly disapproving, or even on balance negative; see ibid., pp. 20–21.

10. LIBERAL VIRTUES

1 Leo Strauss, *Natural Right and History* (Chicago: University of Chicago Press, 1953); C. B. Macpherson, *The Political Theory of*

Possessive Individualism (London: Oxford University Press, 1962).

2 Martin Diamond, "Democracy and *The Federalist:* A Reconsideration of the Framers' Intent," *American Political Science Review* 53 (March 1959): 52–68; Gordon Wood, *The Creation of the American Republic, 1776–1787* (New York: Norton, 1969).

3 Robert Dahl, *A Preface to Democratic Theory* (Chicago: University of Chicago Press, 1956); Theodore Lowi, *The End of Liberalism* (New York: Norton, 1969).

4 J. G. A. Pocock, *The Machiavellian Moment* (Princeton: Princeton University Press, 1975); Quentin Skinner, "The Idea of Negative Liberty," in Richard Rorty, J. B. Schneewind, and Quentin Skinner, eds., *Philosophy in History* (Cambridge: Cambridge University Press, 1984).

5 Charles Taylor, "Atomism," in Alkis Kontos, ed., *Powers, Possessions, and Freedoms: Essays in Honor of C. B. Macpherson* (Toronto: University of Toronto Press, 1979); Alasdair MacIntyre, *After Virtue* (Notre Dame: Notre Dame University Press, 1981), and "Is Patriotism a Virtue?" *The Lindley Lecture* (University of Kansas: Department of Philosophy, 1984); Michael Sandel, *Liberalism and the Limits of Justice* (Cambridge: Cambridge University Press, 1982); and "The Procedural Republic and the Unencumbered Self," *Political Theory* 12 (1984): 81–96.

6 Irving Kristol, "The Adversary Culture of the Intellectuals," in Michael Novak, ed., *The Moral Basis of Democratic Capitalism* (Washington, D.C.: American Enterprise Institute, 1980).

7 Albert Hirschman, *The Passions and the Interests* (Princeton: Princeton University Press, 1977).

8 Immanuel Kant, "Perpetual Peace," in Lewis White Beck, ed., *Kant on History* (Indianapolis: Bobbs-Merrill, 1963), pp. 111–12.

9 Judith Shklar, *Ordinary Vices* (Cambridge, Mass.: Harvard University Press, 1984), p. 5.

10 Rogers Smith, *Liberalism and American Constitutional Law* (Cambridge, Mass.: Harvard University Press, 1985).

11 Nathan Tarcov, *Locke's Education for Liberty* (Chicago: University of Chicago Press, 1984); see also his "A 'Non-Lockean' Locke and the Character of Liberalism," in Douglas MacLean and Claudia Mills, eds., *Liberalism Reconsidered* (Totowa, N.J.: Rowman and Allanheld, 1983).

12 Ronald Terchek, "The Fruits of Success and the Crisis of Lib-

eralism," in Alfonso Damico, ed., *Liberals on Liberalism* (Totowa, N.J.: Rowman and Littlefield, 1986), p. 18.

13 J. Budziszewski, *The Resurrection of Nature: Political Theory and the Human Character* (Ithaca: Cornell University Press, 1986).

14 Harvey Mansfield, Jr., "Constitutional Government: The Soul of Modern Democracy," *The Public Interest* 86 (1987): 59.

15 James Q. Wilson, "The Rediscovery of Character: Private Virtue and Public Policy," *The Public Interest* 81 (1985): 15–16.

16 Thomas Spragens, Jr., "Reconstructing Liberal Theory: Reason and Liberal Culture," in Damico, ed., *Liberals on Liberalism*, p. 43.

17 Shklar, *Ordinary Vices*, p. 5.

18 Thomas Hobbes, *Leviathan* (New York: Macmillan, 1962), p. 124.

19 John Rawls, *A Theory of Justice* (Cambridge, Mass.: Harvard University Press, 1971), pp. 436–37.

20 See Chapter 6.

21 This virtue should not be confused with Roberto Unger's much broader strictures against identifying personality with external structure. See Chapter 3.

22 Thomas Jefferson, Letter to John Adams, October 28, 1813, in Alpheus T. Mason, ed., *Free Government in the Making* (New York: Oxford University Press, 1965), p. 385.

23 For a parallel account, see Mansfield, "Constitutional Government," p. 60.

24 Smith, *Liberalism and American Constitutional Law*, p. 200.

25 Shklar, *Ordinary Vices*, p. 233.

26 John Stuart Mill, *On Liberty*, ed. David Spitz (New York: Norton, 1975), p. 56.

27 George Kateb, "Democratic Individuality and the Claims of Politics," *Political Theory* 12 (1984): 343.

28 See Nancy Rosenblum, *Another Liberalism: Romanticism and the Reconstruction of Liberal Thought* (Cambridge, Mass.: Harvard University Press, 1987), ch. 2.

29 Kateb, "Democratic Individuality," pp. 356–57.

30 Daniel Bell, *The Cultural Contradictions of Capitalism* (New York: Basic Books, 1976).

31 Stephen L. Elkin, *City and Regime in the American Republic* (Chicago: University of Chicago Press, 1987), p. 149.

32 Elkin, *City and Regime*, pp. 159–64.

33 Elkin, *City and Regime*, ch. 9.
34 Richard Dagger, "Metropolis, Memory, and Citizenship," *American Journal of Political Science* 25, 4 (November 1981): 715–37.
35 George Kateb, "The Moral Distinctiveness of Representative Democracy," *Ethics* 91, 3 (April 1981): 359–61.
36 Kateb, "Moral Distinctiveness," p. 358.
37 Kateb, "Moral Distinctiveness," pp. 369–74.
38 Robert E. Lane, "Markets and Politics: The Human Product," *British Journal of Political Science* 11, 1 (January 1981): 3–6.
39 Lane, "Markets and Politics," p. 15.
40 Lane, "Capitalist Man, Socialist Man," in Peter Laslett and James Fishkin, eds., *Philosophy, Politics and Society*, 5th series (New Haven: Yale University Press, 1979), pp. 57–77.

11. CIVIC EDUCATION

1 See Robert K. Fullinwider, "Civic Education and Traditional American Values," *QQ* 6, 3 (Summer 1986): 5–8.
2 See especially Rogers Smith, *Liberalism and American Constitutional Law* (Cambridge, Mass.: Harvard University Press, 1985); Nathan Tarcov, *Locke's Education for Liberty* (Chicago: University of Chicago Press, 1984); and Harvey Mansfield, Jr., "Constitutional Government: The Soul of Modern Democracy," *The Public Interest* 86 (1987): 53–64.
3 James Q. Wilson, "The Rediscovery of Character: Private Virtue and Public Policy," *The Public Interest* 81 (1985): 3–16.
4 Charles Glenn, Jr., *The Myth of the Common School* (Amherst: University of Massachusetts Press, 1988).
5 "Education for Democracy: A Statement of Principles" (Washington, D.C.: American Federation of Teachers, 1987), p. 8.
6 For the fuller statement and argument, see Chapter 10.
7 Amy Gutmann, *Democratic Education* (Princeton: Princeton University Press, 1987), p. 39.
8 Gutmann, *Democratic Education*, pp. 44–46.
9 Other important contrasts between representative and direct democracy are offered in George Kateb, "The Moral Distinctiveness of Representative Democracy," *Ethics* 91, 3 (April 1981): 357–74.

10 As we saw in Chapter 10, Thomas Jefferson strongly endorsed it.
11 See Chapter 12.
12 Gutmann, *Democratic Education*, pp. 30–31. Don Herzog has also advanced a version of this thesis: "Parents need to teach their children to be critical thinkers or at least to tolerate others' so teaching them. . . . [C]hildren taught the skills of questioning their own commitments are better off. They can sculpt their own identities" (*Happy Slaves: A Critique of Consent Theory* [Chicago: University of Chicago Press, 1989], p. 242). And Stephen Macedo has also endorsed such a thesis: "Liberal persons are distinguished by the possession of self-governing reflective capacities. Further developing these reflective capacities leads one toward the ideal of autonomy. . . . Striving for autonomy involves developing the self-conscious, self-critical, reflective capacities that allow one to formulate, evaluate, and revise ideals of life and character, to bring these evaluations to bear on actual choices and on the formulation of projects and commitments" (Macedo, *Liberal Virtues: Citizenship, Virtue, and Community in Liberal Constitutionalism* [Oxford: Clarendon Press, 1990], p. 269).
    My objection to all these views is more or less the same: Liberalism is about the protection of diversity, not the valorization of choice. To place an ideal of autonomous choice at the core of liberalism is in fact to narrow the range of possibilities available within liberal societies. It is a drive toward a kind of uniformity, disguised in the language of liberal diversity. In this respect, at least, I agree with Charles Larmore: "The Kantian and Millian conceptions of liberalism [which rest on autonomy and individuality as specifications of the good life] are not adequate solutions to the political problem of reasonable disagreement about the good life. They have themselves become simply another part of the problem" (Larmore, "Political Liberalism," *Political Theory* 18, 3 [August 1990]: 345).
13 For a very different way of drawing this line, see Bruce Ackerman, *Social Justice in the Liberal State* (New Haven: Yale University Press, 1980), ch. 5.
14 For a nuanced and carefully argued defense of a similar position that unfortunately came to my attention too late to have an appropriate impact on my own formulation, see Brian Crit-

tenden, *Parents, the State and the Right to Educate* (Burwood, Victoria: Melbourne University Press, 1988), chs. 5, 7, and 8.

12. PUBLIC VIRTUE AND RELIGION

1 See Chapters 4 and 5.
2 John Locke, *A Letter Concerning Toleration*, ed. James H. Tully (Indianapolis: Hackett, 1983).
3 Locke, *Toleration*, p. 32.
4 Locke, *Toleration*, p. 27.
5 Locke, *Toleration*, pp. 23–24, 34–35.
6 Locke, *Toleration*, pp. 26, 43–44, 46–48.
7 Locke, *Toleration*, pp. 33, 42, 52–53.
8 For another analysis that focuses on the sociological under-pinnings and innovative character of Locke's *Letter*, see Don Herzog, *Happy Slaves: A Critique of Consent Theory* (Chicago: University of Chicago Press, 1989), pp. 156–71. As my discussion in Part II and the rest of this chapter should make clear, I agree with Herzog's contention that Locke's reformulation of the relation between religion and government, his account of religion as "private," is both transformative and contestable. I am less comfortable with the crucial role the bare fact of increasing social differentiation plays in Herzog's account. At some point, I argue, differentiation becomes an unmanageable problem, even within a liberal context. So our theoretical and practical challenge is to find an appropriately liberal relation between unity and diversity – that is, to distinguish between religious diversity and the kind of moral agreement necessary for a liberal society. And to do that, we need an account of the distinctiveness of religion that goes beyond the sociolog-ical, an account Locke quite properly supplies.
9 Locke, *Toleration*, p. 27.
10 Locke, *Toleration*, p. 49.
11 Locke, *Toleration*, p. 51.
12 Locke, *Toleration*, p. 54.
13 Chapter 11 provides one example of liberal persuasion, in the context of civic education. But there are many other arenas within which it can and should be practiced, including the rhetoric of public officials.
14 Part III of this book sketches the minimum moral commitments and requirements of the liberal state.

15 For these quotations (and much else), I am indebted to Walter Berns, *The First Amendment and the Future of American Democracy* (Chicago: Gateway, 1985), ch. 1; and A. James Reichley, *Religion in American Public Life* (Washington, D.C.: The Brookings Institution, 1985), ch. 3.

16 These quotations are drawn from Tocqueville, *Democracy in America*, ed. J. P. Mayer (Garden City, N.Y.: Doubleday, 1969), vol. 1, part II, ch. 9. For a fuller discussion, see my "Tocqueville on Liberalism and Religion," *Social Research* 54, 3 (Autumn 1987): 499–518.

17 Berns, *First Amendment*, p. 67.

18 See especially Gordon Wood, "The Democratization of Mind in the American Revolution," in Robert H. Horwitz, ed., *The Moral Foundations of the American Republic* (Charlottesville: University Press of Virginia, 1977), pp. 102–28.

19 Quoted in Philip B. Kurland, *Religion and the Law: Of Church and State and the Supreme Court* (Chicago: University of Chicago Press, 1978), pp. 18, 26.

20 Quoted in Mark DeWolfe Howe, *The Garden and the Wilderness: Religion and Government in American Constitutional History* (Chicago: University of Chicago Press, 1965), p. 13.

21 Robert N. Bellah, Richard Madsen, William M. Sullivan, Ann Swidler, and Steven N. Tipton, *Habits of the Heart: Individualism and Commitment in American Life* (Berkeley: University of California Press, 1985), pp. 32–35.

22 Walter Mondale, speech to the B'nai Brith International Convention, Washington, D.C., September 6, 1984.

23 Howe, *The Garden and the Wilderness*, ch. 1.

24 Quoted in Richard John Neuhaus, *The Naked Public Square: Religion and Democracy in America* (Grand Rapids, Mich.: William B. Eerdmans, 1984), p. 10.

25 Mondale, speech to the B'nai Brith.

26 At this juncture I want to emphasize the obvious: To grant traditionalists this point – that substantive judgments are unavoidable – is not by itself enough to secure the conclusion they urge. To say that public discussion must reach the merits of the issue is not to predetermine the outcome of that discussion.

27 See Judith Shklar, *Ordinary Vices* (Cambridge: Harvard University Press, 1985), pp. 4–5.

28 See Chapters 4 and 7.

29 Howe, *The Garden and the Wilderness*, pp. 151–52, 153, 155. See also Michael J. Malbin, *Religion and Politics: The Intentions of the Authors of the First Amendment* (Washington, D.C.: American Enterprise Institute for Public Policy Research, 1978). I am not unaware of the contrary conclusions of respected scholars such as Leonard Levy *(The Establishment Clause: Religion and the First Amendment* [New York: Macmillan, 1986]) and Thomas J. Curry *(The First Freedoms: Church and State in America to the Passage of the First Amendment* [New York: Oxford University Press, 1986]). As Levy himself suggests, "No scholar or judge of intellectual rectitude should answer establishment clause questions as if the historical evidence permits complete certainty. It does not" (Levy, *The Establishment Clause*, p. xiii). Without entering into the full discussion, let me just say that it is my judgment that Howe's position is supported by the preponderance of the evidence.

Common to all the scholars cited in the previous paragraph is the premise that it matters what the Founders thought or intended. One might object to this premise on two grounds, constitutional and sociological: The gradual "incorporation" of the Bill of Rights into the Fourteenth Amendment may affect the interpretation of specific rights; and the growing diversity of American religious belief and practice should lead us, as it has led the Supreme Court, to give greater weight to the broader over the narrower reading of the Establishment Clause. Suffice it to say here that I disagree with both of these arguments. I do not see why incorporation should necessarily make a further substantive difference. And the "functionalist" (Washington/Tocqueville) case I have presented is not weakened by the fact of growing diversity; if anything, it may be strengthened.

30 Quoted and discussed in Richard John Neuhaus, "What the Fundamentalists Want," *Commentary* 79, 5 (1985): 41–46.

31 David Martin, "Revised Dogma and New Cult," *Daedalus* (Winter 1982): 53–71.

32 Harvey Mansfield, Jr., "The American Election: Entitlements Versus Opportunity," *Government and Opposition* 20, 1 (Winter 1985): 3–17.

33 See H. L. A. Hart, "Immorality and Treason," and Ronald Dworkin, "Lord Devlin and the Enforcement of Morals," both

in Richard A. Wasserstrom, ed., *Morality and the Law* (Belmont, Cal.: Wadsworth, 1971).

34 See Chapter 5.

35 105 S. Ct. 2479 (1985).

36 For a fair-minded, though strongly argued, defense of this thesis, see Douglas Laycock, "Equal Access and Moments of Silence: The Equal Status of Religious Speech by Private Speakers," *Northwestern University Law Review* 81, 1 (Fall 1986): 1–67. For the standard contemporary liberal objections, see Ruti Teitel, "When Separate Is Equal: Why Organized Religious Exercises, Unlike Chess, Do Not Belong in the Public Schools," *Northwestern University Law Review* 81, 1 (Fall 1986): 174–89. A useful summary of this issue in its institutional and political context is John A. Murley, "School Prayer: Free Exercise of Religion or Establishment of Religion?" in Raymond Tatalovich and Byron W. Daynes, eds., *Social Regulatory Policy: Moral Controversies in American Politics* (Boulder, Colo.: Westview Press, 1988), ch. 1.

37 See William A. Galston, "A Liberal-Democratic Case for the Two-Parent Family," *The Responsive Community* 1, 1 (Winter 1990–91): 16.

38 In fact, the rate of out-of-wedlock births has not risen significantly since the 1960s. The ratio of out-of-wedlock births to other births has increased dramatically, however, because of declining rates of births to married couples (David Ellwood, *Poor Support* [New York: Basic Books, 1988], pp. 67–71).

39 Mary Ann Glendon, *The Transformation of Family Law* (Chicago: University of Chicago Press, 1989), p. 35.

40 David Blankenhorn, "American Family Dilemmas" (unpublished), p. 15.

41 To be sure, as many analysts have argued, similar trends may be observed in virtually every advanced industrialized country except Japan. But it has proceeded further in the United States. Even today, French and (West) German divorce rates are actually lower than U.S. rates were in 1960, and Swedish rates (popularly believed to be stratospheric) are in fact less than half the U.S. rates (Glendon, *Transformation of Family Law*, p. 193). As Constance Sorrentino of the Bureau of Labor Statistics summarizes the situation, "Based on recent divorce rates, the chances of a first American marriage ending in di-

vorce are today about one in two; the corresponding ratio in
Europe is about one in three to one in four" (Spencer Rich,
"U.S. Isn't Only Place Where Modern Family Is Being Trans-
formed," *Washington Post* [June 22, 1990], A25).

42 Ellwood, *Poor Support*, p. 46.

43 Ellwood, *Poor Support*, pp. 83–84.

44 Karl Zinsmeister, "Raising Hiroko," *The American Enterprise* 1,2
(March–April 1990), p. 53. See also Judy Mann, "Tracking the
Broken Homers," *Washington Post* (October 10, 1986), B3; Ju-
dith S. Wallerstein and Sandra Blakeslee, *Second Chances: Men,
Women, and Children a Decade After Divorce* (New York: Ticknor
and Fields, 1989).

45 See Gilbert Y. Steiner, *The Futility of Family Policy* (Washington,
D.C.: Brookings Institution, 1981), Part One.

46 Marilyn Gardner, "Putting Children First – the New English
Precedent," *Christian Science Monitor*, March 30, 1990, p.14.

47 Mary Ann Glendon, *Abortion and Divorce in Western Law* (Cambridge, Mass.: Harvard University Press, 1987), pp. 93–95.

48 James Q. Wilson, "The Rediscovery of Character: Private Virtue and Public Policy," *The Public Interest* 81 (1985): 3–16.

13. PARTISANSHIP AND INCLUSION

1 Charles Larmore, *Patterns of Moral Complexity* (Cambridge:
Cambridge University Press, 1987), p. 43.

2 John Rawls, "The Priority of Right and Ideas of the Good,"
Philosophy and Public Affairs 17, 4 (Fall 1988): 262.

3 Larmore, *Patterns of Moral Complexity*, chs. 4–5; and "Political
Liberalism," *Political Theory* 18, 3 (August 1990): 349–51.

4 Stephen Macedo, *Liberal Virtues: Citizenship, Virtue, and Community in Liberal Constitutionalism* (Oxford: Clarendon Press,
1990), ch. 2.

5 For a particularly trenchant critique, see Walter Berns, *The First
Amendment and the Future of American Democracy* (Chicago: Gateway, 1985), pp. 35–44.

6 Larmore, "Political Liberalism," p. 357.

7 Waldron, "Theoretical Foundations of Liberalism," *Philosophical Quarterly* 37, 147 (April 1987): 145–46.

8 Kent Greenawalt, "Rescuing Liberal Democracy from Its De-

fenders" (unpublished), p. 13; Waldron, "Theoretical Foundations," p. 139.

9 Stephen Holmes, *Benjamin Constant and the Making of Modern Liberalism* (New Haven: Yale University Press, 1984), pp. 146–47. Don Herzog offers a parallel "sociological" account of neutrality in his *Happy Slaves: A Critique of Consent Theory* (Chicago: University of Chicago Press, 1989), ch. 5. The standard philosophical arguments against neutrality have force, Herzog suggests, but they are largely beside the point. Within a differentiated liberal society, each of the many roles and choices possesses an internal distinction between relevant and irrelevant considerations. It is wrong for the legal system to take the political beliefs of defendants into account, for academic departments to make appointments on the basis of personal connections rather than merit, and so forth. Liberal society is neutral in the only practically significant (and feasible) sense of the term when it honors this diversified logic of relevant reasons.

Herzog's thesis is attractive in many respects. Without entering into a full discussion here, let me just note two complications. First, this thesis represents a shift of focus so dramatic as to constitute in many respects a discussion of a new topic rather than a new answer to an old question. Neutrality no longer means (as Ackerman, Dworkin, and Rawls would have it) a one-valued state macroabstention from a particular kind of argument (about the good life) but rather an open-ended set of microabstentions (from forms of discourse inappropriate in specific cases). Second, as Amy Gutmann has pointed out, consensus about relevant reasons in particular spheres is frequently lacking, and discursive strategies consistent with the relevant-reasons approach can call liberalism into question as well as support it. To resolve these difficulties, she argues, it is necessary to advert to the substantive values underlying liberal democracy. But of course, different individuals within the liberal community disagree about these values, or at least about their relative weight and priority in cases of conflict. So the relevant-reasons approach leads inexorably to the kind of substantive debate that liberal neutrality theories were designed to screen out (Gutmann, *Liberal Equality* [Cambridge: Cambridge University Press, 1980], ch. 4).

10   Larmore, "Political Liberalism," pp. 343–46.
11   Stuart Hampshire, *Innocence and Experience* (Cambridge, Mass.: Harvard University Press, 1989), p. 188.
12   See William A. Galston, *Justice and the Human Good* (Chicago: University of Chicago Press, 1980), p. 284.

Index

Index

cultural interpretation, 16–17, 44–5, 136, 155–8

Dagger, Richard, 234
Dahl, Robert, 213
Daniels, Norman, 325n13
Declaration of Independence, 9, 312n66
democracy, 42–3, 235–6; Walzer on, 50–4, 209–11, 246–8
Democratic party, 270
Descartes, René, 11, 24, 34–5, 46, 50, 66
desert, 10–11, 26, 131–2, 166, 185–7, 199–200; *see also* liberal justice; opportunity, equality of
dialogue, 105–7, 111–13; *see also* procedure, neutrality of
Diamond, Martin, 213, 262
diversity, 4, 6, 10, 27–8, 181–2, 222, 228, 302; *see also* pluralism
divorce, 283, 286, 333n41
Dr. Seuss, 107
Douglas, Stephen, 115, 274
Douglas, William O., 267
Dworkin, Gerald, 110
Dworkin, Ronald, 7, 9, 80–1, 90–1, 100, 101, 109, 184, 280

Elkin, Stephen, 233–4
Ellwood, David, 283
Emerson, Ralph Waldo, 230, 269
Enlightenment, 50, 55, 153, 294
equality, 42–3, 90–1, 115, 138–9, 166; American conception of, 160; liberal, 182–3, 192–3; *see also* opportunity, equality of

family, 195–6, 222, 233, 253–5, 280, 293; breakdown of, 283–7
Federalist, 214–6, 225, 244, 263–5
Feinberg, Joel, 314n12
Fishkin, James, 26, 40–1, 195, 210, 325n12

Flathman, Richard, 8, 9, 169, 172, 174, 175
Forster, E. M., 27
foundationalism, 35–7
Franklin, Benjamin, 269
freedom, 43, 89; American conception of, 160; as autonomy, 252–5; and good, 87–9; Kant on, 83–6; as liberal good, 175; and liberal unity, 143, 145; positive and negative, 82–7; Taylor on, 86
fundamentalism, 111–12, 130–1, 258, 270–2, 279

Gauthier, David, 98
Glendon, Mary Ann, 287
Gramsci, Antonio, 45, 48
Great Britain, 21
Greenawalt, Kent, 113, 298
Griffin, James, 167, 171, 172, 173
Gunneman, Jon, 117
Gutmann, Amy, 113–15, 152, 246–8, 252–4, 335n9

Habermas, Jürgen, 304
Hampshire, Stuart, 39, 167, 168, 172, 300
Hart, H. L. A., 38, 280
Hartz, Louis, 17
Hegel, Georg Wilhelm Friedrich, 11, 32, 45, 136, 304, 319n18
Heidegger, Martin, 24
Herzog, Don, 329n12, 330n8, 335n9
hierarchy, 62–3
Hinduism, 183
Hirschman, Albert, 214
Hobbes, Thomas, 66, 94, 168, 218–20
Hochschild, Jennifer, 17
Holmes, Stephen, 299
Howe, Mark DeWolfe, 271, 278, 282
Hume, David, 49, 172

338

Index

liberalism, 18–19; and affluence, 5,
21; ascendancy of, 4–5; and civic
education, 243–5; and civil
peace, 107–8; and coercion, 53–
4, 108–10, 179–80; as community, 45–6, 183; communitarian
critique of, 150–1; conception of
individuality in, 151–4; and conflict, 69–70, 72–5, 183; enemies
of, 5–6; and family, 283–6; and
fear, 11–12; and good, 7–11, 19,
70, 72–5, 79, 124–7, 143–4, 165,
173–4, 195; and government authority, 12; inclusion in, 21; juridical, 257–8, 269–70, 272, 273,
279; MacIntyre's critique of, 65–
8; and moral culture, 6; and
moral traditionalism, 17–18,
274–9; and perfectionism, 79,
89–90, 94–5; perfectionist, 80, 98;
political, 98–9, 117–18, 140, 149–
50, 290–1, 299–300; pragmatic,
98; public institutions of, 19–20;
and public morality, 257–9, 288–
9; relation of public and private
in, 291–6; and religion, 12–13,
20, 276–9; and self-interest, 213–
17; Unger's critique of, 61, 65;
and virtue, 71, 79, 154, 212–17;
Walzer on, 53–4; see also liberal
goods; liberal justice; liberal
neutrality; liberal virtues
liberationists, 14–15; see also
traditionalism
Lincoln, Abraham, 115, 274
Locke, John, 125, 179, 213, 215,
229, 249–50, 269; on toleration,
115–17, 249, 253, 259–63, 275,
293
Lowi, Theodore, 213

Macedo, Stephen, 291–3, 329n12
Machiavelli, Niccolò, 56
McGuffey, William, 266

MacIntyre, Alasdair, 19, 22–3,
308n19, 311n54; on bureaucracy,
69; on conflict, 69–70, 72–5; as
critic of liberalism, 65–8; on
emotivisr., 68–9; on good, 66–8,
70–2; on virtue, 66–8, 70–2
Macpherson, C. B., 213
Madison, James, 130, 263–4
Malbin, Michael, 278, 282
Mansfield, Harvey, Jr., 215–16,
279
Mapel, David, 40, 180, 187, 323n32
markets, 189, 212, 235–6
Marx, Karl, 45, 56, 67
Marxism, 4–5, 42
Mead, George Herbert, 320n20
Mill, John Stuart, 95, 215, 218-20,
230, 243
minimal code, 49, 167–9; see also
Hampshire, Stuart; Walzer,
Michael
modernism, 59–60
Mondale, Walter, 271, 272
Montesquieu, Baron de, 266
morality, 38–41; see also Aristotle;
Kant, Immanuel; minimal code
Mormons, 293
Muncie, Indiana, 278

Nagel, Thomas, 24, 110–13, 172
Nazi Germany, 25
need, 10, 167, 184–5; see also liberal
justice
neutrality: and good, 9–10; and
liberalism, 7–8, 269, 273–5, 296–
7; and religious toleration, 7,
261; see also liberal neutrality;
procedure, neutrality of
New Deal, 75
Nietzsche, Friedrich, 67, 158, 177
Nozick, Robert, 26, 176, 208
Nussbaum, Martha, 40, 168, 170,
172, 178

340

Index